GN00984642

The Essential Guide to Portraits (Vol.4)

Produced by *Digital SLR Photography* at:
6 Swan Court, Cygnet Park,
Peterborough, Cambs PE7 8GX
Phone: 01733 567401. Fax 01733 352650
Email: enquiries@digitalslrphoto.com
Online: www.digitalslrphoto.com

Editorial
To contact editorial phone: 01733 567401
Editor **Daniel Lezano**
daniel_lezano@dennis.co.uk
Art Editor **Luke Marsh**
luke_marsh@dennis.co.uk
Deputy Editor **Caroline Wilkinson**
caroline_wilkinson@dennis.co.uk
Features Writer **Jordan Butters**
jordan_butters@dennis.co.uk
Designer **Luke Medler**
luke_medler@dennis.co.uk
Editorial Co-ordinator **Jo Lezano**
jo_lezano@dennis.co.uk
Editorial contributors:
Brett Harkness, Ross Hoddinott, Paul Stefan,
Bjorn Thomassen, Paul Ward & Donna Willingham

Advertising & Production
Display & Classified Sales: 020 7907 6651
Group Advertising Manager
Alex Skinner
alex_skinner@dennis.co.uk
Sales Executive **Peter Smith**
peter_smith@dennis.co.uk
Production Controller **Daniel Stark**
daniel_stark@dennis.co.uk
Digital Production Manager **Nicky Baker**
nicky_baker@dennis.co.uk

Management
MAGBOOK PUBLISHER **DHARMESH MISTRY**
OPERATIONS DIRECTOR **ROBIN RYAN**
MD OF ADVERTISING **JULIAN LLOYD-EVANS**
NEWSTRADE DIRECTOR **DAVID BARKER**
COMMERCIAL & RETAIL DIRECTOR **MARTIN BELSON**
PUBLISHING DIRECTOR **JOHN GAREWAL**
CHIEF OPERATING OFFICER **BRETT REYNOLDS**
GROUP FINANCE DIRECTOR **IAN LEGGETT**
CHIEF EXECUTIVE **JAMES TYE**
CHAIRMAN **FELIX DENNIS**

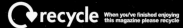

recycle When you've finished enjoying this magazine please recycle

Welcome...

"I enjoy all forms of photography, but nothing comes close to the passion and enthusiasm that I feel for shooting portraits. Whether it is photographing family or friends, taking contemporary lifestyle images or capturing candids, I always enjoy the challenge of delivering high-quality, creative and appealing portraits. I've been lucky in my job to work with many of the UK's leading portrait photographers, who have provided me with a wealth of expert advice, techniques and skills that have improved my own photography. Many of these leading pros helped create the tutorials and guides in this *Essential Guide to Portraits*, so you too will benefit from their mastery of portraiture. As you'll discover, taking great portraits doesn't demand you have the most expensive and extensive camera kit: a modest outfit made up of a camera and 50mm lens is all you need to take brilliant images. The more important factors are having a good eye for composition and detail, knowing the basic techniques of lighting, whether you're using daylight, flashguns or studioflash, and above all, developing strong interpersonal skills with your subject. Don't underestimate this latter point – a relaxed, happy subject will always make for better portraits, so ensure you are confident, friendly and have fun while you're taking pictures. All the best!"

DANIEL LEZANO, EDITOR

Meet our portrait experts

All our portrait experts are regular contributors to *Digital SLR Photography* magazine. For further advice and inspiration to help you improve your photo skills, pick up the latest issue, available on the second Tuesday of every month. For more information, visit: www.digitalslrphoto.com

DANIEL LEZANO
An enthusiast photographer for over 25 years, Daniel specialises in portraiture and is author of several books, including *100 Ways to Take Better Portrait Photographs*.

BRETT HARKNESS
Brett is one of the UK's leading portrait and social photographers and runs regular workshops. For further details, visit: www. brettharknessphotography.com

BJORN THOMASSEN
Bjorn is a successful portrait photographer, a master of lighting and leading speaker at seminars and courses. For more information, visit: www.bjornofinspire.com

PAUL WARD
Paul is a professional portrait and fashion photographer who specialises in location and studio shoots. For more details, visit: www.paulward.net

CONTENTS

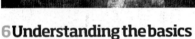

TURN TO PAGE 150 TO FIND OUT ABOUT OUR FANTASTIC SUBSCRIPTION OFFERS

Setting up your camera

Your digital camera has a bewildering array of features and while this is great in some respects, the choices can be confusing. Here we explain the tools that you need to know when photographing portraits

Exposure mode Don't think about using the Portrait program mode – you're more than a happy snapper if you're reading this guide. Instead, select aperture-priority AE mode (A or Av), which lets you choose the aperture, while automatically setting the appropriate shutter speed. For most types of portraiture, you'll want to use a wide aperture to throw the background out of focus. To start off, use f/5.6, as this gives enough depth-of-field to keep the entire face (eyes, nose and ears) in focus. By selecting aperture-priority, you'll be using ambient light only. While flash has its uses, controlling daylight will give you more natural results and help you learn to manipulate available light.

ISO rating & the reciprocal rule In terms of quality, the lower the ISO the better, so start by setting ISO 100 or 200. Handholding your camera allows you more freedom to move and shoot candids, but watch out for camera shake. The simplest way to do this is to use the reciprocal rule. All this means is you shouldn't let your shutter speed drop below the reciprocal of the lens you're using. For example, if you're using the lens at 100mm then ensure the shutter speed is above 1/100sec to reduce the risk of shake. If you're using the lens at 200mm then make sure the shutter speed is above 1/200sec, etc. Increasing the ISO rating is an easy way to achieve a faster shutter speed to avoid shake. Try not to go above ISO 800 as otherwise you'll notice increased noise in the image. In low light, whenever possible, we'd recommend you use a tripod. It allows you to use a lower ISO rating as shutter speeds aren't such a concern.

White Balance You should set the White Balance to match the lighting conditions you're shooting in. If you're working in mixed light and are a little unsure, then Auto (AWB) is the best compromise. Of course, if you're shooting Raw, you can always change the White Balance when you open the image on your computer. Something to bear in mind is that setting the wrong WB preset can be used to purposely shift the colour balance. For instance, setting Cloudy in daylight adds warmth to the tones, while selecting Tungsten will result in a very cool, blue cast – so be creative.

Image quality We would recommend you shoot Raw, as it allows you to play with settings, particularly White Balance, later. If your camera has a facility to shoot Raw + JPEG, use it with JPEG set to Small/Basic. Then when you're reviewing images, you can go through the small JPEGs quickly, choose your favourites and work on the appropriate Raw files. If you're confident in your ability, and don't expect to need to make tweaks to the exposure or White Balance in post-production, opt for the best quality JPEG for optimum results and to save room on your memory card.

Autofocus With the vast majority of portraits, it's important that the subject's eyes are in focus as, more often than not, they're the focal point. Your camera most likely has multi-point AF, which allows you to choose between leaving all the AF points active or to select individual AF points. You could leave all the AF points active to ensure you don't miss a great shot, but you run the risk of missing the eyes and focusing on the nose as it's the nearest object to the camera. A better option is to select a single AF point and use this to focus on the eye. The central AF sensor is usually the most sensitive, so you can use this to lock the AF by placing the point over one of the subject's eyes, then pressing the shutter button halfway down. Once the AF is locked, recompose and fire. It sounds tricky, but with practice it becomes second nature. Another option is to select the AF point that sits over the subject's eye – this means you don't have to recompose, allowing you to work quicker. If you intend to rattle off a sequence of shots with a very similar composition, this is the best option. If you do intend to lock focus, make sure your camera is set to single-shot AF as otherwise you won't be able to lock on your subject's eye.

Metering Your camera's multi-zone metering should be capable of exposing portraits perfectly in most situations. Take a test shot, check the screen and use the exposure compensation facility to add/subtract a little exposure if you feel the shot is too dark or light. Where your camera's multi-zone meter may falter is if your subject has very light or dark skin tones, is wearing light or dark clothing, or is strongly backlit. In these situations, use exposure compensation or select the spot meter and use the AE-L (Autoexposure Lock) button to take a reading from a mid-tone in the scene, or from an 18% grey card that you place near the subject.

Setting up your digital SLR for portraits

A little unsure how to select the exposure, White Balance or AF on your DSLR? Let us show you the way via five popular cameras

CANON EOS 450D/500D/550D

(1) Set the top-plate dial to Av to select aperture-priority.
(2) Press ISO button to set a rating.
(3) Use the WB button to choose WB and the AF button to set One-Shot AF.
(4) Press MENU and select the metering option on the second tab: we recommend Evaluative.
(5) To set image quality, press MENU and select Quality in the first tab. EOS 550D and EOS 600D only: Press Q and use the four-way control buttons as a shortcut to all these key functions.

NIKON DSLRS

(1) Set the top-plate dial to A to select aperture-priority.
(2) Press the info (i) button and scroll to metering mode and select your choice with the four-way control. We'd suggest you start with Matrix. Press the info (i) button again and select AF Mode to AF-S.
(3) Set the ISO rating, White Balance and image quality using the same procedure.

OLYMPUS E-SERIES

(1) Set the top-plate dial to A to select aperture-priority. The other settings are made using the Fn button, four-way controller and the OK button.
(2) To set the autofocus, press OK, select AF and set S-AF. For metering, press OK, go to the metering icon, select multi-zone and press OK. Set the ISO rating, White Balance and image quality using the same procedure.

PENTAX K-SERIES

(1) Set the top-plate dial to Av to select aperture-priority.
(2) Press the Fn button and press right on the four-way control to select an ISO, followed by OK to set.
(3) Press left to set the White Balance in the same way.
(4) To choose the AF mode, press MENU and the Rec. Mode tab, go down to AF mode, then right to set (we recommend AF-S). Set the metering mode in the same way (we recommend multi-zone).

SONY ALPHA: MOST MODELS

(1) Set the exposure dial on the top-plate to A for aperture-priority.
(2) Press MENU and select Image Quality (preferably Raw & JPEG).
(3) The following settings are selected using the Fn button and the four-way control. Press Fn, go to Metering and select Multi segment. Press Fn, go to AF mode and set AF-S. Press Fn, go to White Balance and choose a setting.
(4) Press the ISO button and set the ISO rating you wish to use.

OUR RECOMMENDED CAMERA SETTINGS FOR SHOOTING PORTRAITS
Exposure mode: Aperture-priority set to f/5.6 to begin with
Metering Pattern: Multi-zone
Autofocus: Use a single AF sensor with AF mode set to single-shot (AF-S)
White Balance: Match lighting conditions
Image Quality: Raw + JPEG
ISO rating: ISO 100 or 200

PAUL WARD

The basics of exposure

Our jargon-free guide about exposure provides everything you need to know to get to grips with apertures and shutter speeds

IF YOU'RE NEW TO photography, you need to understand exposure. Every exposure you take is made up of a combination of an aperture and shutter speed that determines how much light reaches the sensor. The aperture is the iris in the lens, much like the pupil of the eye, which can widen to allow more light through or contract to restrict the amount of light that enters the lens. Use a wide aperture and more light is able to pass through during a set time span than if you had selected a small aperture.

The shutter is a barrier in front of the sensor that moves out of the light's path when you press the shutter release, allowing light to reach the sensor and expose an image. The duration of the exposure is determined by the shutter speed. There is an obvious relationship between the aperture and the shutter speed in determining the correct exposure and this is selected by the exposure mode. While full-auto mode provides point-and-shoot simplicity, the beauty and enjoyment of photography is to take control over how your final picture looks.

The first step is to select one of the exposure modes that allows for far more creative photography. Before you know it, you'll be creating imaginative images rather than just shooting snaps.

Exposure controls

Many beginners believe it's difficult to use aperture- or shutter-priority mode, but in fact it's very easy to do. Once you've selected the exposure mode (1), it's simply a case of rotating the input dial (2) until the aperture or shutter speed you'd like to use appears on the top-plate (or rear) LCD panel (3). Depress the shutter button halfway and the camera works out the rest. Easy!

Understanding shutter speeds

Exposure settings are made by changing either the aperture or the shutter speed. The increments at which you change these settings are normally referred to as 'stops'. When you change a setting by a 'stop', you are either doubling or halving the exposure. So, for instance, changing from 1/500sec to 1/250sec doubles the duration of the exposure. As well as full stops, you can also vary exposure in 1/2 or 1/3 stops depending on the camera model you use. The diagram below shows shutter speeds from one second to 1/4000sec.

Full stops	1sec	1/2sec	1/4sec	1/8sec	1/16sec	1/30sec	1/60sec	1/125sec	1/250sec	1/500sec	1/1000sec	1/2000sec	1/4000sec
Half stops		0.7sec	1/3sec	1/6sec	1/10sec	1/20sec	1/45sec	1/90sec	1/180sec	1/350sec	1/750sec	1/1500sec	1/3000sec

Understanding aperture settings

The illustration below shows the iris at one-stop increments, ie each step from left to right halves the amount of light passing through the lens. The maximum aperture setting refers to the iris wide open (in this instance f/2.8) and the minimum aperture is the iris at its smallest setting (f/32 in this case). An explanation of where the f/number derives from would require an extensive scientific explanation, but the key to you understanding apertures is to learn how f/numbers correlate with the size of the aperture.

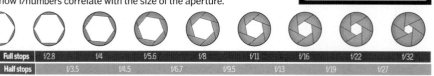

Full stops	f/2.8		f/4		f/5.6		f/8		f/11		f/16		f/22		f/32
Half stops		f/3.5		f/4.5		f/6.7		f/9.5		f/13		f/19		f/27	

Perfect exposure
Learning the basics of
exposure is key to ensuring
your portraits have the
perfect combination of
shutter speed and aperture.

Understand your camera's metering system

Before you can influence the exposure, you need to understand how your camera's metering works. Here are some essentials that you need to know to pick the best metering mode for different shooting conditions

DIGITAL CAMERAS BOAST complex exposure systems and offer a choice of metering patterns, each working out the exposure in a way to suit various lighting conditions. A camera's exposure system works on the assumption that the area of the scene that is being metered is a mid-tone, or 18% grey to be exact; the average if all dark, lights and mid-tones were combined. It's a tried-and-tested method and the basis of all metering patterns. It's important to be aware of this when you're taking pictures as it helps you to know when you may have problems with exposure.

While this system is fine in the majority of shooting situations, it can lead to incorrect exposures when the scene or subject is considerably lighter or darker in tone than 18% grey. For example, very dark subjects or scenes can fool the metering system into thinking that the general scene is much darker than it really is and, as a result, overexposes the image. Similarly, very light subjects or scenes can fool the camera into underexposing them – making them appear darker than they are – as the light meter takes a reading designed to render them as a mid-tone. It's in these trickier lighting situations where the popular multi-zone pattern, which provides the correct exposure for around 90% of shots, struggles as it tries to meter the entire scene. It's in cases like this where using the other patterns such as partial and spot are useful as they offer more control.

As a camera is trying to render an image grey, it's your job to ensure you compensate to keep the tones true to life. To do this you have to overexpose the camera's reading to give a lighter result than the camera wants, or underexpose to give a darker result. With a portrait in a dark scene, for instance, the camera will overexpose the image, bleaching the face, therefore you will need to reduce the exposure. With a light scene, it's giving less exposure than you need, darkening the subject, so you have to add exposure to make it record correctly.

If you're still unsure, don't worry – when you start shooting light or dark scenes and then try to override the camera's readings, you'll soon get to grips with it. By following our expert advice you should also increase the chances of keeping any exposure errors to a minimum.

Multi-zone metering

In theory, you could take every picture using multi-zone metering and never have a bad exposure – well almost... The multi-zone pattern is the newest and most sophisticated type of metering pattern and the one most photographers stick to for the majority of their shots. While every manufacturer has their own type of multi-zone meter, each with varying numbers and shapes of zones, all work in much the same way. The entire image area is divided into a number of zones and, when activated, individual meter readings are taken from each one of them. The camera's microprocessor then evaluates all these individual readings and uses complex algorithms to calculate the final exposure. To improve accuracy, many cameras also boast a library of tens of thousands of images taken in various lighting conditions, which are compared in a micro-second with the new scene to produce the exposure value. This system has proven highly reliable and gets the exposure correct more than 90% of the time. Its weak spots, however, are unusually light or very dark scenes or subjects. Multi-zone meters can also have trouble with very high-contrast scenes, in particular backlit subjects. This is why there are other metering patterns available, as well as a choice of exposure overrides, to help you ensure the perfect exposure.

Recognising the multi-zone pattern icon

Every camera brand has their own icons for metering patterns and below we show you what to look for on four popular brands

How to choose metering patterns

Selecting a metering pattern is a straightforward procedure, but we've provided a guide on how to do it for a number of leading digital SLRs from the six most popular brands

CANON EOS DSLRS
EOS 500D users press the SET button, while for EOS 550D and EOS 600D users, press the Q button and select the metering icon. For older models, like the EOS 1000D and EOS 450D, press the metering button on the four-way control.

CANON EOS 30D/40D/50D
Some older EOS models, such as the EOS 20D and 30D, have push-button controls. With these models, (1) press the metering button and (2) rotate the dial until the top-plate LCD shows the relevant metering pattern.

SONY ALPHA MODELS
Press the Fn button (1) and select the metering mode icon by pressing the AF button (2). Choose the pattern you'd like to use and press AF again to set.

NIKON DSLRS
For newer models like the D3100: Press the info (i) button and scroll to Metering and select your choice with the four-way control. Some older models like the D80 have a metering button you press to set your choice.

OLYMPUS E-SERIES
You can go through the MENU system but a quicker way is to press OK, highlight the metering icon using the four-way controller, press OK. Select the pattern with the dial or four-way controller and press OK to confirm.

PENTAX K-SERIES
Most Pentax DSLRs select the metering mode in the same way as the K100D. Press MENU to get to the Rec Mode display and use the four-way controller dial to go down to AE Metering, select the required pattern and press OK.

Metering options
Understanding how metering patterns work can help you when shooting in tricky lighting conditions, such as backlighting.

Centre-weighted average

Despite the arrival of newer patterns, this veteran still has its place on DSLRs and CSCs. This is the oldest metering pattern and was the number-one choice until the multi-zone pattern was introduced. As its name suggests, it takes an average reading from the entire frame, with a slight emphasis given to the central area. While less sophisticated compared to the more recent patterns, its past popularity means it is still featured in most digital cameras, as many experienced photographers feel more comfortable using this pattern. It is a good option when used in combination with the AE-Lock exposure override (which is covered in more detail later), but if given the choice, we'd recommend that you stick to multi-zone metering

Recognising the centre-weighted icon

You will find the centre-weighted pattern on your camera but you rarely need to use it in preference to multi-zone metering

Spot and partial metering

This is a great pattern when you want to take a reading from a specific area of the frame – but it must be used with care. While multi-zone metering takes measurements from the entire image area, spot and partial metering concentrates on the central area of the frame (you can see the measuring circle at the centre of the viewfinder screen). This allows you to precisely control where the exposure reading for the scene is taken from, as only the area of the frame within the measuring circle will be used to determine what's the 'correct' exposure.

Spot and partial metering is a great way to ensure that you get the proper exposure when you're shooting in difficult lighting conditions. Spot and partial are very similar in how they work. The main difference is spot offers a very precise measuring circle (usually around 3% of the image area), while partial usually measures the central 9% of the frame. The more precise spot meter is found on most cameras, while partial is less common, and a handful of cameras boast both. You must take great care when using spot or partial metering: always take a reading from a mid-tone, like grass or concrete, and not a light or dark subject, otherwise you will get an inaccurate reading.

Recognising the spot/partial icon

You need to select spot or partial by pressing the metering selector button and picking the respective icon. The spot icon is shown as a single dot at the centre of the rectangle, while partial is two small curved lines that form the outline of a circle. Some models offer both metering options

Remember: Position the spot/ partial meter over a mid-tone to get the correct exposure. Spot-meter off a dark subject and you'll overexpose it and vice versa. Try some practice shots to get used to how it works.

ISTOCK

Exposure compensation

+1.5EV

Master the easiest and most commonly used override for increasing and decreasing your exposure

ONCE YOU ARE AWARE of how metering systems work, and had some experience with using your camera, the times when the exposure system is likely to make mistakes becomes easier to recognise. The simplest way to override your camera's metered exposure is to use exposure compensation, allowing you to dial in a set exposure increment to increase (+) or decrease (–) the exposure. For instance, a subject that is significantly lighter than a mid-tone, like a white wedding dress, is likely to be underexposed by your camera, so you need to select positive (+) compensation. If the subject is much darker than a mid-tone – ie is wearing very dark clothing – then it is likely to be rendered overexposed, so negative (–) compensation is needed. Applying exposure compensation is quite straightforward and with experience you'll be able to judge how much is needed. All DSLRs have a dedicated exposure compensation button to make it a quick process in automatic or semi-automatic exposure modes. The compensation you set is often shown as + or – EV (Exposure Value) – ie if you add a half-stop of exposure it will display as +1/2EV.

PAUL WARD

-1.5EV
PAUL WARD

How does exposure compensation work?

Exposure compensation functions differently depending on the exposure mode that you are using. In aperture-priority, the compensation is applied by changing the shutter speed, but when using shutter-priority, it's the aperture that's adjusted. In program mode, the camera automatically decides between the aperture and/or shutter speed depending on the light levels to minimise camera shake.

No compensation

+1 EV applied

Exposure compensation
This is a typical example of when a subject deceives a metering system. The camera attempted to record the scene as a mid-tone and as a result it's underexposed. Positive compensation of +1EV was applied to correct the exposure in the adjacent shot.

Exposure compensation

Set a **+** *value* to compensate for an underexposed scene, eg if it's a light-toned subject.
Set a **-** *value* to reduce the exposure, eg when shooting a darker than average scene.

Using exposure compensation

Your camera's exposure compensation facility is useful when you wish to make a picture brighter or darker than the exposure set by the camera. While exposure compensation is designed for corrective purposes, the effect can be used creatively. It's extremely easy to use: try applying '+' and '–' settings on subjects with different tones and see the effect it has. Here's how to do it:

1) Press and hold your camera's exposure compensation button (normally indicated by a +/- icon).
2) Rotate the input dial to select the amount of compensation. A negative value means you're decreasing the exposure, a positive value means you are increasing it.
3) The exposure compensation scale is displayed in the camera's viewfinder and/or control panel.
4) The compensation you apply will affect all subsequent shots unless you reset it to +/- 0 EV.

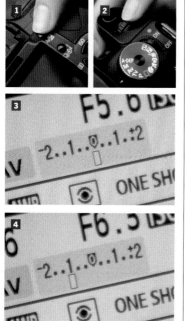

Autoexposure Lock (AE-L)

Use this function to 'lock' your exposure independently from the focusing system to help avoid exposure error

AE-L PRACTICALLY EVERY DSLR AND CSC has an AE-L button, which is normally found on the top right of the camera's rear, or near the LCD monitor. AE-L is an abbreviation for Autoexposure Lock. It is designed to secure the current exposure setting so that it doesn't change when you recompose your image, even if the incoming light levels change. AE-L can be used in any exposure mode, although it is pointless if you are shooting in manual.

When you press the shutter button down halfway, you engage the autofocus and the metering system to take a reading. This is ideal most of the time, but what about when you want to focus and meter from different subjects or parts of the scene? This is where AE-Lock comes in. It allows you to take an exposure reading independently of where you're focusing, which is ideal if your subject is very dark or light, or positioned in a bright or dim area of the scene. AE-Lock is most commonly used with the spot or centre-weighted metering pattern to secure the reading taken from a specific area of the frame. This is particularly useful in tricky lighting conditions that can fool your metering system, such as backlit objects or subjects with very dark or light backgrounds. For instance, if you are shooting a scene containing a bright light source, your camera's multi-zone metering mode could be fooled into reading the scene as brighter than it actually is and will underexpose as a result.

To achieve the correct exposure, you want to take a meter reading that excludes the light region. This is possible by taking a spot/partial meter reading from the subject itself or an area of the scene that is a mid-tone and saving the result with the AE-Lock button, before recomposing the shot and taking the picture. Using the same principle, AE-Lock is useful when shooting subjects that are positioned off-centre or when you want to photograph a series of images using exactly the same exposure settings. An instance of this might be if you want to stitch together several shots to create a panorama; it is important that the shooting parameters employed for each frame are consistent – using the AE-Lock facility ensures constant exposures for each shot.

The AE-Lock button is an essential exposure aid when shooting subjects with very dark or light backgrounds that can easily fool your camera's multi-zone metering into over or underexposure. In this instance, the very dark backdrop fooled the camera into thinking the scene was darker than it actually was. As a result, it has set a shutter speed longer than was required and so the subject is overexposed. In order to achieve the correct exposure, a spot-meter reading was taken from a wall to the side of the stairs. This reading was then locked using the AE-Lock button. The picture was recomposed and the image taken. The result is perfectly exposed.

Using AE-Lock

The AE-L button, combined with spot or centre-weighted metering, is one of the most accurate ways to achieve the correct exposure settings for any given subject.

1) Select your camera's spot (or partial) meter.
2) Direct the camera so that the metering circle is positioned over the area you wish to meter from.
3) Activate AE-Lock by pressing the button. On some models you have to keep it depressed, so consult your user's manual. AE-L may display in the viewfinder to indicate the lock is activated.
4) Move the camera and recompose the image as you want. Your exposure settings will not change, even if the incoming light levels alter as a result of changing composition.
5) Finally, fully depress the shutter release button to take the shot.

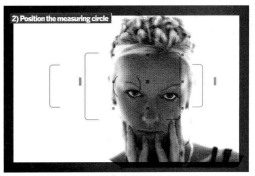

Master your exposures for backlit subjects

Learn the best way to correctly expose a backlit portrait using the spot meter, a reflector and fill-in flash

Paul Stefan: Shooting a backlit subject (ie with the sun behind them) certainly comes with its challenges. Unless you know what you're doing, your results can be unpredictable and, more often than not, your subject looks flat and underexposed. This tutorial will help you to understand how to use the techniques you need to achieve great results.

It's easy to stick your camera on full-auto mode and let it decide the exposure for you. And for portraits where the light shines on the subject's face, or off slightly to the side, auto mode often works fine as the exposure levels aren't too extreme. However, if you position your subject so that the light source is behind them (so you're shooting towards them and the sun or light source), your camera is likely to get

confused and set the wrong exposure. What tends to happen is that your subject gets underexposed, sometimes silhouetted. The reason for this is that the camera's multi-zone metering mode evaluates the overall scene. Given that you are pointing the camera towards the light source, it will always look to expose the shot for a bright scene, causing the darker areas – in this case the person – to be underexposed.

Taking more control over your camera will greatly improve the image and enable you to get the exposure you really want. One of the easiest ways to do this is to set your camera to aperture-priority mode and to use the spot meter along with AE-Lock to fix the light reading. With this method, you take a spot-meter reading from the person's face, almost always resulting in a perfectly exposed person. The only time that

this technique may be tricky is when your subject is very dark-skinned. If that's the case, use the same technique but take a spot-meter reading off a mid-tone in the same lighting conditions; this could be a piece of clothing, grass or ideally an 18% grey card.

While spot metering is quick and easy, it may cause your subject's surrounding scene to be overexposed if it's lighter than your subject. If you want to include the environment in the shot, one way around this is to take a meter reading from an in-between subject and then use your camera's flash to fill in the foreground with light, balancing the scene's overall exposure. Equally, a reflector can help as it bounces light back towards your subject for a similar fill-in effect. If you're feeling really adventurous, why not try a mixture, using both flash and a reflector?

1 Take a shot with your camera set to full-auto I am keen for my portrait to have a picturesque backdrop, so I choose a south-facing hillside near my home, with a view looking out to Robin Hood's Stride and Cratcliffe in the Peak District. My first shot is to see how the camera's auto mode handles the exposure of my subject with the sun directly behind and above her. With this set-up, I am shooting towards the sun, which will certainly challenge the camera's multi-zone metering system.

Try spot in manual You can use the spot meter in manual mode. Change apertures and shutter speeds until the exposure scale reaches the correct setting. This saves you having to use the AE-Lock function

2 Using spot metering and a reflector The shot taken in full-auto isn't a disaster, but it could certainly be improved with spot-metering. By switching my DSLR to aperture-priority and setting the metering mode to spot, I'm able to meter from Emily's face and lock the reading using AE-Lock. I do this by looking through the viewfinder and placing the central circle over the her face then pressing the AE-Lock button to ensure a perfect exposure. I then focus on her face, recompose and take the shot.

The result isn't too bad as the face of my subject, my eldest daughter, Emily, isn't completely underexposed, but it could be improved. This would have been much worse if the sun was lower and in direct view of the shot. Other DSLRs may not have coped as well as my Canon EOS 5D Mk II either.

Spot-metering improves the scene greatly, but to make it even better, I place a portable reflector just out of shot, perched on a stick, to throw some warm sunlight back onto Emily's face. This makes a big difference, revealing more detail, adding depth and contrast to her face and clothes.

3 Use fill-in flash
I like the natural look of the spot-metered and reflector shot, but you could make it more dramatic by using flash. I hook up my flashgun to my camera with a sync lead so I can hold the flash unit away from the camera and over to one side. This is a useful technique that causes your flash to give a more flattering look to the subject, rather than blasting them directly in the face. With this set-up, I also leave the reflector in place, use the same exposure settings from the previous shot and point the flashgun towards Emily's body, rather than her face.

The flash has made a big impact on how she's lit. Her face is brighter, but because I aimed the flashgun towards her body and feet, the shot has exposed her lower half so much better than the previous shot. Her hair is also really well-exposed and she now has catchlights in her eyes from the flash.

240-4788 ISO100
5.0 ±3⅓. 0. 0. 0 sRGB
1/200 Av RAW+iL 5.84MB 13/04/2009 16:08:41
176/274

Portrait composition

There are no rules, only guidelines when it comes to composition but, like lighting, it has the potential to make or break a portrait. Consider these aspects…

1) Landscape or upright orientation?

It's natural to tilt the camera upright when you're shooting a portrait as it allows you to fill the frame with the subject's head and shoulders or entire body. It's a good format to adopt when you're trying to exclude as much of the background as possible to concentrate attention on the subject. Because this format is used so often when shooting people, the upright format is often termed the portrait format. Photographing portraits with the camera held normally to produce a landscape-orientated image often allows you to employ more creative compositions. For one, it means you can place the subject off-centre to include some of the backdrop in the frame. It also allows you to crop tightly into the face, which can add drama and impact to the image. Both options are worth trying while looking through the viewfinder to see which works best and, if in doubt, take a shot using both formats!

We have cropped the same image (see right) into a landscape and portrait format. Which do you prefer? The orientation you choose each time you compose a shot has the potential to strength or weaken your portrait.

Landscape

Portrait

2) Viewpoint

It's natural when taking a picture to shoot from your normal eye-level. However, while there is nothing wrong with this, shooting from your standard viewpoint is a little unimaginative. Also, it's not always the most flattering angle for your subject – you'll find that by shooting from slightly above and down on your subject, you'll capture a better and often more flattering picture. It pays to think outside of the box – experiment by shooting from a much higher or lower viewpoint to your subject and see how the results turn out.

Shooting a subject from halfway up some steps provides a very high viewpoint and produces an unusual and quirky result. Give it a try!

3) Breaking the rules: New angles to try

Use a wide-angle lens
Set your standard zoom to its widest focal length (or, better still, use an ultra wide-angle zoom) to photograph portraits with a difference. Because wide-angle lenses distort perspective, it's possible to create some very unusual images, where the part of the subject closest to the lens appears much larger than the parts of the body that are further away. It's not very flattering but definitely fun!

Eye contact
Yep, we harp on about making sure you get both eyes in focus with the subject looking at the camera, yet there are many stunning examples where the subject's looking away or their eyes are obscured. A lack of eye contact can add intrigue to your portrait or give it a candid feel, so don't be afraid of having your subject looking away from the camera.

Look how the wide-angle lens used on this shot has distorted perspective. You can get some quirky portraits from using unconventional techniques.

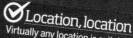

✓ Location, location
Virtually any location is suitable for taking portraits. You'll find you can take great portraits anywhere as long as you use the light correctly. Make it a project to walk around your local neighbourhood trying to spot decent backdrops

Shoot on a slant
Shooting images at an angle can add energy to an image as it displaces the balance of the scene. Give it a try, whether shooting with the camera in an upright or landscape format, and see how it can inject life into the image.

BRETT HARKNESS

Frequently asked questions

Q Why should I not use my camera's Portrait mode?
A While it takes the fuss out of taking a picture, scene modes like Portrait remove any opportunity for being creative. As with all scene modes, the Portrait program automatically activates certain picture-taking options. Depending on which camera you use, you'll find that setting Portrait mode results in the following: White Balance: Auto; Autofocus: Multi-point AF/One-shot mode; ISO Rating: Automatically selected; Metering pattern: Multi-zone; Built-in flash: Auto.

While these settings are suitable for those looking for point-and-shoot simplicity, for those of you wanting to develop your photographic skills, it's quite prohibitive and the fact that you can't control aspects such as the flash and White Balance can really affect the result you're trying to achieve. Instead, learn how to get the best from semi-automatic modes such as aperture-priority.

Q What should subjects wear?
A The most important thing is that your subject feels comfortable. So don't get them to overdress or wear items that they don't like.

Ideally, ask to see a selection of clothing and talk through what they like the most and the types of portraits they want. You don't want colours, logos or patterns to dominate the image, so a plain neutral top is usually a good starting point, along with casual trousers or a pair of jeans. Tastes change so, if possible, opt for a timeless look that encourages them to love their portrait even longer.

Q How should they pose?
A It's vital that they appear natural and comfortable, whether they're sitting, standing or lying down. You'll find that subjects are normally unsure of what to do with their hands, resulting in them looking clumsy or awkward in the frame. A good starting point is to have them keep their hands in their trouser pockets if standing, hanging over their knees or between their legs if sat down. Buy fashion and lifestyle magazines and tear out pages where a model has a pose that you like, then show it to your subject and ask them to recreate it.

Q Any tips on make-up?
A We asked professional make-up artist Fay Bacon for expert advice:
1) Always thoroughly cleanse, tone and moisturise the skin before applying make-up. It will help the products to sit better on the skin.
2) Apply an illuminator over the top of a moisturiser. This helps lift the skin and increase its radiance underneath the foundation, so skin appears more youthful.
3) Always apply foundation with a foundation brush as it reduces the amount of foundation used on the skin and prevents patchiness or lines on the face, making the skin appear extra-flawless and natural.
4) Use a translucent, loose powder and dust it lightly over the 'T-Zone' area. This reduces the appearance of shiny, oily skin.
5) Always use concealer for disguising dark circles and unwanted blemishes. There is an enormous difference between foundation and concealer; foundation evens out the skin tone while concealer covers. You need to use both for flawless-looking skin.
6) In terms of colour such as eye shadows, blushers and lipsticks etc, always consider the colour contrasts of skin tone, eyes and lips. Dependent upon the style and theme of the photography shoot, certain make-up rules do not apply. However, most make-up artists would advise using lighter and more intense shades such as purples, blues and greens on darker skin and eyes, as this helps echo the beauty and vibrancy of the skin tone.

Pastel, neutral and darker shades are better suited for paler skin as they help intensify the eye area and the skin tone by allowing both to stand out more.

Capture wide-angle portraits

Distortion, exaggerated perspective, huge angle-of-view – you'd have to be crazy to try portraits with a wide-angle lens. So, let's go a little crazy

SHORT TELEPHOTO LENSES are so popular for photographing people that they're sometimes referred to as 'portrait' lenses. They produce images with flattering perspective and allow you to fill the frame from a comfortable distance. The shallow depth-of-field they offer makes it easy to throw the background out of focus and achieve a professional-looking result.

So why would you turn your back on such wonderful qualities to shoot portraits with a lens that offers none of them? Because, although it's unconventional, if used well, wide-angle lenses can yield very creative and dramatic results. Wide-angle portraits are not the easiest to master but, by learning how to turn their so-called disadvantages into image-enhancing features, your photographic skills will improve enormously.

Wide-angle lenses have a focal length of 35mm or less. The shorter the focal length, the more pronounced the distortion and wider the angle-of-view, with around 24mm being the point where you might start to see some distortion in the form of curving. As these types of lenses have such an extensive coverage, you need to carefully consider your subject's environment. A full-length shot will also capture a lot of the surrounding area, so you need to be sure that it all works together and is enhancing rather than distracting, by keeping it as simple as possible. For this reason, wide-angle lenses often make good environmental portraits as the choice of location can often be used to add context to a portrait that says something about the subject: their job, a hobby or interest, for instance.

Dramatic perspective is also a feature that can make or break a wide-angle portrait. Anything close to this type of lens appears massive, but falls away rapidly in size as it gets further away and distant objects appear tiny with a really wide sweep. The relative difference in size is exaggerated the shorter the focal length and the closer the camera is to the subject, plus compounded by the front-to-back sharpness you get with the type of lens. Used recklessly, they can produce unnatural-looking, big-headed, long-nosed people with short legs and enormous hands. Used intelligently, they can create exciting, dynamic images where dramatic effect more than make up for any lack of realism.

✓ Sense of proportion
The perspective trick played by a wide-angle lens can make parts of an image seem disproportionately large. Move in too close with a wide-angle and you'll give your model a big nose and a face like the reflection in the back of a spoon. Keep your distance

Take an extreme view

Look at the image of our model below. Fun, isn't it? Quirky. By taking a high viewpoint and getting close to the subject with an ultra wide-angle lens (approx 10mm), perspective has been distorted and the features closest to the lens have been grossly exaggerated. See how her hand looks bigger than her head and her feet are really small in comparison. It can create some novelty portraits, especially if you introduce props like glasses and hats in to the shot, too.

You can create a similar effect, but a very different-looking image, by reversing the angle and shooting upwards so the subject has huge feet and a tiny head. Used deliberately and thoughtfully, it can create fun portraits, but be careful not to overuse it so all your portraits look gimmicky. Give it a go and see what you can come up with.

1 Take a test shot Pick your location and take a test shot. We set the DSLR to aperture-priority mode and our lens to f/5.6. We chose to frame our model with columns and arches as the lines will help exaggerate perspective. From this distance, the subject is too small and it looks as if it could have been shot with a portrait lens for the lack of drama in the perspective. We need to get a little closer.

2 Find a low viewpoint By getting closer to the model and shooting from lower down, the perspective-bending characteristics of the wide-angle lens are coming into play with converging vertical lines. The girl looks taller and the archway taller still. From the lower viewpoint, the whole scene looks grander. This is certainly a stronger shot but there's room for it to become more dramatic still.

3 Go even lower Get as close to the subject and as low to the ground as possible to exaggerate perspective. We've had to tip the camera back to keep the arches in the frame. See how combining a dramatic viewpoint and a wide-angle lens stretches the model's legs and shrinks her top half. Be careful not to cross that line between dramatic and comical, though.

4 Use a frame Foreground interest can work well with a wide-angle lens as it exaggerates whatever is closest to it, like this archway. To keep the subject in proportion move them further away from the camera so you can still use the widest focal length to include the foreground. In this image, the way the repeated archways frame the subject strengthens the composition.

Final image
By changing position to rid the scene of distracting elements, zooming in to the subject and experimenting with different focal lengths to control distortion, you should be able to capture a relatively natural-looking portrait with a dramatic perspective.

5 Make the subject larger To get the subject bigger in the frame, move in closer but zoom the lens in (in this case, from 10mm to 20mm) to control distortion. To find the balance between perspective and keeping the model naturally proportioned, place her in the centre of the frame where distortion is minimal from a distance and shooting at head height but from an angle.

6 Use a shorter focal length Moving in closer to the subject using a shorter focal length (we used 16mm) means the model dominates the frame but is central enough for her head not to be distorted. However, keep an eye on the surrounding area. Here, the scope of the wide-angle lens means the archways and greenery are included, which distracts from the portrait.

Take a turn for more creative portraits

Learn how to abandon the rule that tells you to keep your pictures' horizontal and vertical lines level and still have the skills to produce perfect portraits with a twist

WE LOVE KEEPING things level. The picture on the wall has to be straightened, the cutlery must be arranged 'just so', the leaning garden shed can cause insomnia. We like right angles: up, down and straight across. Neat British fields, no converging verticals and straight sunsets.

So when we arrange elements within the rectangular frame of a camera viewfinder, our default setting is to level things out. Lines and edges that are horizontal in the physical world run parallel to the top and bottom of our viewfinder frame. Anything vertical follows the sides. That's neat. That's ordered. That's the way it should be. Now ignore that urge. Just for once, or maybe for a short while, add a little skew into your picture-taking. Try coming at a portrait from a different angle and be rewarded with a fresh perspective.

Breaking with this composition convention is probably the easiest and most forgiving way to break the rules. It takes a second to twist the camera and then correct it if you wish. So what have you got to lose? Look for scenes where there are strong horizontal and/or vertical lines and then decide how dramatic you want the slant based on the subject by controlling depth-of-field and the angle of the skew.

By doing this, you'll gain longer diagonals that give your picture more height and a sense of drama and energy that avoids the composition looking static. Okay, it might play havoc with some deep-rooted obsessive compulsive disorder that you keep in check, but fight the urge. Turn off that composition grid in the viewfinder, discard the spirit level on your tripod and try shooting on a slope.

Dramatic versus subtle

Compare the main image of the girl on the right to the one of the two little girls jumping below. The skew in the image of the little girls is what makes the image work so well. Without the angle it would be a good but relatively static action shot. The close to 30° slant adds energy and enhances the subjects' movement to make it a great picture, full of life.

The skew in the image on the right is a lot more subtle. An untrained eye might not even comment on the angle because the telltale stonework is out of focus. But with an angle of approximately 15°, it's still enough to elevate the shot from a good portrait to a great photograph by adding extra interest to a head-and-shoulders shot. However, although it might be less obvious, both examples shown here go way beyond what might be produced by mistake. You'd have to be extremely careless to shoot at 15° from the horizontal by accident. So, that seems to be the secret to the success of this rule-breaking technique – be bold and deliberate when trying it out.

1 First shot The image above is a nice picture of an attractive subject and would do fine as a simple snapshot. However, to turn this image into a more striking portrait it needs a little more work and some breaking of the rules. The background is fairly cluttered, showing grass, flowers and all the stonework of the building. Plus the composition is too wide.

2 Zoom in Using a telephoto lens to zoom in really improves the image as it compresses the background and a large aperture of f/4 throws it out of focus, bringing all the viewer's attention to our model. However, the image still isn't breaking any rules and, although the model's pose is relaxed, the shot looks static and needs an injection of energy.

3 Tilt the camera This is where the idea of twisting the camera can pay off. Although our focal length, aperture and the model's overall pose have stayed the same, by simply twisting the camera, the new, slightly jaunty angle has added a sense of energy to the portrait. The strong vertical lines enhance the skew, but the pillars look as if they're falling towards her.

Final image
By reducing the columns to a blur and cropping closer in to the model's face, we've made a dramatic 15° twist into a subliminal effect. The viewer is aware of the skew as it makes the portrait more dynamic but isn't overpowering. The success is in its subtlety.

✓ Twist, then stick
The dramatic slant could become a staple of your style. It's so simple to create a twisted variation on any picture idea, you'd be crazy not to use it all the time. Or you might want to save it for when nothing else is working to make the portrait a little more dynamic

4 Zoom in further A tighter crop adds more prominence to our model by blurring the background even more and eliminating some of the distracting stonework. Although we've broken some rules with the slant, we've still placed our model on an intersecting third. Placing our model too far to the side of the frame would have unbalanced the image.

5 Tilt the opposite way As a final refinement, we've tilted the camera in the opposite direction so the pillars look like they're falling away from the model, rather than on top of her. The best practice is to try all sorts of angles to see what works best for your subject and scene. Unlike film, digital files cost nothing, so feel free to fill those memory cards up.

Take great portraits with no direct eye contact

It changes the connection between the viewer and subject, alters the mood of a portrait and gives you the chance to show your subject in a different way. So give it a go: break the rules and try avoiding eye contact

WHEN A SUBJECT looks straight at the camera, it creates an immediate connection between them and the viewer that's defined by the expression on the subject's face. Whether they seem happy, seductive or angry, all elicit very different reactions in the viewer. Focusing on the eyes and using direct eye contact has become one of the golden guidelines for good portraiture, as it grabs the attention of the viewer. However, if it's mood and mystery you really want to evoke, your images could become stronger if you choose to break this rule.

Photographs without eye contact can also look less posed and more natural. When someone makes eye contact, it's obvious that they're aware of being photographed but when they look past the camera, it takes on the curiosity of a candid and makes the viewer feel as if they're gaining a glimpse into a private moment. The two adjacent photos are good examples of this. The photograph below right has a sense of the unknown as it leaves us wondering what's got her attention and what she's thinking about. While the top photo, with the girl looking into the camera, has none of this mystery. When the subject doesn't connect with the viewer, the viewer is no longer involved in the picture, but rather takes on the role of the observer. Another example would be two people looking at each other, as the camera depicts their relationship with each other, rather than with the viewer.

As well as trying portraits without eye contact, why not combine it with some of the other rules we have suggested you break in this section? It's unlikely that an image breaking all the rules will succeed, so for each broken rule, complement it with a powerful obeyed rule. We've shot our model in a landscape format, instead of portrait, but we've obeyed the rule-of-thirds. We've also skewed the camera to the left to create a more interesting shape – but we've used a telephoto lens to get a compressed and out-of-focus background. Try mixing and matching these rules to see what you can do.

Right: Only the faraway look in her eyes and the half-smile differentiate these two photographs. But, while both are equally as powerful, they elicit very different feelings and connections with the viewer.

Direct eye contact

The eye contact in this image creates an instant connection between the viewer and subject.

No eye contact

It's not eye contact that connects us to this image but its inquisitive nature and mystery.

Ideas for images without eye contact...

■ Sleeping babies
Capturing the peaceful yet fleeting moments of repose can create some cherishable images. Images like this wouldn't have the same appeal if the baby's eyes were open. Use soft window light and a wide aperture to preserve memories like this.

■ Reflections
Normally an image with no eye contact leaves you wondering what's caught the subject's attention. But with the subject wearing sunglasses, you're able to reflect the rest of the scene in the shades and bring some context to the photograph.

■ A private moment
By becoming the observer, the viewer experiences a glimpse of the subject uninhibited by the camera. Imagine this shot but with the child looking at and reacting to the camera; it would have a totally different feel.

■ Facing away
One of the easiest and most powerful ways to take a picture with no eye contact is to have the subject turn their back to the camera, so, again, the viewer feels as if they're not observing but sharing in the subject's private moment.

Subtle seduction
The fact that the subject isn't looking at the camera gives this image a stronger sense of seduction than if she had looked straight at the camera.

Focusing fundamentals

While the autofocus systems of cameras are highly responsive, we can help to improve their accuracy

AUTOFOCUS IS ONE OF THOSE THINGS that all photographers take for granted at one time or another. Half-press the shutter release and it does its job quickly and quietly. While everything is working well, you don't really need to think about what's happening and why, but taking control of the autofocus (AF) can help you improve, especially when your camera struggles to interpret what you are trying to do. Understanding how this highly advanced technology works will ultimately help you to use it more effectively in your photography.

How autofocus systems work There are two main kinds of autofocus system used in modern cameras: contrast-detection AF and phase-detection AF. In DSLRs, the latter of these is used most of the time. Phase-detection AF works by taking some of the light entering the camera through the lens, splitting it into two and directing it onto a pair of sensors. The point where it hits the sensor tells the camera if the image is in focus or not, and if not by how much it's out and in what direction. This means that the camera can find the correct focus very quickly. The downside of phase-detection AF is that it needs contrast to work. Phase-detection AF also requires a DSLR's mirror to be down, meaning it doesn't work well in LiveView mode. This is when we need contrast-detection AF – the same system that is used in CSCs. It works by continuously monitoring the overall contrast in a scene while focusing, the idea being that an image has the most contrast when it's at its sharpest. It was initially a slower method, but in the last couple of years has developed to rival phase-detection.

Autofocus modes The most popular AF modes are Single-Shot AF (known as One-Shot on Canon EOS DSLRs) and continuous autofocus mode. With Single-Shot AF, you press the shutter release halfway down to engage AF and lock focus until you release the button. This mode also prevents the shutter firing unless the subject is in focus. Continuous autofocus mode, on the other hand, lets the shutter fire regardless of whether the scene is in focus or not, and carries on focusing even when your finger is half-pressing the shutter button. It's the mode best suited to shooting moving subjects, as we'll see shortly. It's worth mentioning good old manual mode, too. There are times when autofocus is simply not the best option, and focusing manually produces better results, such as with night photography, where low light confuses AF, and macro, where focusing is so critical that it is often best to focus manually.

Multi-point autofocus Early AF systems used a single sensor at the centre of the frame. Cameras now use multiple AF points grouped to occupy much of the frame area. As a result, AF systems can now handle off-centre subjects and objects that move in the frame, not just those in the centre. The most focusing points in a DSLR is currently 61 (Canon) but the average is 11. Shoot with all points activated and the camera will focus on what is closest to you – handy in most situations, but with portraits, can result in the lens focusing on the tip of the nose rather than the eyes. You usually have the option of reducing the number of active focus points, which increases focusing speed and allows you to focus on a precise point.

There are two distinct types of focus point. Line-type sensors are the most common, but least sensitive. They work in one direction and look for detail that crosses them perpendicularly (left to right) to focus accurately. Cross-type sensors look for detail in both directions, and are faster and more sensitive. The central focus point is usually a cross-type sensor, though advanced DSLRs have a number of them clustered together.

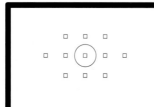

Single-point AF Select single-point AF and focus precisely on your chosen subject. Choosing the central point is usually best.

Multi-point AF Multi-point AF activates all the sensors and usually focuses on whatever is closest to you. It's ideal for tracking subjects such as a child running.

Setting autofocus modes on your DSLR

Selecting the autofocus mode and the number of active AF points differs from camera to camera. Here we show how it works on five popular models, but most cameras work in a similar way

CANON EOS (MOST MODELS)

AF mode: Press the AF button (located on the right side of the four-way control) and choose from One Shot, AI Focus or AI Servo mode.
AF points: Press the AF point selection button on the top-right of the rear of the camera and use the input dial by the shutter release button to choose the AF point.

NIKON DSLRS

AF mode: Press the info (i) button and scroll to Focus mode. Use the four-way control and OK button to select AF-A, AF-S, AF-C or manual focus.
AF points: Press the info button and scroll down to the AF-area mode. Choose between Closest Subject, Dynamic Area (where you can select a focus point for tracking), or Single Point.

OLYMPUS E-SERIES

AF mode: Press OK and scroll to the AF mode option. Press OK again and choose between S-AF (single-shot AF), C-AF (continuous AF) and MF (manual focus).
AF points: Press OK and scroll to the AF Area option. You can then use the command dial to select all the AF points or select an individual point.

PENTAX K-SERIES

AF mode: Press the MENU button and use the four-way control to select AF Mode. AF.S is the single-shot AF mode, while AF.C is continuous AF mode.
AF points: Press the MENU button and use the four-way control to go down to Select AF point. Choose from Auto, multi-point or spot AF (the camera uses the central AF point only).

SONY ALPHA SERIES

AF mode: Press Fn and choose the Autofocus mode option using the four-way control. Choose between AF-S, AF-A or AF-C mode.
AF points: Press the Fn button and then choose the AF area option using the four-way control. Choose between Wide (all points), Spot (centre point) and Local (manual selection of any AF point).

Focus on off-centre subjects

When you are out shooting, it's not often that your subject will be slap-bang in the middle of the frame. In fact, we often go to great lengths when taking pictures to avoid placing the subject at the centre to ensure the image has the best possible composition. If your camera has multiple focus points spread across a wide area then, chances are, these will manage off-centre subjects very well. For the ultimate control though, try selecting one individual AF point to take charge of exactly where your camera is focusing. The traditional way of handling off-centre subjects with a single focus point comprises three steps: using the central AF point to focus on the subject; locking the focus using your camera's AF-lock function; and recomposing the frame so that your subject is off-centre. Your camera's AF-Lock is easy to use. Providing your camera is set to Single-Shot AF mode, a half-press of the shutter release will tell the camera to focus and then lock-in this distance for as long as the button is held down. It's an intuitive process, you'll soon find yourself performing the focus-lock-recompose routine without realising it. By default, on the majority of cameras, pressing the shutter button halfway not only locks the focus, but also takes an exposure reading, too. Try it yourself and see how your camera performs. You'll find you can usually use a custom function to set the shutter release to lock AF and the exposure together, or just the AF. Some models have a separate AF/AE-lock button, meaning it's possible to customise the AF so it's just the way you like it.

Use depth-of-field to give your portraits much more impact

By altering your shooting distance, considering your choice of aperture and focusing creatively, you'll stand a great chance of taking outstanding portraits

THERE ARE FEW, if any, more rewarding feelings in photography than capturing a portrait that not only pleases you, but has the subject over the moon with how they look in the shot. Most people have had their picture taken, but few get the chance to have their portrait shot. There is a subtle difference to the two: one is a quick snap, with little attention given to anything but basic composition and the other is far more creative and carefully considered.

It's often said that a good portrait captures a little bit of the person's personality and it's true. But what it also does is record the sitter in a different way from other pictures taken of them. By using a couple of simple techniques based around depth-of-field and focusing, you can produce distinctive results, as you will discover shortly.

The general rule for portraits is that you should focus on the eyes and set a wide aperture of at least f/5.6 to throw the background out of focus, while keeping the face sharp. The 'f/5.6 rule' is one that is used frequently by many professional lifestyle photographers who like to work fast and prefer to concentrate on their interaction with the subject rather than changing settings. If you want to include more of the environment, however, a smaller aperture (usually with a wider lens) is required to keep the background, as well as the subject, in focus.

While ambient light is quite often sufficient – and sometimes ideal – you should also consider using studioflash. As well as allowing you to control the direction of the light, you can also adjust the intensity to provide the exact amount of light that you need for any given aperture. Once you learn how to use it correctly, a one- or two-light set-up can also offer scope for creative opportunities.

Portraits can look exceptionally flattering when there's a shallow area of sharpness. The easiest way to do this is to use a telezoom set to its maximum aperture with a relatively short shooting distance. The result is a tight crop of the face where, bar a small sharp area, much of the frame is thrown out of focus. The result is a very 'soft' image that, with some

thought given to lighting, can look romantic if lit by diffused light, or more arty and striking if used with strong directional light. When using this technique, be sure to focus on the appropriate part of the face, usually an eye but sometimes the mouth, depending on where you want the viewer's gaze drawn to. It's certainly worth giving it a go with a friend or family member and seeing how you get on.

Lens choice
You can use most lenses for portraits, from the tele-end of an 18-55mm kit lens to telezooms like a 55-200mm. Using a longer focal length provides a more flattering perspective than using a wide-angle and also produces a shallower depth-of-field, making it ideal for eye-grabbing portraits.

Portrait top tips
1) Shoot handheld It will enable you to move more freely and frame quicker. Better still, use a monopod. Using the maximum aperture provides the fastest possible shutter speed, but if it's still low, use the image stabiliser if your DSLR or lens has it and/or raise the ISO rating.
2) Check your distance At very wide apertures, you have to be careful not to move forward or backward after focusing as this will lead to an unsharp shot.
3) Eye contact Ensure that the subject's eyes are clean and make-up has been carefully applied. Try some shots with the subject looking into the lens and others with them looking away.
4) Use the shadows Pay attention to the lighting and to where the shadows fall, as they can add drama to an image.
5) Consider mono It's always worth converting your portraits to black & white and seeing how they compare to colour images. You may find them more striking.

Shooting distance
Both shots were taken using the same lens and aperture, but depth-of-field was altered by changing the shooting distance. The shorter distance gives less depth-of-field, which blurs the window blinds.

Differential focusing
Another popular technique when using shallow depth-of-field is differential focusing. It's a simple one to master but the secret is knowing when to use it. The basic principle is to use a very wide aperture to emphasise a particular subject within the frame by having it in focus while the rest of the scene (background or foreground) is out of focus. It's particularly effective when there is a lot of depth in the scene and you're using a wide aperture that blurs elements in the frame to the point that it's still recognisable. Use it to pick out a particular person in a crowd or to produce a creative portrait with a story to tell.

Hide and seek: These images illustrate the effect differential focusing has on an image. The same exposure was used in both shots but the focus was changed to reveal different elements in the scene.

Focus on nearest person

Focus on furthest person

4th Edition | The Essential Guide to Portraits

Understanding the basics | 27

Creative use of depth-of-field
Depth-of-field is one of the most creative in-camera tools, so think how you can use it to add an extra dimension to your images.

ISTOCK PHOTO

Master the art of selective focusing

Take control of your camera's point of focus to make your images more interesting. Here's how…

Caroline Wilkinson:
Part of the beauty of digital SLRs and CSCs is arguably the ability to control depth-of-field and determine what areas of a scene you want to appear in focus. You do this by adjusting your camera's aperture (the wider the aperture, the shallower the depth-of-field) and by manually selecting your autofocus point. Unless you take control of the AF system and select an individual point, the camera automatically uses whichever AF point(s) it decides is best, normally to focus on the subject closest to you. By being selective about what you focus on and how much depth-of-field you use, you can greatly improve your images, especially if it's a busy scene and you want to isolate a point of interest. It's a useful, aesthetically pleasing technique when done right, but very unforgiving if done wrong. If you use a wide aperture and your focusing isn't pin-point, the result can look awful.

Selective focus can be used almost anywhere and on anything to highlight the area of interest in your image, by blurring the rest of the surroundings. For portraits, you could use this technique to focus on the eyes, but that's rather conventional. Instead, add meaning, context and creativity to your portrait by making something else the point of interest, and the person a secondary feature. Both elements have to work together for it to become a quality portrait, so you need to find the correct aperture that doesn't blur the background (ie the person) out of recognition, but enough depth-of-field to isolate the focal point from the background. It's a tricky balance.

The point of interest doesn't have to be the closest thing to the camera either, but, on

Camera settings

(Av) **Exposure:** Set your camera to aperture-priority mode so that you can concentrate on finding the right aperture for the scene, letting the camera take care of the shutter speed. If you're handholding the camera, however, be careful that the shutter speed doesn't get too slow, causing camera shake. If this happens, increase the ISO rating and, if possible, place the camera on a tripod for extra stability.

□ AF-S **Focusing:** Set your camera to single-point AF and AF-S/S-AF mode so that when you partly depress the shutter release, the lens locks focus and remains locked on the subject until you release the shutter. As long as your subject stays still and you don't move forward or backwards, you'll get a sharp result. As default, the centre focus point is usually activated. To use it, focus lock and recompose (see panel) or select a point that's over the area of the frame you aim to keep sharp.

this occasion, it suited the image. Hands are very telling, especially those of an elderly person, and can be very photogenic subjects, with great detail and tonal range in the wrinkles and lines. Rarely are they made the focal point of an image, though. Here you can see that, by focusing on the hands with a wide aperture, using a standard 50mm lens and getting close to the subject, it's made them the feature and the person secondary. It's a far more creative and interesting image than if a small aperture was used to give front-to-back sharpness.

Focusing techniques

If your point of focus is off-centre, there are two ways you can handle it. As the central focusing point is the most sensitive, some photographers prefer to place it over the subject, lock focus and then recompose. However, if you or your subject moves slightly, they'll be rendered out of focus, unless you repeat the process. The alternative is to manually select the autofocus point that covers the point of interest in the scene. With this technique, you can concentrate on the aperture selection as you won't need to recompose the frame once you've set the AF point over the area of the subject you want sharp. Whichever method you use, ensure your camera's set to single-point AF and One-Shot or Single-Shot mode (S-AF/AF-S).

Here, the subject was placed by a window to create soft contrast with side-lighting. If it's too bright, a net curtain can diffuse the sunlight, or use a reflector on the other side of your subject to fill in the shadows. Set your camera to its widest aperture and stop down until you find the right balance for adequate depth-of-field.

❎ **Depth-of-field:** This is an average snapshot: taken at f/6.3 there's good depth-of-field making it unclear what is meant to be the focal point. Putting more thought into the composition can also help emphasise the real focal point – in this case the hands.

❎ **Focusing:** By opening the aperture to f/2.8 and distancing the book from the subject, depth-of-field is shallower but it means the plane of focus is much thinner, too. Here the focus point is on the book, resulting in the hands appearing unsharp.

❎ **Subject distance:** A change of viewpoint makes the picture more interesting but at f/5.6 there's still too much depth-of-field. As well as altering the aperture, you can also reduce depth-of-field by putting more distance between the focal point and the background.

❎ **Background clutter:** Before you press the shutter, remember to check the background for anything that can distract the eye from the subject. Adjust the viewpoint to exclude any unwanted elements in the frame, in this case the picture on the wall in the top left.

Final image
To finish this image (shot at f/1.4), a High Pass filter was applied to bring out detail in the lady's hands. First, duplicate the image and go to *Filter>High Pass*, setting 5 pixels, and then change the layer's *Blend Mode* to *Soft Light*. Follow this with a simple black & white conversion (*Layer>New Adjustment Layer>Black & White*).

D5200

I AM IMAGINATION

I AM THE NIKON D5200. I am your creative eye. With a vari-angle monitor, Full HD movie function and wireless connectivity with smart devices.* Experience superior image quality thanks to a 24.1 MP image sensor, an ISO range up to 6400 and 39 focus points. I am turning your imagination into images. **www.nikon.co.uk**

At the heart of the image

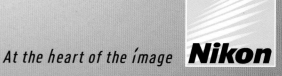 **Nikon**

NATURAL-LIGHT PORTRAITS

LEARN TO CONTROL YOUR CAMERA AND DAYLIGHT FOR FLATTERING PORTRAITS

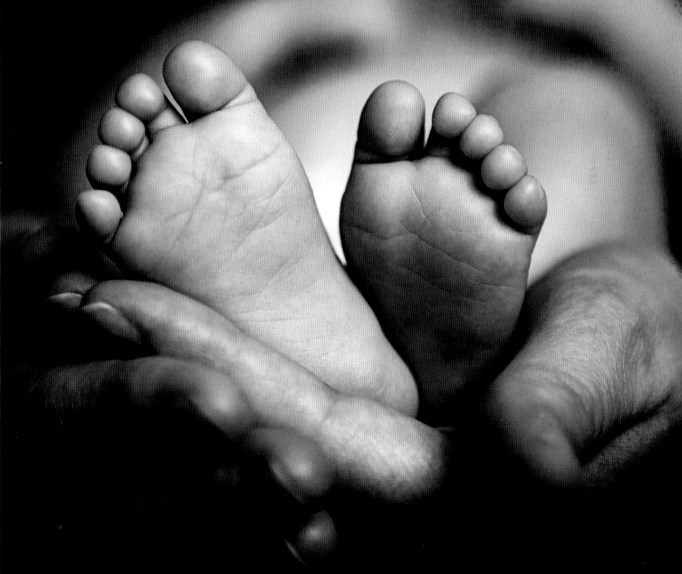

CONTROLLING SUNLIGHT

DAYLIGHT PORTRAITS

SHOOT SILHOUETTES

How to control daylight

Learning how to manipulate available light is an essential skill for portrait photographers to master

WORKING WITH DAYLIGHT has several advantages and disadvantages for the portrait photographer compared to artificial light sources such as studioflash and flashguns. Daylight is incredibly versatile: the range of images that are possible, depending on the weather and the time of day, and the wide variety of lighting effects are tremendous. And, let's not forget it's free! However, available light also has the problem of being unavailable – both at night or on days of particularly poor weather when light levels are too low to justify the effort.

One of the most wonderful things about working with daylight is that it allows you the chance to shoot outdoors in any location. Whether it's in the local park, a scrapyard or down by the coast, the options for great daylight portraits are limited only by your imagination and the ability you have to control daylight. And in the respect of the latter, despite the light source being millions of miles away, you still have plenty of control over how daylight falls on the subject simply through the use of basic lighting aids such as reflectors and diffusers. Over the following pages we'll show you how using the most basic lighting accessories and techniques can transform your daylight portraits. As you'll discover, investing in a reflector or two and a diffuser – should you be really keen on shooting outdoor portraits – will really help to improve your portrait pictures.

Setting up your camera for daylight portraits

Exposure Before you head outdoors, take a minute to prepare your DSLR so that once you're on location, you can begin shooting without delay. First, you should set your camera to aperture-priority mode as you'll want to ensure that depth-of-field is limited. We'd recommend you start by shooting at f/5.6. If shutter speeds are low enough to risk shake, raise the ISO rating to 400 and switch on image stabilisation if you have it.

Metering In terms of metering, you should find the multi-zone pattern to be perfectly adequate, but if you're shooting a dark-skinned person close-up, be prepared to add +1 to +2 stops of exposure compensation.

Focusing We'd suggest you switch from multi-point AF to central-point focus as otherwise you risk focusing on the subject's brows or nose, rather than the eyes. Point the central AF point over the eye and half-depress the shutter button to lock focus, then recompose and shoot.

Also consider... While you can shoot with the White Balance set to Auto (AWB), you're better off setting it once you've arrived at the scene to the most suitable preset, especially if you're shooting in only JPEG. We'd strongly recommend you shoot in Raw + JPEG, though; this way you can review the smaller JPEG images on your computer. Then open and process your Raw files for ultimate quality, including any adjustments to White Balance or exposure that you need to make.

Which lens is best?

Using a telephoto focal length, which flattens perspective, is the best choice as it gives the most flattering portraits. You can get away with using the tele-end of your standard zoom, but you'll find a telephoto zoom, such as a 55-200mm, is a far better choice. Alternatively, you could go 'old-school' and shoot with a prime lens such as a 50mm f/1.8 (effectively 75mm with APS-C sensors), which has the advantage of a wider maximum aperture than zooms.

Setting your camera for daylight portraits

Select aperture-priority, set the White Balance for the shooting conditions and centre-point AF. You're now ready to shoot!

CANON EOS DSLRS

1) Set the mode dial on the top-plate to Av to select aperture-priority mode.
2) Press the WB button and use the four-way control to select White Balance. Select the WB preset you want and then press the OK button.
3) Press the AF points button and select central-point AF.
4) Press the AF button and set AF mode to One Shot.

NIKON DSLRS

1) Set the mode dial on the right of the top-plate to A to select aperture-priority mode.
2) Press the i button and use the four-way control to select White Balance. Select the WB preset you want to use and then press the OK button.
3) Press i again and set the AF mode to AF-S and the AF-area mode to central-point only.

OLYMPUS E-SERIES

1) Set the mode dial on the right of the top-plate to A to select aperture-priority mode.
2) Press the OK button and use the four-way control to select White Balance. Select the WB preset you want to use and then press the OK button.
3) Press OK and set the AF mode to S-AF and the AF points to central-point only.

PENTAX K-SERIES

1) Set the mode dial on the top-plate to Av to select aperture-priority mode.
2) Press the OK button and use the four-way control to select White Balance. Select the WB preset you want to use and press the OK button.
3) Press the MENU button, then select the Rec. Mode tab and set the AF mode to AF-S. Then select the central AF point.

SONY ALPHA SERIES

1) Set the mode dial on the left of the top-plate to A to select aperture-priority.
2) Press the Fn button and use the four-way control to select White Balance. Press the AF button and select the WB preset you want to use. Now press the Fn button again, select Autofocus mode and select Spot in AF area and AF-S in Autofocus mode.

The great outdoors

Shooting portraits with daylight is a great way to get to grips with the fundamental techniques of lighting and to learn how to use aids such as reflectors and diffusers.

Main lighting accessories for daylight portraits

Unlike when shooting with studioflash, you cannot control the light's direction or intensity when working with daylight. But while you can't control the sun itself, by using reflectors, diffusers or a combination of the two, you can control the amount of daylight reaching your subject. Reflectors and diffusers come in various forms, with the most common covered here.

Reflectors This simple accessory is incredibly effective at filling in shadows and can make a major improvement to your portraits. The standard type – and the one you should begin with – has a white side and a silver side (1). The white side reflects a clean, neutral light and is ideal when you can place it relatively close to the subject, as it reflects an even spread of light. The silver is far more efficient, producing a stronger result, so can be overpowering in bright sunlight or if placed too close to the subject, but is ideal in very overcast conditions or when shooting in shade. Gold reflectors are also available and, like silver, are very efficient, but add a warm golden glow to the light. Look for collapsible reflectors as they're light and easy to store. The larger the reflector, the wider the area they cover – look for a

minimum diameter of 80cm and don't go too big as they can be cumbersome. Those with grips, such as Lastolite's TriGrip, are great when you have no assistance, as you can hold it with one hand. Other reflectors to check out are those with a silver and gold slip-on sleeve (2) or with a lightweight frame, such as the California Sunbounce (3).

Controlling bright sunlight

A bright summer's day may seem the ideal time to shoot outdoor portraits, but only if you know how to diffuse harsh sunlight to produce flattering results

THERE ARE MANY BENEFITS to taking photos outdoors on a day when the sky is blue and the sun is beaming. Light levels are very high, so you've a full range of apertures and shutter speeds to choose from, even with the ISO rating set to a low sensitivity for maximum image quality. Also, because the weather is warmer, subjects are happier to sit and pose for you and you've a full choice of outfits for them to wear. Plus, because the light is so bright, colours tend to be punchier and saturation higher, which all helps to add extra impact to images.

However, there are also drawbacks to take into account. The first is the most obvious: sunlight is very bright and direct, so if your subject is facing it, they will most likely be squinting and their face and chin will have harsh shadows, which amounts to a very unflattering portrait. Facing them away from the sun is one solution, but you'll then need to watch out for flare, as well as cope with a subject whose face is in deep shadow. The high contrast between the bright background and the subject also means that you'll have to be careful with metering to ensure that the subject isn't underexposed.

The other solution, which we illustrate here, is to use a diffuser panel, placed between the sun and the subject, to bathe the model in a far more flattering light. In effect, you're shading the subject from the sun, but using a diffuser offers a number of differences to placing the subject within a shaded location. The nature of light passing through a diffuser is very non-directional, much like shade, but because the light has passed through a white material, it's neutral, clean and retains a relatively high level of illumination. Whereas in the shade, the light is reflected off surfaces, which, if coloured, will influence the light falling on the subject. And, because the light has bounced off one or more surfaces, it will be dimmer, meaning you have less choice with exposure settings.

The other key difference is that by diffusing direct sunlight, you're not limited in terms of location. You can shoot from the middle of a garden, beach or park, or anywhere else that suits your fancy, as you're able to use the diffuser panel to control the light falling on the subject. And as the diffused light is even, you can shoot from any direction, therefore being able to place the subject against a backdrop of your choice.

Shooting into light

If you don't have a diffuser, you can try shooting with the sun to your subject's back and to find a position where the sun is obscured from view. Using the leaves of a tree is one option, or, as in this example, a wide-brimmed hat provides a very photogenic solution. Use a white reflector to bounce light back towards the subject and either use AE-Lock to take a reading from their face, or add between +1 to +2 stops of exposure compensation.

Sunlit step-by-step

For this simple step-by-step, Daniel Lezano took some pictures in a garden using a Lastolite Skylite, which is a large diffuser panel that requires at least one person to hold it. Smaller panels that are easier to handhold are available, but bear in mind that the area of diffused light will therefore also be smaller. For a truly budget-conscious diffuser, look at our suggested 5-in-1 reflector kit on page 159 for further details. As you'll see, reflectors also have their part to play in manipulating the light to help better illuminate the subject and produce the effect that you want. In this shoot, the camera was set to aperture-priority mode at f/5.6 (ISO 100) and White Balance to Daylight.

1 Set-up Here's the basic set-up for the pictures. We're shooting around 3pm so the sun's still very high in the sky, and the diffuser has to be held over Ruby's head. You can see the large area of diffused light it produces beneath her.

2 Test shot This is the result of this basic set-up. Because the sun is obscured by the panel, Ruby isn't squinting and as the diffuser is just above her head, her hair has an attractive highlight. However, while the light on her face is fairly even, there are still some faint shadows that need removing.

3 Add a reflector To add a little colour to the diffused light, I place a Lastolite Sunfire reflector on the grass within the diffused shade, angled up towards Ruby's face. It's a powerful reflector, but as I'm positioned under the panel, its effect doesn't cause Ruby to squint.

4 Spot-on lighting The resulting image is much better than the shot captured using the diffuser alone. The light from the Sunfire's surface has added warmth to Ruby's skin and has evened out the shadows. The result is more than satisfactory, but I'm not happy with the pose so I want to try something else.

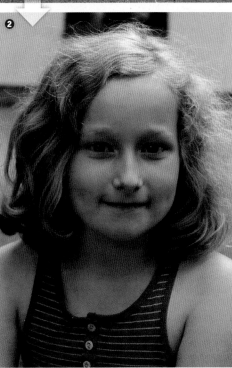

Final image

I ask Ruby to lie down on her front and I do the same. As she's very close to the Sunfire reflector, the effect is too strong, so I turn it over to the white surface. Its effect is far softer and more neutral and, along with the pose, gives a better result.

Shooting in overcast conditions

Cloudy days are a blessing in disguise for portrait photographers.
We show you how simple it is to manipulate Mother Nature's softbox...

ANYONE WHO LIVES IN THE UK will know we're blessed with more cloudy days than clear skies and sunshine, even in the summer months. For most, this might not sound an ideal scenario, but for a portrait photographer it's perfect; a blanket of grey cloud acts as a natural diffuser, providing even, malleable light for you to control with ease using lighting aids such as reflectors. A cloudy day offers the greatest scope for manipulating sunlight as the angle, strength and tone of the light hitting your subject simply depends on what type of reflector you choose to use and how it's positioned. As there is no direct sunlight to contend with, you're also free to place your subject anywhere you please, even at high noon, without having to worry about harsh sunlight creating unsightly shadows and stark highlights. As you're dealing with flat lighting, to add a summer feel to your shots, try to have your subject dress in brightly coloured clothing and find an environment with lots of colour impact, like a lush green field, or head to a garden filled with summer flowers.

How well your subject is lit doesn't always depend on your environment, but often your skill in using lighting aids. As the light will be descending through the clouds, it is a good idea to position the reflector below and angled upwards towards the subject to fill in any shadows. Also try varying the distance of the reflector from the subject to get the light intensity you're after. If you're dealing with young children, why not have them sit on the reflector? It will fill in any shadows by bouncing the maximum amount of light back onto the subject from the sky and it doubles up as a 'magic carpet' – ideal for keeping those little ones occupied long enough to rattle off a couple of frames. Looking around your environment for reflective surfaces, such as marble or white-coloured walls, can also be useful for bouncing light onto your subject: watch out for colour surfaces, though, as they will reflect coloured light.

There are several types of reflectors to choose from, with a 5-in-1 kit being the best option for beginners, as they include a gold, white and silver side that vary in reflectance. In some scenarios, though, you may find the silver reflector is too harsh and cool, while the gold is too warm. In cases like this, you may want to invest in a mixed reflector such as Lastolite's TriGrip Sunfire/Silver reflector, which Brett Harkness uses here in the following step-by-step.

BRETT HARKNESS

Create backlighting with flash

More often than not, bright sunshine won't make an appearance when you want it to. So, the next best thing is to use a flashgun. Mixing daylight with flash can, from a practical point of view, help fill in any shadows and, from a creative point of view, catapult your images to a new level of dynamism. It's a more advanced technique to tackle, but if you continue to practise it, you'll find it opens up a whole range of possibilities. One technique that you could try is placing a flashgun behind your subject to mimic a sunlit backlight. As your flash is off-camera, you'll need to be able to fire it wirelessly with a remote trigger. If you're trying this technique for the first time, set your camera to program mode and your flash to TTL. If you find that the flash effect is too low, boost its power by dialling in (positive) flash exposure compensation.

Handling overcast light

Working with kids is tough at the best of times, so shooting in overcast conditions is ideal because you can allow them to move around freely knowing you don't have to worry about harsh shadows or squinting in direct sunshine. We helped Brett Harkness on a typical lifestyle shoot as he worked his magic in very overcast lighting conditions.

Brett's model is a typical eight-year-old boy, unable to sit still for more than a few frames before running off to explore and play. The beauty of a cloudy sky means Brett can let him do this and then, when the opportunity arises for a good shot, simply manoeuvre a reflector to improve the quality of light. When photographing your kids, or someone else's, remember to have fun: you're more likely to get better shots of them if you succumb to a few games than if you force them to comply with your shoot.

1 Set up Having scouted the location for suitable backgrounds, Brett starts by sitting his subject in front of a green door and sets an aperture of f/5.6. As the light levels are low, we position a Lastolite Sunfire/Silver reflector to the side of him to create a little contrast from the flat, low light.

2 Test shot With his face in focus, Brett rattles off a few frames, encouraging the subject to give a few different expressions and to mess around with the grass. To get a more dynamic picture, Brett twists his camera to get a diagonal composition.

3 Alter position After letting the subject play for a while, Brett sits him on top of a mesh cage to stop him moving around. We hold two Lastolite TriGrip reflectors below and to the side of him to bounce the light descending from the sky. We use one close to him and the other further away to create slight contrast in his face.

Final image
Brett's series of images
captured a variety of
expressions and poses.
The reflectors worked a treat
with the lighting and we used
Levels to slightly boost contrast
to give us this final result.

How to take portraits under cover

If you're ever struggling to work with direct sunlight, an easy way to control the light is to shoot you subject in the shade. We show you how to go about it...

WHEN THE SUN IS STRONG and high in the sky, there's often nowhere to escape its harsh rays and high-contrast conditions. So if you're after a wide, smooth tonal range with limited contrast and better control but you don't have a diffuser, your best chance for success is to find cover in a spot of shade, such as under a tree or beside a building.

Placing your subject in some shade instantly improves lighting and gives you more control over the strength and direction of the ambient light. Just remember that the light will be softer, cooler and more diffused, so you'll also have lower light levels to consider, as well as potential colour casts.

As shade is naturally cooler than sunlight, as well as setting your White Balance to Shade, you may want to opt for a reflector that adds warmth, such as a gold reflector or Lastolite's Sunfire/Silver reflector. You will also need to be aware of surrounding colours, because dark surfaces absorb light while pale ones reflect it. Watch out for strong coloured surfaces, too, as they may reflect coloured light, so don't place your subject too close and be aware that you may need to adjust your White Balance settings appropriately, or shoot in Raw so you can correct any colour cast later.

When shooting in shade, you need to be aware of where the light is coming from, which can be tricky as it's likely to be bouncing off different surfaces like walls and floors at various angles, but with practice you'll learn how to master it. By placing your subject in the shade, an easy way to control the strength and direction of light is to vary the subject's distance from the shade and sun; the closer they are to leaving the shaded area, the stronger the light. You can further control light by moving a reflector towards or away from the subject. You can also control the contrast by where you position your subject – for instance, half in the light and half in the shadow, or with their back to the sun so that they're backlit. If you try the latter technique, position a reflector in front of your subject to reflect light onto the face to fill in any shadows. You could also try turning your back to the sun, and have your model face you – it will cast a very flattering, soft and low-contrast light over their face.

Learning how to work with shade is useful when shooting on sunny days, especially if you're dealing with subjects who are wearing clothes that are near white or black in tone, or are dark-skinned, as bright conditions can be an exposure nightmare.

White Balance

Most beginners keep their White Balance set to Auto and normally get good results, but selecting the White Balance to match the lighting conditions will provide a more accurate result. For instance, by setting AWB, a photograph in shade looks very blue, but changing the WB to Shade will provide a warmer result. You can take things even further by using the Custom WB setting or one of the other presets to produce images that deliberately have a warmer or cooler tone.

Shooting in shade

We asked pro photographer Brett Harkness to show us his process for shooting in shade. This alleyway was perfect; it offered some shade and the contained light meant it was soft and easily controllable. To get the right level of light on Emma, his model, he had her walk very slowly from inside the alley, towards him and the light until he was happy with how her face was illuminated.

1 Try different settings As light levels were low, Brett started with a wide aperture of f/4 and cranked up his ISO to 640 to generate a fast enough shutter speed to shoot handheld. The first few shots he took were good but even though the background is blurred, there's still a lot going on. Brett zoomed his lens in closer to make a tighter head-and-shoulder crop. Much better!

2 Experiment with poses For a different shot, he positioned Emma leaning against a wall but by moving her, the light on her face was reduced, so he brought in a reflector. We opted for the silver-strong side of the Lastolite reflector as it gave the strongest reflectance and filled in a lot of the shadows.

If you're using a wide aperture you need to be very careful where you place your focus point. Here, Brett has focused on Emma's eyes using selective focusing, which has thrown the foreground and background out of focus. The wall also provides useful lead-in lines to Emma's face, strengthening the composition.

Final image
We picked our favourite and converted it to black & white. Note how the shaded light produces beautifully smooth skin tones.

Shooting late in the day

Daniel Lezano reveals the challenges and rewards of shooting in the final minutes of the day's light

Daniel Lezano: The 'magic hour' is a phrase commonly used by landscape photographers to describe the period of time early in the morning or late in the day when the sun is so low in the sky that the light has a strong golden hue. For landscape images, this light can give scenes a three-dimensional feel as it creates shadows that reveal the depth and contours of the scenery. For portrait photography, this golden light adds warmth to a subject's skin tone and backdrop. You have to work fast, though, as you literally have minutes to take advantage of the setting sun before it disappears. You also need to be aware that you're at the mercy of the weather as, if it's cloudy, you will have little or no golden light to play with. However, if you are lucky enough to have this wonderful light appear, as well as shooting with the subject facing the light, it's also worth using the sunset as a colourful backdrop.

You're guaranteed soft light once the sun is low in the sky, as the entire scene will be in shade. This means you can work without any lighting aids, although even with low-light levels, you'll find reflectors still produce some illumination. The extra reflectance will come in useful when trying to avoid camera shake, as the very low light results in a longer shutter speed.

To provide an example, I headed to a park to capture some shots of a friend's daughter. Ruby has blonde curly hair – perfect for backlighting. Rather than go for colourful clothing, I arranged for Ruby to wear neutral tones to complement the natural colours of the scenery.

With such a short time period to work in, arrive at your location ten minutes ahead of when you plan to shoot to spot potential viewpoints and backgrounds. I decided on the bank of a pond, as it meant the horizon was unobstructed and I'd have the light for longer than if I was to shoot within the park where trees block the falling sun.

I took a white, silver and gold reflector, which Ruby's mum was happy to hold in position. The white reflector, while a favourite for most daylight shoots, might be too inefficient to bounce enough daylight when light levels fall very low. In which case, the silver or gold reflector could prove more useful, although care would need to be taken with the gold reflector when combined with the already golden light from the low sun that it doesn't create too warm a cast.

As with the majority of my portrait shoots, I used my DSLR (with 50mm f/1.8 lens) set to aperture-priority, with the initial aperture setting at f/5.6. The White Balance was set to AWB and I shot in Raw + JPEG to allow me to tweak WB if necessary in post-production.

Avoiding camera shake

Due to the relatively slow shutter speeds that occur when shooting at this time of day, avoiding camera shake should be at the forefront of your mind. The easiest way to do this is to use image stabilisation if your camera or lens has it, stick to a wide aperture of around f/4-5.6 and set the ISO rating to at least 400. You should also use a moderate telephoto lens of between 50mm and 100mm, rather than a longer telephoto, which increases the risk of shake. Using the reciprocal rule can help you determine when you run the risk of shake. To do this, ensure your shutter speed is at least equal or faster than the reciprocal of the lens in use. For instance, if you are using a focal length of 100mm, ensure the shutter speed is at least 1/100sec; at 200mm use 1/200sec or faster; and so on.

With the sun's orb still visible in the sky, I position Ruby in front of a pond, with her back to the sun, to make the most of the golden colours of the backdrop. While the low sun creates a glow in her hair, the glare effect is too strong, reducing contrast and adversely affecting the image.

I move Ruby to stand in front of a tree and try shooting from a variety of viewpoints, remembering to alternate the format by taking portrait and landscape images. The texture of the tree adds interest and the golden light from the sun, to Ruby's left, adds a lovely warmth to her skin.

Before the sun has completely set and the scene becomes totally shaded, the light still has a very slight touch of gold to it, adding colour to her hair. Positioning a white reflector to Ruby's left side allows me to bounce a little extra light in to fill any shadows, yet retain the skin's natural tones.

Going too gold!

Take care with the gold reflector: using it with a setting sun can overdo the warm effect, especially if the reflector is positioned too close to the subject. Save the gold for when the subject is in deep shade and try a silver or white reflector instead.

Final image
By moving further away from Ruby, I can use some of the scenery to add visual interest to the image. By shooting in an upright format and placing Ruby off-centre, I used the line of trees to lead the eye through the scene towards her.

Add flare to outdoor portraits

Pro photographer Paul Ward shows how deliberately letting the sun encroach in the frame to add a touch of flare can work with portraits

Paul Ward: Few things divide opinion like lens flare. Some photographers love it, while others abhor it, going to great lengths to avoid it. Lens flare is caused by direct light travelling through a lens and bouncing off its glass elements, usually having one of two effects: bleaching colours with a white haze, reducing contrast, and creating rings of colour (known as artefacts) that dart across the frame from the sun. Using a lens hood or shooting with your back to the sun helps avoid it, but lens manufacturers have developed such effective lens multi-coatings that it's difficult to create flare with some lenses. If you struggle, try an older uncoated lens: good quality secondhand manual-focus lenses can be picked up for just a few quid. Artefacts vary depending on the type of lens, too: flare from a

zoom will look very different from that of a prime lens, so experiment a little.

When using aperture-priority mode, you'll find that every time you change position, your exposure changes. You can avoid this by working in manual mode, but for the sake of beginners I'll show you how to achieve it in aperture-priority mode. Start with a test shot using between f/3.5-f/5.6 to get a shallow depth-of-field. The trick is to then position the model in front of the sun. Depending on how high the sun is, you might need to kneel and shoot from a lower than normal perspective. Winter, or early morning and evening, is perfect, as the sun is never that high in the sky. Nearly every lens produces flare if it's aimed in the direction of the sun, but it takes the right kind of lens to give artefacts, which gives pro photographers that stylised finish they like.

Old lenses can create flare

Often older lenses create better flare because they lack anti-flare multi-coatings. If you're lucky enough to have only new kit that's not proving very effective, have a look on eBay for a lens adaptor so you can buy an old lens to fit to your camera. I bought an 'M42 for Canon' adaptor and a 28mm Vivitar lens for £15 each. Car boot sales and secondhand stores are also good places to pick up a bargain lens.

1 Use a reflector As the subject is backlit, you can expect the multi-zone metering of your camera to produce an underexposed result. You could add positive exposure compensation, but there is another option. Using a reflector is an easy and effective way to bounce the sun's rays back on to the subject's face. A gold reflector gives a warmer light than a silver or white reflector, which suits this technique. If the model squints, have them close their eyes and then open them moments before you take the shot.

2 Focusing It can be tricky to autofocus on a subject when the sun is in the frame, as it causes a lack of contrast. To get around this, use the subject to block the sun and focus, keep the shutter button half-depressed to lock focus, and then move slightly to the side so the sun enters the frame. This can mess around with your exposure, so it takes a little trial and error. Depending on where you put the sun in the frame, it may cause too much flare, leading to blown-out highlights, so be patient and keep trying.

3 Exposure If the shots look too bright, dial in a couple of stops of negative exposure compensation or don't let as much sun encroach into the frame. If the shots are too dark, but the sun is in the frame as much you want it to be, dial in a couple of stops of positive exposure compensation. For this image, as the sun is just peeping past her head, I used two stops of positive exposure compensation to overexpose, but it's slightly too much. For the next shots, I try to replicate the position of the sun and use one stop of positive exposure compensation.

4 Different optics The Canon EF 24-70mm f/2.8L USM lens I've been using is so efficient at blocking flare that I'm struggling to get any artefacts in the picture, and am only getting the haze. The more I overexpose the shot, the more streaks of white flare expand across the subject's face, which is not the effect I want. I switch to my new, 20-year-old 28mm Vivitar lens (not anti-flare coated) to see if it does a better job. With the model in the same position, I take another shot that produces some excellent artefacts running across the picture, giving me the stylised effect I'm looking for.

Final image
There's a beautiful balance to the flare in this image, it's got the lens artefacts and a subtle whitewash that gives it a stylised spring finish.

Have a ball with backlighting at the beach

Silhouettes are graphic and simple to achieve: read on to get expert advice on how to capture your own

Ross Hoddinott: There's no better place to spend a warm, summer's evening than at the seaside. Maybe you like to surf, paddle or play – or simply relax by reading a book or topping up your tan. However, if you are heading to the beach with the family, whatever you do, don't forget your camera as there are endless photo opportunities to be had. Colourful skies are highly seductive and sunsets are particularly photogenic by the sea. With the sun so low in the sky, anything between you and the sun will be cast in silhouette. Personally, I love the simplicity of silhouetted subjects as they're rendered without colour or detail. Therefore, bold, easily recognisable shapes and outlines work best.

People are particularly photogenic silhouetted at sunset. The warm, evening light can create a romantic mood, so think about photographing a couple kissing with the sun setting behind. Children also make great subjects – holding hands with a parent, or just playing and having fun. You could try shooting candids on the beach, but ask permission first – particularly if photographing minors. However, you can apply far more control over the look of your results by photographing a family member or someone you know. Using a willing 'model' gives you the opportunity to experiment more, perfect your exposure and try again if your first attempts are unsuccessful.

With this in mind, I asked my sister if I could borrow my eight-year-old nephew for the evening. She enthusiastically agreed and while she poured herself a glass of wine and relaxed for an hour or two, Tom and I headed to the local beach with the promise of a large ice cream if he would happily let me photograph him having fun…

Exposure compensation

TTL metering systems are highly sophisticated and reliable. However, that doesn't mean that they don't make mistakes. In awkward lighting conditions – for example, backlighting – they can easily be deceived. By regularly viewing the histogram, any exposure error is easy to spot, as there will be a spike of data at one end of the graph. Correcting under- or overexposure is easy using your camera's exposure compensation button. If your images are too light, dial in negative (–) compensation; this will make the image darker. If your images are too dark, dial in positive (+) compensation to lighten results. You do this by pressing the +/– (exposure compensation) button and rotating the command dial until you have set the desired level of compensation. However, the way you select compensation will vary from camera to camera. Most cameras allow you to set compensation at up to three or five stops in 1/3 or 1/2-stop increments. Note: it doesn't automatically reset itself to 0 when you switch the camera off. Therefore, remember to reset compensation after you have finished shooting. Fail to do so and you will apply the compensation to future images, too.

1 Planning If you are visiting the beach to shoot silhouetted portraits, then plan carefully. Check the time of sunset, and its position, by visiting http://photoephemeris.com (or download the app The Photographer's Ephemeris). For safety, also check the time of high tide. Arrive an hour before sunset to give yourself time to set up before the best light and colour appears.

2 Set up Use a standard zoom as it's very versatile. I use a Nikon 24-70mm as its fast maximum aperture of f/2.8 provides a bright viewfinder image, aiding focusing and composition – perfect for low-light photography. Using aperture-priority, I set f/8 and opt for a low ISO of 200. With this image, shooting handheld allows you more creative freedom than using a tripod.

3 Posing By adopting a low angle and carefully aligning your model with the sun, you will be able to use your subject to obscure the sun's intensity and create an inky-black silhouette. However, with Tom standing on the wet, reflective sand and looking out to sea, the result is too static and posed. Overall, the shot is too dark, being at least a stop underexposed.

4 Exposure When shooting backlit subjects, the sun's intensity can fool multi-zone metering patterns into believing the scene is brighter than it is. As a result, the camera selects a faster shutter speed than required, resulting in underexposure. To compensate, I dialled in a stop of positive (+) exposure compensation. I also asked Tom to jump up to add motion to the image.

5 Composition Use trial and error or your camera's histogram to fine-tune the amount of exposure compensation needed. Once you're happy, turn your attention to composition. Props work well when photographing kids and help them to relax in front of the camera. I asked Tom to play catch with a ball, tilting the camera at a slight angle to add energy to the composition.

Final image
The combination of a beautiful sunset and an interesting pose makes this great image.

Use daylight to shoot a high-key portrait

Master a popular lighting technique with nothing more than a reflector and natural light

Caroline Wilkinson: Bright, fresh – even romantic – are all words that have been used to describe high-key portraits; shadowless images with an emphasis on highlights. But if you don't take a stylistic approach and use the correct technique, your final image might be more akin to a passport photo with a smile. This type of lighting suits the soft features of females and babies, and the bleaching effect hides a multitude of sins as it evens out skin tone, washes out blemishes and hides wrinkles.

If you were to use studioflash for this effect, you'd set up the lights to overexpose a white background and to fill in shadows on the model's face. But you can get equally good results with natural light and a reflector by sitting your subject in front of a window or open doorway and metering for their skin. You don't need a bright day, though it's easier if it is – this image was taken inside on an overcast day; you just need to be careful not to let your shutter speed get too slow. Pick a window or door facing east or west in the morning or afternoon; light from a north-facing window is usually ideal any time of day. Lastly, ask your subject to wear summery, soft colours like light pink and white.

1 Pick your window Choose a window large enough to give you sufficient background, with the view outside of the window clear and distant. If you have foliage or buildings nearby, your background will be coloured, not white. I used a large north-facing window, but had the subject sit on the windowsill so more of her torso is illuminated. I stood on a chair to get a more flattering downward viewpoint – take care if you do the same. You may need a reflector to bounce some light on to your model's face.

2 Dial in your settings Set your camera to shoot in Raw in case you need to recover detail in the highlights. In aperture-priority mode, dial in a starting aperture of f/5.6 and ISO 200. Switch to single-point AF and set the metering mode to spot. Compose your portrait, focusing on the eye closest to the camera to take an exposure reading. If the shutter speed is 1/60sec or slower, you need to open the aperture, increase the ISO rating, or both, to avoid camera shake. Once you're happy, take a test shot.

3 Add exposure compensation You may find that the background isn't bleached enough; if so, dial in one or two stops of positive exposure compensation. Always be aware of your shutter speed – increasing the exposure will lengthen your shutter speed. The amount of exposure compensation you add comes down to personal taste: do you want wraparound highlights or just a glowing backdrop but still with a defined outline of the subject? Experiment until you get the photo effect you want.

4 Post-process There shouldn't be much that needs to be done in Photoshop, other than a slight contrast boost using Levels, or maybe a bit of highlight recovery in Adobe Camera Raw if you've overexposed the image too much, and some sharpening. I converted my image to black & white, too, by adding a Black & White adjustment layer (*Layer>New Adjustment Layer>Black & White...*). Use the channel sliders, particularly the Red and Yellow, to adjust contrast and lighten skin tone.

Common errors to watch out for...

✗ Metering If you use multi-zone metering, the camera will take an average reading of the whole scene to get the 'correct' exposure. By using spot metering and taking a reading from the subject's skin, the face is correctly exposed but the background will be overexposed, as it's already brighter than the subject.

✗ Focusing Always make sure the eye closest to the camera is in focus, especially if you have to open up the aperture for minimal depth-of-field. Use the LCD monitor between shots to zoom in to the eyes to make sure they're sharp – especially if shutter speeds are low. Don't let it drop lower than 1/60sec as it will be very difficult to avoid camera shake.

✗ Background Objects such as trees by the window will give you a coloured background and restrict the light, resulting in longer exposures. If you don't add enough exposure compensation, you may find that areas of colour appear from distant objects. Increase the exposure if it doesn't ruin your lighting, or paint over these areas later in Photoshop.

Capture bath-time portraits

Use your bathtub as a makeshift giant softbox to capture beautiful natural-light portraits of the little people in your lives

Caroline Wilkinson: Short on studio space to shoot your little ones or trouble keeping them still long enough by a window to get a decent shot? You'll be surprised at the solution. If bath time is a happy time in your household, you can use this to your advantage as the bathtub is a great locale for capturing studio-esque portraits – unless you have a peach or avocado suite, that is. Finding an area of the house with clean, natural light where unflattering shadows, colour casts and messy backgrounds aren't a problem can be difficult, and getting your child to sit in that spot long enough to capture an angelic portrait makes it that much more challenging. As long as they're old enough to sit up on their own, a white bathtub keeps them contained and the tub works like a giant softbox and reflector; bouncing natural light off the white surfaces for bright, even illumination with a clean studio-like background. If your bathroom has limited light due to frosted or small windows, you could also use the sides of the bath to bounce flash off for similar results.

The toughest part of this technique is getting the child to interact with the camera and to compose a good portrait; standard bathtubs don't leave much room for negotiation. Bathrooms can be quite cold, too, especially if you've no water in the tub, so make sure the heating is on and/or your child's wearing clothes. They might think it's odd to have no water in the bath, so if they start acting up, run a shallow one for them to play in – just make sure you have a second adult on hand out of frame to prevent accidents as your attention will be distracted by the camera. Use whatever means necessary to get a smile from them, too: chocolate bribery works well, as does someone pulling faces or playing with toys behind your head for getting eye contact. But above all, make sure they have fun, otherwise you'll be lucky to get more than three frames off before bath time is over.

1 Set up Very little is needed for this technique: your camera, subject and perhaps a flashgun with a bounce function and tilting head, if light levels are low. You'll need a portrait lens, if not a macro lens, for this shoot, as you'll find space is limited and you'll need to crop out any handrails and the edge of the bath. For this shoot, a 50mm f/1.8 worked well, but a longer lens, such as a 100mm macro, would have made it even easier.

2 Assess the exposure A lot of white in your image may fool the camera into underexposing the picture. Set the camera to spot metering rather than multi-zone for better results, as the exposure will be based on where you focus: the face. Use aperture-priority mode and dial in a wide aperture of f/2.8-f/5.6 to maximise the light and blur the background. Use single-point autofocus and pinpoint the eye closest to the camera.

3 Change your angle Depending on how tall your child is and the focal length you use, you may need to alter your viewpoint to crop out any unwanted elements like tiles, toys or handrails. Even if you don't need to change your view, try it anyway by getting low so you get their eyes peeping over the bath, high for a more flattering angle or simply alternate between portrait and landscape orientation for different looks.

4 Edit the shots If you've exposed the image well enough, very little should need to be done, other than basic editing. To improve the contrast, I duplicated the image layer (*Layer>Duplicate Layer*) and changed the *Blend Mode* to *Soft Light*. A small adjustment to Levels (*Layer>New Adjustment Layer>Levels*), the addition of a High Pass filter (*Filter>Other>High Pass*) set to no more than 4px and a quick crop was all that was done.

Common errors to watch for...

✕ Inaccurate metering If your background is rendered grey rather than seamless white, make sure you've switched to spot metering. If that alone doesn't work, dial in a stop or two of positive exposure compensation. Use your camera's histogram to determine if the image is underexposed: you want to see the peaks biased to the right and a little to the left of the histogram.

✕ Bad focusing Using shallow depth-of-field means your focusing has to be pinpoint. As multi-point autofocus locks onto the closest subject to the camera, which for portraits is often the nose, manually placing a single AF point on the eye closest to the camera produces the best results. If you want both eyes in focus, you'll need to use at least f/5.6 for sufficient depth-of-field.

✕ Not enough light If shooting wide open and increasing your ISO as high as your camera's noise control allows doesn't give you a shutter speed fast enough to freeze movement or illuminate the bathtub sufficiently, you'll need a flashgun. Keep it simple by using TTL metering for a fill flash and turn the head so it bounces off the white ceiling or sides of the bath.

All smiles!
Who'd have known your bathtub could be used as a mini-person's studio? The bathroom in general is a great place for utilising natural softbox-esque light for any type of portrait.

Keep it simple and use daylight

Daniel Lezano shows how – with a few little tricks to make the most of the daylight – you can create fantastic lifestyle shots in your own home…

Daniel Lezano: Many leading lifestyle portrait photographers use nothing more than ambient daylight for the vast majority of their portrait shoots. So, when we have the benefits of bright, sunny days at our disposal, we should use it to capture some simple yet effective portraits of family and friends. The best thing about shooting lifestyle portraits is that you can do it with the minimum amount of equipment – your DSLR or CSC with a kit lens is enough – although I'm using my favourite optic, the humble (and cheap!) 50mm f/1.8 lens. Due to the unpredictable nature of daylight, lighting aids such as a reflector and a diffuser can come in handy, too, but aren't essential. The key thing to remember is that you want to capture a 'clean' image: in other words, try to keep the subject and the setting as simple as possible. I've opted for the classic combination of having my subject, Bethany, wear a white top and jeans, and shot her lying on my dining room's laminate flooring.

Shoot at a slant

One compositional trick that most lifestyle photographers apply to their images is to slant the camera so that the images are captured with an uneven horizon. This simple technique adds a little energy into the image and is very effective – just take care not to tilt the camera too far.

Focus with care!
You need to ensure your focusing is precise, as using a wide aperture – which gives limited depth-of-field – leaves little margin for error. Select single-point AF, lock the focus on the eye and recompose

My dining room is quite small, so I've had to clear it completely of furniture. As my subject will be lying on the floor, I vacuum it to ensure it's as clean as possible. Due to the cramped space, I open the patio doors in case I need to shoot from the patio. However, I'll start by shooting from within the room and use the white walls as a neutral backdrop. Using a wide aperture to give a shallow depth-of-field is ideal for this type of shot and I'll be trying out my 50mm's maximum aperture of f/1.8, although I'll take most of the images at f/2.5-3.5 as it will improve sharpness.

Diffused daylight

For flattering portraits, the light should be as diffused as possible to avoid your model squinting in direct sunlight or having the light on their face too harsh. In this instance, try to reposition them so they're in the shade or use a diffuser to shade the scene (inset right). If neither of these work, you may need to wait until the sun's position changes or shoot when the sky is more overcast. A silver reflector is handy, even when shooting in non-directional light, to fill in shadows.

1 Test shot My first frame is just to test composition and exposure. I've a clear idea of the type of shot I'm looking to get with Bethany lying down with her lower legs and feet bent back towards her head. This shot isn't bad, but the side-lighting causes her right side to be too dark.

2 Use a reflector I place a silver reflector to Bethany's right, just out of frame, and it makes a noticeable difference; bouncing back enough light to even out the light on her face. The lighting's better, but the wall behind causes the whole scene to appear a little too cramped for my liking.

Final image
My next shot is perfect and all I need to do is apply minimal post-production. I've boosted the contrast in Curves and cropped the image slightly to give me the result I set out to shoot. Give it a try – you'll be surprised just how easy it is to shoot a great lifestyle portrait at home.

3 Change backgrounds I shift Bethany and my position so that I'm now shooting into the room from the patio. I close the blinds in the room behind to darken the background. The empty space created behind her is an improvement over the original set-up, but my viewpoint is too high.

4 Different viewpoint I crouch down and the lower viewpoint is far better. However, the multi-zone meter has bleached Bethany's face due to the dark background causing it to overexpose the scene. To correct this, I dial in negative exposure compensation. I find -2/3EV is ideal.

How to shoot baby portraits

The ups and downs, techniques and tools for photographing those special bundles of joy

THE ARRIVAL OF A new baby is one of those special moments in life that any proud parent will want to capture and cherish. Before you know it they will be walking and talking, and those first months will be confined to memory. Babies stay small for a surprisingly short period of time, so take a moment to capture the details while they are tiny. Concentrate on hands, feet and facial features, such as their eyes, ears and nose, using a wide aperture to isolate the details. A nice touch is including the parents in some of these shots to give a sense of scale – for example, the baby gripping Mum or Dad's finger, or holding the baby's foot in their hands as our step-by-step over the page shows. You'll need patience, understanding and a bit of luck on your side, but persevere and you can capture some great images.

Working with babies

When photographing babies, patience is a valuable asset. Rarely will you get the shot you want when you want it. Come prepared with a bank of different ideas and be prepared to change direction at any moment; very often, your session will not go to plan. Ultimately, the shoot will be dictated by the baby's mood, temperature, whether they are hungry, tired or need changing. Sometimes you feel like you are along for the ride, and the truth of it is, you are. The best you can do is be prepared, patient and work quickly within the baby's schedule.

Top tip

To keep the baby, or babies, comfortable, crank up the room temperature and avoid draughty areas. It's popular to photograph babies semi or fully naked, but check with the parents first to make sure that they are happy for you to do this.

Two in a bed...
Twins present an interesting challenge but can lead to some great results.

Choosing the correct lens

Prime lens: A 50mm prime lens is a must-have for any portrait photographer. The Canon EF 50mm f/1.8 II or original Nikon NIKKOR 50mm f/1.8D AF can be picked up for £100, whereas the newer Nikon NIKKOR AF-S 50mm f/1.8G comes in at £150. For a little bit more, consider the £370 Sigma 50mm f/1.4 EX DG HSM, which allows you to shoot handheld in very low light. Prime lenses with large maximum apertures allow you to achieve a shallow depth-of-field, ideal for baby portraits.

Zoom lens: A zoom lens is more versatile than a prime lens as you're not restricted to a single focal length, but if you want a high-quality optic with a large maximum aperture, equivalent to a prime lens, be prepared to part with some serious cash. The Canon EF 24-70mm f/2.8L is a popular choice but costs around £1,500. The £320 Tamron 28-75mm f/2.8 XR Di LD is a good alternative, but you can still get good results using your 18-55mm or 18-105mm kit lens; you'll just lack the extreme shallow depth-of-field.

 Wide-angle lens: You can capture some really fun shots with a wide-angle lens, but you need to be careful because it can stretch perspective, which isn't very flattering for portraits. The £370 Sigma 10-20mm f/4-5.6 EX DC HSM is a popular choice and is available to fit most cameras. Other options include the Canon EF-S 10-22mm f/3.5-4.5 USM at £625 and the £600 Nikon AF-S DX NIKKOR 10-24mm f/3.5-4.5G ED. All three offer a 24cm minimum focusing distance, so allow you to get nice and close to your subject.

My baby portrait...

Jordan Butters: Photographing babies is best suited to soft, diffused lighting conditions. If you are using window light, try to position both parent and child near a large north- or south-facing window to avoid direct sunlight. If necessary, use a reflector to bounce some light back onto the baby to fill in shadows. If you can't avoid direct light then you can use net curtains or hang some muslin or a bed sheet in front of the window to soften the light. Alternatively, some reflectors double up as diffusers, too. Avoid using on-camera flash if possible – however, if this unavoidable, bounce the flash off a wall or ceiling.

Remember when shooting at wide apertures that your band of focus is very narrow, making it easy to miss your mark, especially if the baby moves and kicks their feet. Pick your moment and be prepared to take several shots before you get your final image.

1 Position the baby Babies tend to kick and wriggle when they are awake, so asking for the help of a parent or friend to occupy their attention is often a good idea, allowing you the freedom to concentrate on getting the shot. For this image, I asked baby George's mother to sit back with him in her lap, cupping his feet in her hands. Not only did being in his mother's arms put him at ease and stop him from moving about too much, it also helped create a sense of scale between her hands and his feet.

2 Experiment with apertures Using aperture-priority mode, select a wide aperture and single-point autofocus in order to selectively focus on the area of interest before recomposing the shot. Choose too wide an aperture and you might not get both feet in focus; too small and the background could become distracting. I chose a final aperture of f/2.8, which allowed me to get both feet in focus whilst achieving a shallow depth-of-field, rendering the background out of focus.

3 Be careful of the exposure As I wanted a low-key image, I asked George's mum to wear a dark top, which acted as the backdrop. If you choose multi-zone metering, the camera will try to compensate for the dark background, overexposing the image. If this happens, you can dial in a touch of negative exposure compensation to correct it, or use spot metering to take an exposure reading from the baby's skin, ensuring that the most important areas are metered for.

4 Finishing touches Use a Gradient Map in Photoshop to convert the image to black and white. In the Layers palette, click on the **Add new adjustment layer** button and select **Gradient Map**. In the Adjustments palette, choose the **black to white** gradient. You can alter the strength of the gradient to adjust the dark, mid-tone and light areas of the image independently. The mono conversion should hide most skin blemishes, but I also use the Healing Brush Tool to tidy up any remaining marks.

Baby details: More great ideas to try

■ Try using Props
Props are very on-trend in baby photography at present. Hats are a popular choice – not only do babies look adorable in them, but they can also help to disguise a misshapen head or patchy hair; common issues with newborns. Also consider sitting or laying the baby in items that add interest to your shots, such as a basket or an old vintage suitcase.

■ Differential focusing
Try switching focus between two points from the same viewpoint by aiming at the area you wish to be in focus and half-depressing the shutter button before recomposing the shot. Use a wide aperture for a shallow depth-of-field. The results can be combined as a diptych to display both the baby's portrait and a detail shot in the same frame.

■ Background
The best solution is often a soft blanket or throw draped over a settee for the baby to lay on. You could choose to inject some bold colour by laying them on a bright throw. Use cushions as support under the blanket, or ask one of the parents to sit with the blanket on their lap, so they can support the baby. A newborn's skin is sensitive, so choose a soft fabric.

■ Include the parents
Remember to include the parents by gathering the family together to fuss over the child. People can quickly forget you are there when they are cooing over the new baby, allowing you to get some fantastic natural shots of the family together. Alternatively, try a wide-angle lens for a fun family portrait, or how about a mono shot of Mum and baby?

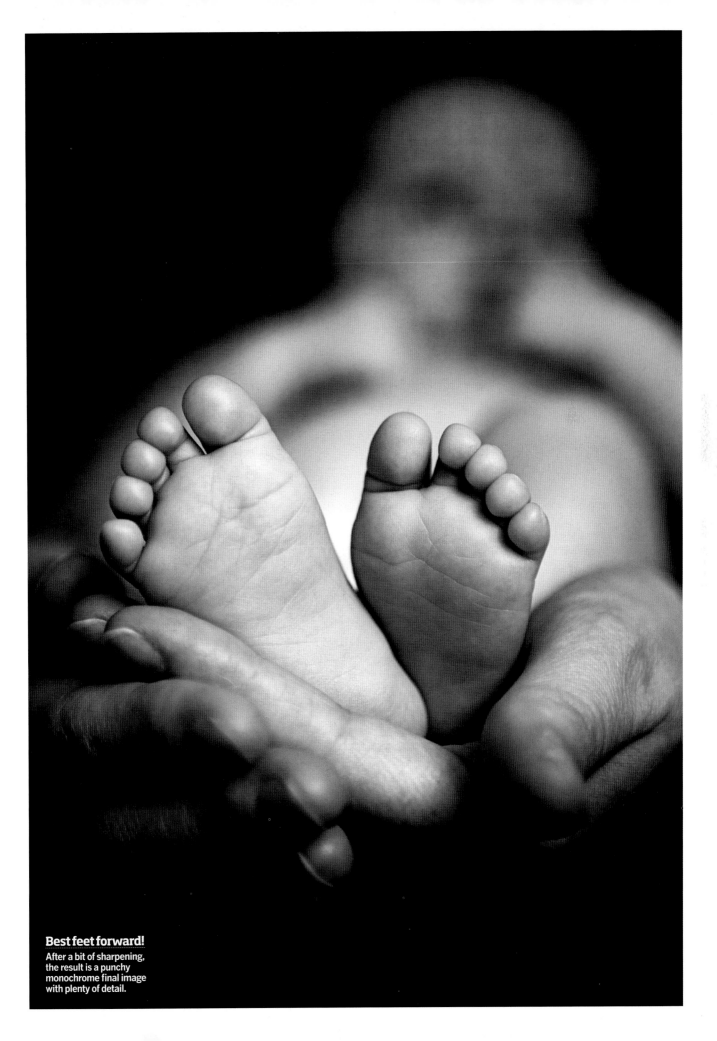

Best feet forward!
After a bit of sharpening,
the result is a punchy
monochrome final image
with plenty of detail.

CHILD PORTRAITS

Portraiture is one of the most popular types of photography and also one of the most exciting and fluid, as new styles and techniques are developed and introduced by innovators in the field. Professional photographer Brett Harkness is fast gaining a reputation as one of the UK's most creative portrait photographers and in this guide, he shares some of his favourite techniques for capturing wonderful contemporary lifestyle portraits of children

Get ready for lifestyle portraits

First things first, Brett reveals the professionals' tips to producing the best lifestyle portraits, so you can recreate the mood for yourself...

"SIT UNDER THESE LIGHTS in front of the white background and smile" may sound interesting and fun if you are photographing your grandparents, but in the manic world of children's photography, you should ensure the shoot is as far away from this scenario as possible.

At our studio just outside Manchester, we often get asked if we can do shoots in the studio, but once we have sat down with the clients and they see how much fun an outdoor shoot can be, their minds are usually changed. For me, shooting on location is all about getting the most out of the kids with the greatest of ease (or at least making it look that way!). That comes with knowing my equipment inside out, having faith in my assistant, being able to work with the kids and most of all having the ability to keep my patience no matter what happens. With some shoots, the best images may be taken at the end of a three-hour shoot! Because the secret to taking a great set of lifestyle portraits is spontaneity and thinking on your feet, there is no 'tried and tested' way of capturing great images – it's all in the relationship you build, having a sharp eye and knowing your gear inside out. You must work fast, so stick to using a couple of zooms for the majority of the shots. With experience, you get to know which focal lengths you need and when to swap so that you don't miss a shot.

Biography Brett Harkness

From their beautiful converted 'woodmill' studio in the outskirts of Manchester, Brett Harkness and his partner Kristie run a highly successful photography business. Brett has made a name for himself over the years for his brilliant contemporary portraiture and is regarded in photographic circles as one of the most innovative and exciting talents to come from the UK. As well as taking pictures, Brett's studio runs a series of training courses covering a wide range of subjects including portraits, weddings and lighting. He also provides DVD tutorials.

For further information, visit: www.brettharknessphotography.co.uk

☑ Brett's portrait kit
Camera: Canon EOS-1Ds Mk II
Lenses: Canon 70-200mm f/2.8L IS; 24-70mm f/2.8L IS; 50mm f/2.5 macro
Accessories: Lastolite reflector; Canon Speedlite 580EX flash

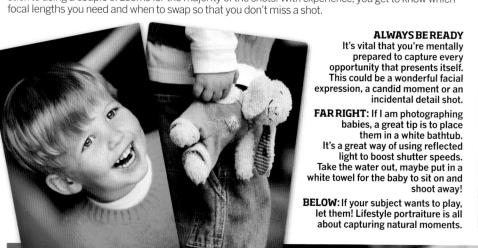

ALWAYS BE READY
It's vital that you're mentally prepared to capture every opportunity that presents itself. This could be a wonderful facial expression, a candid moment or an incidental detail shot.

FAR RIGHT: If I am photographing babies, a great tip is to place them in a white bathtub. It's a great way of using reflected light to boost shutter speeds. Take the water out, maybe put in a white towel for the baby to sit on and shoot away!

BELOW: If your subject wants to play, let them! Lifestyle portraiture is all about capturing natural moments.

Lifestyle case study

Here, Brett recalls a lifestyle shoot that didn't go to plan, but turned out all the better for it...

I THOUGHT I'D RECOUNT a day out to give you an idea of how one session worked so well, even when the weather took a turn for the worse. We had a fantastic shoot on the hills above Yorkshire. We turned up, had a cup of tea and went for a walk to search out locations, so at least we could guide the shoot to another background if need be. The little girl, Molly, had plenty of time to get used to us while we looked around. We started off shooting pictures in a shed at the bottom of the garden. The light in its doorway was perfect and it was a great place to begin.

We then did a few shots by the front door of the house. Front doors give you a great opportunity to bring some colour into your shoot. Here, the step was used to sit the child down and Kristie, my assistant, chatted with her to take her mind off things. Another great way to distract children's minds is to get them to pick flowers – sometimes some of the best moments are when the kids aren't looking at the camera and when they wander off to another place in their minds. For me, photography of this nature is 60% ability, 30% psychology and 10% technical know-how.

It started raining, so we went back to the house to do a few shots inside. Choose a room where there is sufficient light coming through a window to enable you to shoot handheld. You will have to increase your ISO to at least 800 or above or use image stabilisation. This is when shorter focal lengths and faster f/2.8 lenses come into play. Indoors, I tend to use a 24-70mm f/2.8L and a 50mm f/2.5 lens. Once it stopped raining, we moved the shoot outside and headed for a farmer's field up on the hills. I could see the light was changing: the clouds were moving in and the sun was peeping through the gaps – the type of light you can usually only dream of in the UK. I reverted back to my 70-200mm f/2.8L IS lens and lowered my ISO to 400 to give the files better clarity and detail.

This part of the shoot was not planned, it just happened. Sometimes all the planning in the world can't prepare you for backgrounds and light like this. The series of shots were taken in about ten minutes as the clouds swept over and the sky turned black! I had to work quickly while keeping the shoot fun. I wanted to get some good depth-of-field, so used a mid-aperture setting of f/8. The exposure for all of these frames was 1/500sec at f/8 (ISO 400). These images are some of the best lifestyle shots I've ever taken as they encapsulate everything about Molly at this age. They show a time in her life when she is care-free, having pure childhood fun! All we did was put in her in the right light, the right background and let her do the rest!

Let your subject have fun – if they're free to play and enjoy themselves then you'll get better pictures. Here, a low viewpoint worked a treat.

Family fun on the beach

The secrets to success lie in the preparation before the shoot and building a rapport with your subjects, says Brett Harkness

I HAD A GREAT DAY at Fleetwood, which is an hour or so's drive from my studio near Manchester. As I always do for this type of shoot, I had the family come to the studio first, for a coffee and a chat and also to give a chance for the kids to meet me and my wife Kristie, who assists me on this type of shoot. As part of our routine, the parents will have a coffee with Kristie, while I go for a quick wander around the studio with the kids. Their curious nature means they enjoy looking around, so it allows me to establish a bond with them. While walking around, I take a few shots of them, which gets them used to the camera. I'll always take their picture in a doorway by my studio, which I call my 'three feet of magic' as its always beautifully lit.

When it comes to what the kids wear, I leave Kristie to run through the choices with the child's parents over coffee. When they come to the studio, they'll have been asked to literally bring the wardrobe with them! I'll spend a few hours taking pictures and will be looking at a change of outfit after an hour or so. Kristie knows what I like – I prefer strong colours or bold stripes on dark days, while in summer, I like more muted colours so that the clothes have less influence over the images.

The beach here is excellent as the kids are free to roam, allowing me to shoot candids using my Canon 70-200mm zoom. I don't have any preconceived shots in mind. The entire day's shoot depends on the light. If it's overcast I've no problems with harsh light, but when it's sunny, there's a great little pier that makes for an interesting backdrop and provides beautiful shade. To entice the kids here, Kristie places some shells in the shade and leads them there to play games with them. She'll be careful to stay out of shot, but her interaction is essential to take the kids' minds off me taking their pictures. Another trick is to dig a hole in the sand and ask the family to walk towards it. I lie on my belly and take their picture and the shots look natural as their eyes are on the hole and not me. As they reach the hole I ask them to jump over it and capture them laughing and smiling as they're in mid-air.

There are no set rules, as every child acts differently, but I've learned the best ways to manipulate the situation to get the best pictures and I think that's been a key factor in my success at this type of photography. The most important thing is to capture images that the parents cannot produce themselves. A lot of people think they can take great pictures of their kids simply because they own a camera, but it's not that easy. You can't just plonk a kid into a location and get great shots. You have to push your creativity, try using tough lighting, change the backgrounds and so on. You have to make it hard for yourself as a photographer and that way you'll get the most out of your subject. Take the easy route and you won't produce anything different from what other people are doing.

Top: It's easiest to 'Velcro' the kids to a spot by having the parents in the frame and taking a family portrait.

Left: Having a child in shade but backlit by the sun is great for rimlighting hair.

Below: Shoot toddlers exploring the location and don't worry if they're not looking at the camera. Parents love these types of images as they capture 'real' moments.

Once I've gained the child's trust, I swap the telezoom for a wide-angle and get in closer. If there's a good sky, I use fill-in flash and set -2EV on exposure compensation to darken the backdrop.

Beach shoot: Summary

✔ Base your shoot around the toddler's sleeping and feeding schedule. Have everything ready for when they're awake/fed so that you make full use of the time at your disposal.

✔ A female assistant is ideal for helping choose clothes and for bonding with young children.

✔ Don't try to preconceive shots but be ready to grab the shots as they happen.

✔ Shoot a few family shots as the parents will treasure them!

Lifestyle inspiration

To conclude Brett's inspirational guide to kids' lifestyle portraits, he provides an insight into the techniques behind some of his recent shoots

IF THE WINTER IS rolling in, you must organise your lifestyle shoot earlier in the day to capitalise on any light available. Make sure that the kids are well wrapped up – colourful hats and scarves are a great way to frame faces and bring some colour into the shoot.

Allow the kids to do what they want. If you try to sit them down too early to get that 'close-up face shot', then they will be off; sit them down too late and they will lose interest! Timing is essential. You have to constantly change the goal posts and use other stimuli to keep them interested and give you what you need.

Bringing props into the shoot can also work, as in the shot below where we brought the young girl's moped into the frame to give her something to lean on. Using family pets is also a great way to keep the shoot rolling. They mean a lot to the owners and they will almost always love to include them in the shoot.

If you are really struggling with the weather and the kids/family just don't want to go outside, then there is a great way of getting some good indoor shots and keeping it in one room. Go upstairs to the bedroom and open all the curtains, allowing as much light into the room as possible. Clear away any clutter; make the bed! Get the family on the bed and using high ISOs such as 800-1600 and a short focal length lens like a 18-55mm, you will get some fantastic shots. Just let them play and have fun. It is testing for you as a photographer but the results can be fantastic.

You'll find the shoot almost becomes more like a documentary of the family or kids rather than staged, posed images. Sometimes I choose slowish shutter-speeds. I like 1/50 or 1/80sec to give me some movement within the image; any blur is the result of subject movement and not poor focus. This can give the images more atmosphere and emotion.

When I'm working like this, I'm going back to what photography, for me anyway, is all about. Letting the subject do the work, see how they interact with me and what they are willing to give is what makes it special. Making sure I am there, ready: right exposure, right lens, right light, right framing... Not much to get right really! But when I do, it is the best feeling ever.

> "Timing is essential. You have to constantly change the goal posts and use other stimuli to keep them interested and give you what you need"

If you're shooting indoors, have the family play on a bed and capture the fun. Also make sure to record every mood, from pensive thought to tantrums to playful activity.

Family values

Make sure you include the whole family in shots as they will usually prove popular with the relatives. If you're shooting a commission, this could mean several extra sales in prints

Brett's lifestyle portrait tips

✔ **Have fun!** Keep the shoot fun. If it means you have to put down your camera for a while and become the entertainment then so be it! Shoot quickly: bored kids will give you nothing. Take their minds off the fact that they are having their pictures taken!

✔ **Minimise lens choice** Things happen so quickly when photographing children. If you are changing lenses all the time you will miss the best moments.

✔ **Use a reflector when you can** We will always use a reflector when we can on lifestyle shoots. Obviously when the subject is sitting down we can use it to throw some great light back onto their face. Small children can sit on it; not only is it a great way to illuminate the subject but also a magic carpet that can take you to fantastic places!

✔ **Try something different** Once you have taken the usual shots, try something different, either by the way you frame the subject, the lenses that you choose or the backgrounds or light that you use. It is keeping things fresh like this that will take your photography forward and mean that you are a frontrunner in the lifestyle portrait market and not bringing up the rear!

✔ **Keep it simple** Try to have a basic plan as to where you are going with the shoot. Look for different backgrounds and bring some colour in to your images.

✔ **Be quick!** Especially if you are working with babies, as they will lose interest after about 20 minutes if that – they will need to eat, sleep and poo... Maybe not in that order! Make sure you have a flexible plan in mind, although things can change. Know when to bring a shoot to an end as there is no point carrying on if you have the shots anyway.

✔ **Get dirty!** Part of the fun of the shoot and getting the most from the shoot is if you do most of what the kids are doing. If you lie down in the mud then you are going to get the kids on side quicker. You may end up forking out for the dry cleaning bills but it will be worth it!

Props and locations play a very important role in lifestyle portraits and you should always be on the lookout for what you can include in the frame. When I'm out and about with my subjects, I'm always keeping an eye out for suitable places to have children sit or stand: front doors are a favourite of mine! And when it comes to clothing, have your subject change outfits during the shoot to add variety. Try a plain outfit for one session and a colourful or patterned outfit for another.

FLASH& STUDIOFLASH

YOUR COMPLETE GUIDE TO LIGHTING PORTRAITS WITH FLASH INDOORS AND OUT

STUDIOFLASH TECHNIQUES

MASTER OUTDOOR FLASH

CREATIVE LIGHTING TIPS

Fundamentals of flash

If you're looking to take control of your flash photography, the first thing you need to do is discover what flash modes and functions are at your disposal and understand when and how to use them

IN THE PAST, you had the option of two flash modes: on and off. You couldn't really get simpler than that! Today, you've all sorts of modes available that can seem bewildering to beginners and even prove baffling to experienced photographers. What's important for you to remember is that every flash mode has its uses for particular types of subject, so it's essential you know when, as well as how, to use them. The great thing with digital, of course, is that you can try out all the various modes and keep practising until you've got the hang of it. As you'll discover, once you try out each mode in turn, you'll soon learn what it's best for and how you can make the most of it. We've set out the guide to cover all the more straightforward flash modes first and will cover the more creative options later. We've also provided essential information panels that cover flash terminology and useful accessories to help you make the most of your flashgun.

Why you need to buy a dedicated flashgun

Almost all digital SLRs have an integral flashgun, while most CSCs have either a built-in flash or a clip-on unit supplied with the camera. So why buy an additional unit? There are several reasons why, but here are the three main advantages of using a dedicated flashgun:

Power: The output from a built-in flash is good enough for shooting subjects within a couple of metres' range, but won't extend further. Hotshoe-mounted flashguns are far more powerful, allowing you to expose subjects several metres away.

Features: Your built-in flash has several modes on offer, but can't match the sophistication of a separate unit. As well as the bounce head, there are additional modes on offer that allow for more creative flash photography.

Flexibility: The fact you can use a dedicated flashgun off-camera opens up a wealth of possibilities. You can also combine several flashguns for a multiple lighting set-up to rival what's possible from a studioflash system, but in a far more portable outfit.

Anatomy panel: Know your way around a flashgun...

AF assist
Some DSLRs have an AF assist lamp on the body, but this is overridden by the AF assist on a flashgun as it has a better range

1) Flash head: Your flash head will most likely angle vertically and horizontally: an action commonly referred to as bounce and swivel actions. Most flashguns have a zoom head, where the light coverage changes to suit the lens in use to optimise the range.

2) AF assist lamp: In low light, you may see a red patterned beam emitted by the flashgun to help the camera lock focus.

3) Built-in diffuser/reflector: Slide out the diffuser and drop it in place over the flash window to soften the light, or use the reflector to redirect some of the flash output.

4) External power socket: Many mid- to top-end flashgun models accept an external power source.

5) LCD monitor: The sophistication of its features means that many flashguns have an LCD panel offering a wealth of information about what modes have been selected, as well as a flash-distance scale to give you a visual representation of the flash range at your current chosen settings.

6) Control buttons: The advanced features on flashguns mean there are a large number of buttons, with most controlling more than one function. You're advised to spend a little time getting used to the layout, as they're not always straightforward to use.

7) Hotshoe fitting: The hotshoe fitting has pins that touch contacts on the camera's hotshoe to communicate information and trigger the flash when the shutter is released. All DSLR hotshoes follow the same design, with the exception of Sony's Alpha series. Some CSCs have accessory shoes, while others lack this facility.

8) Ready/test lamp: Most models have a two-stage lamp that lights green then red to indicate partial and full charge. With many, you can press this lamp to test-fire the flash.

9) Locking mechanism: This facility prevents your flash slipping off the hotshoe by locking it in place.

10) Stand: Many flashguns that sport a wireless facility come supplied with a stand that allows the flashgun to be positioned, ready for use off-camera. An alternative is to buy a ball & socket tripod head, like the £25 Cullmann CB2 (www.newprouk.co.uk), which allows you to precisely position the flashgun while mounted on a lighting stand or tripod.

Common flash terms explained

■ **TTL flash metering:** Your camera uses Through The Lens (TTL) metering to ensure accurate exposures. Most cameras use the multi-zone pattern as the basis for exposure calculation, with some offering the option via a Custom Function to switch to using centre-weighted metering. Some systems fire a 'pre-flash' to aid exposures and others even boast a Flash Exposure Lock (FE-Lock) facility that allows you to take a spot reading using flash when shooting in particularly tricky shooting situations. For the vast majority of pictures, you can rely on the standard TTL system to give good results.

■ **Red-eye:** We've all experienced red-eye in our flash photos – the red you see is the reflection of the flash off the blood vessels in the retinas at the back of the eyes. If the red-eye reduction mode of the camera doesn't work, you can easily reduce or remove the problem using one of the techniques covered later in this guide.

■ **Flash-sync speed:** Your camera has a shutter speed at which it synchronises with the flash, usually between 1/90sec and 1/250sec. You can select a shutter speed slower than this, but not one faster, as this can lead to part of your image appearing black.

■ **Guide Number:** The Guide Number (GN) is an indication of the flashgun's power: the higher the Guide Number, the more powerful it is. It's often stated as a number followed by (ISO 100, m), which is an indication of its power in metres when used at a particular ISO setting. It's rare that you'll be required to calculate a flash exposure, but if you do, set the camera to manual, the shutter speed to its sync speed and calculate the exposure with this simple formula: Aperture = Guide Number / subject-to-flash distance. So, if your subject is ten metres from the flash and your Guide Number is 40, you need to set an aperture of f/4. Most built-in units have a GN of around 12, while most dedicated flashguns vary from 28 to over 50!

■ **Master and slave flash:** If you're using a multiple flash set-up, you'll use a master flashgun to control the slave flashguns. A switch on the back of the flashguns allows you to set them to either setting.

■ **Flash coverage:** This indicates the spread of light from the flash. It's stated as a focal length (usually around 18mm), so that you're aware that if you use a lens wider than the stated figure, you risk dark corners/edges to your image due a lack of flash coverage.

Flashtastic! Learning to use flash properly can help you capture dazzling results like this.

Where to find flash control settings on your digital camera

Most cameras have a flash button on the body and further options in their menu system. Here are examples of how to access the features

Canon
Press the flash button to pop up the flash. The Flash Control setting on the menu's first tab allows the mode to be set.

Nikon
With some models, press and hold the flash button. You can also access via the MENU and via the i button if available on your camera.

Olympus
Press the flash mode button, make your selection using the four-way control or the input dial, then press OK.

Panasonic
Press MENU and scroll through options in the Rec tab. If your camera has a Q Menu, you can add flash modes as a shortcut.

Pentax
Press the flash button and use the four-way control to choose a mode. Set flash exposure compensation via the input dial.

Samsung
Press MENU and scroll through options in the Camera tab. Alternatively, press Fn and select a mode with the four-way control.

Sony
Press the flash mode button, make your selection using the four-way control or the input dial, then press OK.

Flash accessories

There are various accessories that can be used with your camera's flash and these can be split into the following main categories:

Lighting aids: There are a wealth of softboxes, diffusers, brollies, beauty dishes and other lighting aids available to help soften or direct the output from your dedicated flashgun. They vary in price from under £20 for a simple diffuser to up to £200 for a decent softbox. We recommend you check out the following:

■ Diffuser: Stofen Omni-bounce £17; www.newprouk.co.uk

■ Softbox: Lastolite Ezybox (38cm) £170; www.lastolite.com

■ Beauty dish: Speedlight Pro £70; www.speedlightprokit.co.uk

■ Complete kit: Interfit Strobies £120; www.interfitphotographic.com

Brackets: These hold your flash to the side of your camera, rather than have it mounted on your hotshoe, which improves the lighting effect and frees your hotshoe for dedicated accessories like a remote trigger. Check out the range by Custom Brackets (www.flaghead.co.uk).

Off-camera triggers or leads: If you want to use your flashgun off-camera, you'll need these to retain dedication with your flash (unless they have a built-in wireless trigger). Manufacturers have their own, but Hama (www.hama.co.uk), Hähnel (www.hahnel.ie) and Phottix (www.intro2020.co.uk) offer affordable options.

Gels: Slip a coloured gel over the flash head and you can bathe the scene in colour. Many pros use it with an off-camera flash to illuminate a backdrop. Honl (www.flaghead.co.uk) and Hama (www.hama.co.uk) offer excellent flash gel sets.

Battery packs: If you regularly shoot lots of flash exposures (for instance, at weddings), then a battery pack is a cost-effective option and an alternative to AA rechargeable batteries. Quantum (www.flaghead.co.uk) is the most popular brand.

Slave cell: Pop one on the bottom of a flash and it will fire when the sensor detects a flash output. If you have non-dedicated manual flashguns, it's an inexpensive way of using multiple flash set-ups. Hama's Slave Unit costs £20.

Ball & socket flash platform: If you use the flash off-camera, you'll need a 'foot' to stand it on a surface or a ball & socket head with a flash-compatible platform bracket to hold it securely. Cullmann (www.newprouk.co.uk), 9 (www.interfitphotographic.com) and other independent brands have several options. For more of our recommended flash accessories see p160-161.

Basic flash modes

Auto: DSLRs don't have an autoflash mode as such, but rather have certain exposure modes that pop up the flash automatically. Some CSCs do have an auto setting among their flash modes and this works much like it does on a compact camera, firing the flash when needed in low light and taking pictures without in brighter conditions.

When to use autoflash

■ Leaving your flash set to auto mode makes sense when shooting general snapshots indoors as it's most likely that shooting using ambient light only may result in camera shake ruining images.

Forced-on (fill-in): You don't have to wait for the camera to suggest you need to use the flash – you can pop it up yourself by pressing the flash button. Do this to add a touch of fill-in flash to remove shadows and add catchlights to daylight portraits, or when your subject's face is in shadow. The amount of fill-in flash is determined automatically by the camera, but you can boost or reduce it using flash exposure compensation (explained over the page).

When to use fill-in flash

■ The subject is standing with their back to the sun, so fill-in flash is used to reveal detail.

■ Your subject is positioned under a tree with dappled shadows across the face.

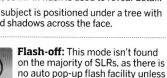

Flash-off: This mode isn't found on the majority of SLRs, as there is no auto pop-up flash facility unless the camera is set to a scene mode where it decides if the flash is needed or not. However, it does exist on some DSLRs as a mode on the mode dial and is designed to be used to prevent accidentally firing the flash in locations where flash photography is not allowed, such as museums or theatres. This mode is found on all CSCs, regardless of whether or not it has an integral flash.

When to turn the flash off

■ When shooting through glass, leave the flash off to avoid reflections.

■ In locations where flash is not permitted, ensure it's switched off.

Red-eye reduction: If you're shooting indoor portraits using the camera's built-in flash and there is very little available light, then you run the risk of the subjects suffering from red-eye. Using this mode sets the flash to fire either a fast burst of 'strobe' flashes or a constant beam of light, with the aim of closing your subject's pupils and reducing the risk of red-eye. As well as this mode, you can minimise the problem of red-eye by using one of the following techniques:

■ **Use bounce flash:** Red-eye is the result of direct flash, so bounce flash instantly removes the problem (see panel opposite).

■ **Move the flash away from the lens:** The risk of red-eye decreases the further the flash is away from the lens. A hotshoe-mounted flash is less likely to result in red-eye, while red-eye is extremely rare when the flash is off-camera.

■ **Avoid alcohol:** Alcohol leads to pupils dilating so your subjects are more likely to have red-eye in your photos if they've already started drinking!

Red-eye reduction OFF — Red-eye reduction ON

■ **Increase ambient light:** If you're using the built-in flash, the previous points won't apply. The best option is to switch on the room lights or shoot in a brighter room, as the higher the ambient light, the smaller the subject's pupils.

■ **Cheat!** If all else fails, use software to remove red-eye from your images. Many packages have a red-eye function that can be used to automatically remove the problem. It's also found on some cameras, too!

Using bounce flash

The light from your flash can be unforgiving for portraits, which is why most hotshoe-mounted flashguns boast a bounce head. In its standard position, the flash head delivers direct flash at your subject, which gives a less than flattering effect as well as producing shadows behind the subject. By bouncing flash off a ceiling or wall, it is more evenly spread to give a better result, while also eliminating the problem of shadows. You don't have to worry about the exposure – the camera takes care of this for you. What you do have to be careful with is how much you angle the head – you want to aim it to bounce off the surface halfway between you and the subject – aim the head too low and the flash will bounce behind the subject; raise it too far and it will fall in front of them. Also make sure you bounce it off a white or neutral-coloured surface –the flash will take on the colour of the surface, so bounce it off a red wall and it will bathe your subject in a red cast. If you have a flashgun with a built-in reflector or diffuser, use it to further improve the flash effect.

DIRECT FLASH   BOUNCE FLASH   BOUNCE WITH REFLECTOR

Choosing the correct exposure mode to use with flash

While the TTL flash exposure system on your camera will aim to give you perfectly exposed images every time, it's worth noting that the actual result varies depending on the exposure mode the camera is set to. How this works depends on the camera brand and model, but our easy reference table provides information on how using flash with each of the core creative modes affects how the image is captured.

Brand	Canon	Nikon	Pentax	Olympus	Sony
Program	Camera sets shutter speed and aperture, but raises shutter speed to avoid camera shake. The background may be dark.	Camera sets exposure, but raises shutter speed to avoid camera shake, unless slow-sync mode is set. Background may be dark.	Camera sets exposure, but raises shutter speed to avoid camera shake, unless slow-sync mode is set. Background may be dark.	Camera sets exposure, but raises shutter speed to avoid camera shake, unless slow-sync mode is set. Background may be dark.	Camera sets exposure, but raises shutter speed to avoid camera shake, unless slow-sync mode is set. Background may be dark.
Aperture-priority	User picks aperture; camera calculates flash exposure accordingly. Shutter speed is picked to render ambient light correctly. Be aware of camera shake.	User picks the aperture and the camera selects flash exposure accordingly. Shutter speed is limited to prevent camera shake, unless slow-sync mode is selected.	User sets aperture and camera sets shutter speed to correctly expose background, up to the maximum sync speed. Risk of camera shake in low light.	User picks aperture and camera selects flash exposure accordingly. Shutter speed limited to prevent camera shake, unless slow-sync mode is also selected.	User picks aperture and camera selects flash exposure accordingly. Shutter speed limited to prevent camera shake, unless slow-sync mode is also selected.
Shutter-priority	User picks shutter speed and camera picks corresponding aperture for ambient light, then calculates flash output according to this aperture.	User picks shutter speed and camera picks corresponding aperture to expose ambient light correctly, then calculates flash output according to this aperture.	User picks shutter speed and camera picks corresponding aperture to expose ambient light properly, then calculates flash output according to this aperture.	User picks shutter speed and camera picks corresponding aperture to expose ambient light correctly, then calculates flash output according to this aperture.	User picks shutter speed and camera picks corresponding aperture to expose ambient light correctly, then calculates flash output according to this aperture.
Manual	You set the aperture and shutter speed (at or below the flash sync) to ensure the scene receives enough ambient light. The TTL flash system ensures the subject is correctly exposed.	You set the aperture and shutter speed (at or below the flash sync) to ensure the scene receives enough ambient light. The TTL flash system ensures the subject is correctly exposed.	You set the aperture and shutter speed (at or below the flash sync) to ensure the scene receives enough ambient light. The TTL flash system ensures the subject is correctly exposed.	You set the aperture and shutter speed (at or below the flash sync) to ensure the scene receives enough ambient light. The TTL flash system ensures the subject is correctly exposed.	You set the aperture and shutter speed (at or below the flash sync) to ensure the scene receives enough ambient light. The TTL flash system ensures the subject is correctly exposed.
Exposure compensation	Affects ambient light exposure only.	Affects ambient and flash exposure.	Affects ambient and flash exposure.	Affects ambient light exposure only.	Affects ambient and flash exposure.
Flash exposure compensation	Affects flash exposure only.	Affects flash exposure only.	Affects flash exposure only.	Affects flash exposure only.	Affects flash exposure only.

* Please note that the stated information relates to most general shooting conditions. However, in certain situations, the camera and flash will operate differently.

Creative flash modes

Second (rear) curtain sync: Your camera is normally set up for first-curtain flash synchronisation, which means that when you take a picture, the burst of flash is at the start of the exposure. With most standard exposures, this system works well, but when using a longer exposure, it can adversely affect the result if there is a subject moving in the frame. What happens is that the burst of flash when you first press the shutter records the subject in its original position, but as it continues to move through the frame, it records a 'streak' across the picture. To make the image more natural, select second-curtain sync (also known as rear-curtain sync) to fire the flash at the end of the exposure. The problem with second-curtain sync is that when shooting a moving subject, you never quite know where it will be in the frame when the flash fires. This isn't an issue if the shutter speed is reasonably quick, such as 1/8sec, but it can present a problem if you're using a very slow shutter speed, especially if the subject is moving quickly.

When to use second-curtain sync flash
■ When you're shooting moving subjects with a slower shutter speed to reveal motion.

Slow-sync: This mode involves combining flash with a slow shutter speed. The longer exposure time allows ambient light to be recorded in the scene, while the flash takes care of the main subject. With the standard flash setting, the camera uses a faster shutter speed to ensure there is no camera shake, but the result is that, while the subject is well-exposed, the background is very dark. Because of the length the shutter remains open, you should place the camera on a tripod to ensure the image isn't spoilt by movement during the exposure. That said, you can capture creative results by purposely moving the camera during the exposure – try rotating the camera clockwise or anticlockwise and note how bright hotspots of light record as streaks. Many cameras have a slow-sync mode that you select, while others automatically set the flash to slow-sync when you use particular exposure modes – check your camera's instruction manual. Finally, it's worth noting that, with some cameras, you can combine slow-sync flash with second-curtain sync.

When to use slow-sync flash
■ Use slow-sync to reveal ambient light in the background and a flash-exposed subject.
■ The relatively slow shutter speed creates unusual effects when moving the camera.

Wireless flash: This facility allows you to fire off-camera flash without the need for any form of wired connection, giving you freedom to experiment with flash. The actual procedure for shooting wirelessly varies from brand to brand, but the basic set-up involves setting your camera to Wireless flash mode and using the integral or hotshoe-mounted flash to set off the off-camera 'slave' flashguns. Wireless flash photography is possible even if your camera lacks a Wireless mode by attaching a wireless trigger to the hotshoe, with a transmitter fitted to the base of your off-camera flash. Branded triggers are expensive, so a far more affordable option is an independent trigger. You can opt for the least expensive triggers, which do not provide TTL flash metering, or more expensive options that give full dedication. The latter option is the best choice for most people, but if you're using older non-dedicated flashguns at manual power settings, the cheaper option is suitable. Our favourite flash trigger is the Hähnel Combi RF Interfit Titan Pro, but also look at those by PocketWizard if you're serious about multiple off-camera flash photography.

When to use wireless flash
■ Multiple flash set-ups or when using a colour gel on an off-camera flash to liven up a backdrop.

FP/High-speed flash: This mode is available on a limited number of cameras and flashguns, and allows the flash to be used at any shutter speed, therefore not restricting it to the standard flash-sync speed. This is particularly useful for sports photographers looking to use flash in bright daylight to freeze action and it's also popular with lifestyle photographers looking to combine flash with wide apertures in bright daylight. It's a highly sophisticated mode suited for specialist rather than general photography types.

When to use high-speed flash
■ Using flash to freeze action in daylight.
■ When you want to use flash in bright daylight.

Manual power settings: Many hotshoe-mounted flashguns, as well as a small number of Compact System Cameras, boast manual power settings. These are set to fire the flash at particular power ratios, in steps from full power to 1/2 power to 1/4 power etc, down to 1/64 power or lower. When used at a manual power setting, the flash output will be consistent, regardless of the camera settings, ambient light or any other variable, so set it to 1/4 or 1/2 power and it will fire the same output every time. This means that, once set up, the flash exposures are consistent – this is useful if you're photographing a variety of subjects that range from dark to light, or are highly reflective. Once you've set the manual power ratio of your flash(es) to give a decent exposure, so long as you don't vary the flash-to-subject distance, every exposure will be consistent. Another instance where manual flash settings is useful is if your flashgun is very old or a different brand from your camera. By using it in manual mode, with either a trigger or a slave cell attached to the mount at the base of the flash, you're able to shoot using a multiple flash set-up. Manual power is also ideal when you want to paint a scene with flash, as shown here.

Creative flash control

Flash Exposure Compensation (FEC)

This isn't a function that you may use too often, but it's important as it provides you with a fast and easy way to control the level of flash output. In the same way that you use exposure compensation to add or subtract from the exposure that the camera has determined is correct, FEC is used to boost or reduce the amount of flash the camera has decided is required. You'll usually want to do this after reviewing an image you've just taken, having decided you'd prefer a little more or less flash. Most often, this is when you've taken a shot using fill-in flash and decided that the flash/ambient light balance isn't quite right. However, with some brands of camera, including Nikon, Pentax and Sony, adjustments made using exposure compensation also affect the flash exposure, so FEC can be applied to compensate for this.

External flash func. setting

Flash exp. comp   ⁻2 . 1 . 0 . 1 .⁺2

DISP. Clear flash settings

No FEC applied

-1EV FEC applied

Flash control
The camera's flash output was too strong for our taste, so reducing it one stop using FEC gave a more natural result.

Simulate low evening sunlight

Learn how to use off-camera flash to create an attractive hairlight

WHEN USING FLASH to light a portrait, most photographers point it at the subject's face, but by placing it behind the model's head you can create an attractive hairlight – adding a different dimension to the image. It's a creative technique to try in the winter months, when you don't fancy going outdoors but want to simulate the look of a low evening sun from the warmth of your home.

To get the best results, the subject should ideally have curly or wavy hair, and be placed in front of a dark background to accentuate the light. You'll also need to experiment with your flash's power to find a balance between overpowering the ambient light and getting the right spread through the hair. For instance, if you're doing a full-body portrait, a burst of flash at 1/2 power would work best, while a head shot might require only 1/4 power. Play with the distance of your flash to your subject's head as well, but make sure the flash is completely hidden so it diffuses through the hair. Also consider your aperture: minimal depth-of-field will soften the spread of light while a narrow aperture will produce a star-like effect from the flash.

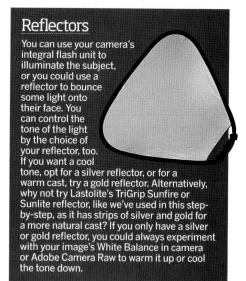

Reflectors

You can use your camera's integral flash unit to illuminate the subject, or you could use a reflector to bounce some light onto their face. You can control the tone of the light by the choice of your reflector, too. If you want a cool tone, opt for a silver reflector, or for a warm cast, try a gold reflector. Alternatively, why not try Lastolite's TriGrip Sunfire or Sunlite reflector, like we've used in this step-by-step, as it has strips of silver and gold for a more natural cast? If you only have a silver or gold reflector, you could always experiment with your image's White Balance in camera or Adobe Camera Raw to warm it up or cool the tone down.

Backlighting a portrait with flash

Professional lifestyle photographer Brett Harkness frequently uses his off-camera flash behind his subjects, whether to create a dramatic burst of light behind a full-body portrait or to add a subtle, attractive hairlight to a head shot. He shows us how…

1 **(Above) Use natural light** To start with, we position Emma in a doorway so we can use natural light to fill in the shadows on her face. During the winter months, however, when light levels are low you may need to use a reflector or a second flash to light the face, held approximately three or four feet away so as not to overpower the backlight. With the camera and flash set to manual, I dial in f/5.6 and ISO 500, because of the relatively low light, and place the flashgun on the step behind Emma.

2 **(Right) Take test shots** I take my first shot at f/5.6 with the flash behind her set to 1/8 power and no reflector. The flash isn't strong enough and her face is underexposed. So I set the flash to 1/4 power and ask my assistant to hold a reflector a few feet from Emma's face to fill in the shadows.

Without reflector

With reflector

3 **(Left) Tidy the background** As I can see the stairs in the background of the pictures, I add a blanket over the steps to get rid of the white line and darken the background to enhance the backlight.

4 **(Above) Try different WB settings** You may also want to try playing with your camera's White Balance settings to see what effect it has on the picture. Normally if you're working with flash, you would set Flash or Custom WB, but why not try Daylight or Tungsten to alter the tone of the image? Alternatively, you could shoot in Raw and play with the WB in post-production.

Final image
With slight tweaks to the contrast in Photoshop and a little skin softening, we're left with a beautiful portrait.

How to add drama to sky for outdoor portraits

Underexposing the scene and using flash to light the subject is a great way to add impact to portraits

MORE OFTEN THAN NOT, flash is used to balance flash and ambient lighting, or to fill in shadows, but now and again, it pays to use flash to overpower the ambient light and completely transform a scene.

A great technique to try is to capture a dramatic sky by underexposing the scene, leading it to appear far darker than it does in reality, while allowing the flash to correctly expose the subject. You can do it two ways: use the exposure compensation facility to dial in a negative value, or work in manual mode, both of which we'll explain in further detail.

Regardless of which you choose, for the best results, avoid using the camera's integral flash or mounting a flash on the hotshoe and instead trigger a remote flash via a slave or off-camera flash cord. Simply reposition the flash to the side of the subject to immediately change the function of the flash from a flat fill-in light to one that's directional and contrast-enhancing. For the purpose of this step-by-step, we'll explain how to do this technique using manual settings rather than relying on your camera's TTL system, as it offers greater control and a chance to learn and experiment.

Different camera and flash systems work in different ways, so if you do want to try the exposure compensation method with TTL, check your camera's instruction manual.

Remember: when working with manual flash, the shutter speed controls the amount of ambient light reaching the sensor, while aperture controls flash output. For this technique, shutter speed is paramount as you're exposing for the sky, not the subject. The faster the shutter speed, the darker the ambience will be; the slower the shutter speed, the more you encourage the influence of ambient light.

Using radio triggers

Most of the time, once a flash is off-camera and triggered by a radio release it loses its TTL capabilities, so it's important your flash has manual settings. To retain TTL, you could opt for a dedicated off-camera lead, but you will be restricted by the length of the cord. However, if you're comfortable using manual flash, the more affordable option is a slave cell (see p70) or a flash remote trigger – there are many available, varying in price and functions. While PocketWizards are brilliant, and a market leader for performance, they're also expensive. Camera manufacturers also have their own remotes but we'd recommend independent versions by the likes of Calumet, Kenro, Hähnel and Seculine as they're cheaper and do the job well enough. The Hähnel Combi TF, for instance, is a bargain at around £60 and doubles up as a remote flash trigger and shutter release. Seculine's highly efficient Twin Link T2D Wireless Radio Flash Trigger Kit can be bought for around £120. Regardless of what remote you buy, remember you need a transmitter to sit on your camera's hotshoe and a receiver to attach to each of your off-camera flashguns for it to work.

Using exposure compensation

Instead of using manual mode, set your camera to aperture-priority mode, your flash to TTL and meter for the background. Dial in the aperture you want and then set a negative value on the camera's exposure compensation to at least two stops to underexpose the scene: the flash will take care of the subject. If you're shooting with a Nikon, you may have to increase your flash exposure compensation by two stops too, as the flash and exposure compensation are linked. Have a play and experiment with results.

Getting a dramatic sky with an outdoor portrait

This is an advanced technique, so requires practice. Pro photographer Brett Harkness, who regularly uses it, explains how to make the most of manual flash and moody skies. On this shoot, it's overcast and there's a mass of detail in the sky to capture. As Brett likes his shots sharp front-to-back, he uses a small aperture of around f/13 and sets his flash to 1/4 power to compensate. If you want shallow depth-of-field, keep the flash close to your subject, set the flash to 1/8 power and open the aperture.

1 (Above) Prepare the flash I ask my assistant to hold the flashgun several feet away from the model, Emma. Because we're not using any diffusion accessories, I have him hold the flash vertically to get a bigger spread of light. Sunglasses and gold fabric add a fashion-shoot feel.

2 (Right) Underexpose the scene To capture a moody sky, I have to dramatically underexpose the scene using a fast shutter speed to retain detail in the sky. As you can see, a fast shutter speed has underexposed the scene, but without using flash it means the subject is also very dark.

3 (Left) Set exposure Once I start using flash, my shutter speed is immediately limited to the camera's sync speed – in this case 1/250sec. With my camera set to manual, I set the aperture that gives the scene the correct exposure for the ambient light. I then set the flashgun to 1/4 power, which exposes Emma well, but the scene lacks drama and mood.

4 (Below) Raise the flash To improve the effect, my assistant raises the flash and points it down on Emma. However, the key to darkening the scene behind her is to close down the aperture (in this instance, by two stops) so that the background is underexposed, resulting in a far moodier result.

Final image
With a few tweaks to
the Curves and Levels
in Photoshop, Brett's
produced a dramatic
portrait with a single
off-camera flash.
Give it a go!

1 Set up your key light The key light is the one that will be illuminating your subject. You can use the on-camera flash for this, but for a more flattering light I have chosen to use an off-camera flash within a small portable softbox to the right of the camera.

2 Find your exposure Select manual mode, choose a low ISO, and select your camera's max sync speed and a mid-aperture of around f/8. Take a test shot to establish the correct power – I've settled on 1/4 power after some adjustments. It's a nice shot, but the background is dark and boring.

Add interest with coloured gels

Transform your background and inject a splash of colour into portraits using coloured flash gels. These four simple steps show you how

Jordan Butters: Shooting portraits using natural light can yield fantastic results, but once the sun goes down, flash really comes into its own. It allows you to continue shooting into the darkest hours, retain control over the direction and intensity of the light, and to use low-ISO and mid-apertures for optimal image quality. As well as illuminating your subjects, a burst of flash to the surroundings can add interest to your images and, paired with coloured flash gels, can give your portraits a creative twist.

In case you don't already know, flash gels are semi-translucent sheets of plastic that, when placed in front of the flash, cast colour onto whatever it illuminates. They needn't cost a lot either; you can even use coloured sweet wrappers to achieve a similar effect!

You will, of course, need at least one off-camera flash and a method of triggering it; this can be done by a dedicated sync lead, or optically (master flash triggering slaves). The other option, as I've used here, is radio triggers. These tend to offer a better range than optical triggering, and don't rely on the

flashguns having to see each other to work. The idea of using two, or three, flashguns at once may sound daunting, but it's relatively simple once you break it down. You first need to concentrate on lighting your subject with one flashgun, as it's the most important aspect of your photograph. If your subject isn't well lit then it's not going to be a great image no matter what colour you add to the background. Once you've got the correct exposure for your subject, you can then add flashguns to the background one by one.

Final image
By adding each flash one by one, the process is simplified. A nice and easy creative portrait using flash gels.

Wall
Flashgun with red gel (30ft away at full power)
Pillar
Wall
Flashgun with green gel (15ft away at 1/2 power)
Small softbox
Pillar
Key light (flashgun 3ft away at 1/4 power)
Camera: 1/160sec at f/8 (ISO 100)

TTL vs manual

Depending on the model of flashgun and trigger that you are using, you may have the option of setting the flash exposure using TTL (through the lens) metering. This means that the camera and flashguns meter the scene and decide on the best output power for an even exposure. The advantage of TTL metering is that it's quick and easy to use, but the results can be hit and miss as the system might not interpret the lighting in the same way that you imagined it. It's also usually only available on the more expensive models of flashgun.

Manual metering, on the other hand, involves setting the power output for each flashgun manually. It takes a bit more time to perfect, but you can easily assess the effect that any changes have on the image. You tend to learn a lot more about what works, and what doesn't, this way, too.

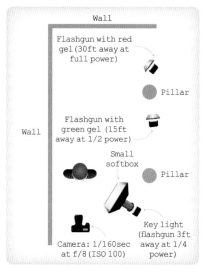

3 Add some colour Position a second flashgun to illuminate the background. I've fitted a green gel to light the pillar on the right. As the flash is a good 15ft behind my subject, I've selected 1/2 power on this flashgun. Take a second test shot to assess the difference this makes.

4 Add a second colour For added interest, I've added a second flashgun, this time fitted with a contrasting red gel pointing at the far wall. As the wall is around 30ft behind my subject, I've selected full power. If the colour is too intense, simply move the flash away from the wall.

Studioflash outfits

Some newcomers find studioflash intimidating, but the truth is, using it isn't as difficult as you think

ALTHOUGH THERE ARE VARIOUS studioflash kits available, ranging in price from under £200 to thousands, most of them have very similar features and all follow basic principles of operation. A studioflash head is designed to fire a burst of flash at a given power setting – the extra functions and accessories are all geared to allow the photographer more control of the flash output. Truly mastering a studioflash system can take years but, thankfully, getting to grips with the essentials is relatively easy. Much like using ambient light, the key factor to success is learning how to control the flash output so your subject is lit the way you'd like it to be. The big difference between studio and ambient light is your level of control – you are able to fine-tune the lighting's intensity and direction, as well as the nature of the light falling on the subject, far more accurately than you could ever achieve with natural light. This makes it an incredibly versatile form of lighting but, obviously, one that does take time to learn to use correctly. Here, we cover the basic workings of studioflash and how the various attachments, such as softboxes and brollies, can be used to control how your subject is lit.

Anatomy of a studioflash head

This illustration is of the rear of an Interfit head, but most brands will have a similar layout, with easy-to-use and well-labelled controls.

Rear of light
You'll normally find controls on the rear of the head, but some models have them on the side, too.

1) Sync socket: Most studioflash outfits are supplied with a sync lead, which connects your camera to your flash head, to allow the flash to fire when you press the shutter button.

2) Slave cell: This sensor detects any flash output, so if your camera is connected to one light in a multiple set-up, its output will trigger the slave cell on other lights, making them fire together.

3) Power settings: A key function of studioflash heads is being able to adjust the power output. Basic heads have fixed settings, eg 1/4 power, 1/2 power and so on, while advanced heads have stepless variable settings.

4) Status lights/beeps: Many heads have lights that indicate when the head has sufficient charge to fire.

☑ Too hot to handle!
Flash heads heat up quickly, so take care not to burn yourself when swapping attachments. The metal mount, as well as the bulb, can get hot, especially when the modelling lamp is turned on

Front of light
Removing the lighting attachment will usually reveal two bulbs, each with different uses.

5) Modelling lamp: This tungsten bulb remains switched on to allow you to compose the image, focus on the subject and to assess the lighting effect.

6) Flash bulb: These provide the powerful flash output. Most brands have specialised bulbs to fit certain heads or studioflash series. They're very fragile, so handle them with utmost care.

Setting up your camera for using studioflash

Set the camera to manual and the correct flash sync speed. Then fit a PC adaptor to your hotshoe to connect to the flash sync lead

CANON EOS DSLRS

(1) Set the main control dial to M to select manual mode
(2) Turn the input dial behind the shutter button and set the flash sync speed
(3) Once you've taken a flashmeter reading, press and hold down the +/- button, then turn the input dial to set the aperture you require

MOST NIKON DSLRS

(1) Set the main control dial to M to select manual mode
(2) Turn the input dial behind the shutter button and set the flash sync speed
(3) Once you've taken a flashmeter reading, turn the input dial on the front of the handgrip to set the aperture

PENTAX K-SERIES DSLRS

(1) Set the main control dial on the top-plate to M to select manual mode
(2) Turn the input dial behind the shutter button and set the flash sync speed
(3) Once you've taken a flashmeter reading, press and hold down the +/- button, then turn the input dial to set the aperture you require

SONY ALPHA DSLRS

(1) Set the main control dial on the top-plate to Tv to select shutter-priority mode
(2) Turn the input dial in front of the shutter button and set the flash sync speed
(3) Once you've taken a flashmeter reading, press and hold down the +/- button, then turn the input dial to set the aperture you require

COMPACT SYSTEM CAMERAS

Very few CSCs sport the exposure mode dial found on the majority of digital SLRs, but it's still very easy to select the exposure mode. With most models all you need to do is press the Menu button or the four-way control dial to display the exposure modes and rotate the wheel to M to select manual mode. With touchscreen models, simply press the M icon on the screen.

Studioflash accessories

Get the best out of your flash system with lighting attachments and accessories

STUDIOFLASH HEADS ARE DESIGNED to produce a high-power burst of light, but it's the lighting attachment you use that dictates the effect of the flash on the subject. If you've ever looked into buying a studioflash system, you'll no doubt have seen various types of attachments available, each having their own way of affecting the intensity and nature of light. While most basic kits are often supplied with a brolly or two and 'spills', there are a huge number of optional accessories available and getting to know which are best suited to your needs is important. In our comparison set below, we have used the most typical types of attachments available for most studioflash kits to give you an idea of how each affects the light.

As well as lighting attachments, other accessories can play a big part in the quality of your final results, or just make the process a lot easier.

For instance, a flashmeter is useful to identify the correct aperture you need to set your camera to for a perfect exposure, and a remote trigger is also handy. Which background you use also affects the final image: there are a variety available, from plain to coloured patterns, to paper rolls that fit on frames and collapsible backdrops. A reflector should not be overlooked either; it bounces light back onto the subject or background as an alternative to using an additional light. Silver is the most efficient, white provides a softer and more natural effect, while a black reflector can accentuate cheekbones!

> ### Flashmeter readings
> When using studioflash, make sure the white dome (invercone) on your flashmeter is set over the sensor so that it takes incident light readings, which will prove to be the most accurate

Umbrella (brolly)

Available in white, silver and translucent, a brolly is one of the cheapest lighting accessories available. Silver is very efficient at bouncing light, white gives a soft, natural effect, while translucent brollies provide the most diffused light.

Softbox

A real favourite, as softboxes provide a very diffused effect that's ideal for flattering portraits. The larger the softbox, the softer the light it produces. The majority are square, but some are rectangular and thin (also called strip lights).

Beauty dish

Beauty dishes are often used, as you may expect, for close-up 'beauty' and make-up shots. They give off a very harsh light in the centre, which has the ability to enhance make-up, but also has the effect of highlighting flaws on a subject's skin.

Spill (spill kill)

Often supplied along with the flash head, a spill will help channel the light in to a concentrated beam. With portraits, they're useful for lighting backgrounds, but can have quite a harsh effect when aimed at a subject's face.

Snoot

This conical lighting attachment provides a hard edge and a directional beam of light that photographers often find is better suited for backlighting or as a hairlight – it can be unflattering if used to provide the key lighting for portraits.

Honeycomb grid

Honeycomb grids provide a soft-edged circle of light and are a popular alternative to a snoot. They act in a similar way to a spotlight, but provide a wider angle spot effect. Honeycombs are available with various sizes of grids.

How to set studioflash exposures

If you want to use studioflash, you'll need to set your camera to manual mode. Paul Ward explains the key factors to ensure that you get set up correctly

Paul Ward: For some photographers, the first time they need to switch their camera to manual mode is when they want to use studioflash. That's because, other than the sync, which triggers the flash, there's no information passing between the camera body and studioflash. It's down to you to set an ISO rating (usually a low 100 or 200), adjust the power of the studioflash, and set an aperture that gives a suitable exposure. The traditional (and best) way to match the studioflash output with the exposure is using a lightmeter that measures flash. However, rightly or wrongly, digital photographers are increasingly doing away with the separate lightmeter and instead using the LCD monitor preview facility to work out the best settings via trial and error.

Both methods have their good and bad points so either technique can be used. Here, we explain what they are and show you how to use these techniques for great studioflash photography.

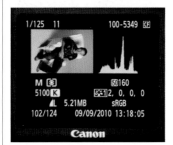

In other photography genres, the histogram can prove a useful tool in the search for a balanced exposure. When it comes to studio photography, Paul suggests it's better to avoid always relying on the histogram: "If you're shooting in a white studio, you're going to get big peaks on your histogram that will look odd, especially if you're used to interpreting a histogram of a landscape image. I think it's much better to judge the exposure on your LCD monitor, or if you're shooting tethered, on your laptop." So, if you choose to use the histogram, be wary of overexposed peaks.

Get connected!

Your camera needs to be connected in some way to the studioflash heads before they can communicate and be told when to fire. There are a number of ways to achieve this and there is a solution to suit all budgets. The cheapest and simplest way to link a camera and flash is with a sync cord. Costing around £10, the lead plugs in to the camera's PC socket at one end and the flash at the other and is very reliable. However, the main drawback is that the photographer is tethered to the studioflash head, so mobility is limited.

A more flexible method is to use an infrared system. A trigger is placed on the camera's hotshoe, while a receiver plugs into the flash head's sync cord socket. No wires means the photographer can wander freely around the studio, but infrared systems can be unreliable if the trigger and receiver are not in sight of each other. They are more expensive than a sync lead, but models from brands like Hama and Hähnel start at around £50.

For the ultimate in flexibility and reliability, most professional photographers opt for a wireless radio triggering system. Like infrared, the radio systems have a trigger and a receiver, but unlike the

infrared versions, they don't suffer from line-of-sight issues as they're triggered by a radio signal. This convenience costs more, with top brands like PocketWizard costing a small fortune. However, third-party brands like Hama, Sekonic, Seculine and Hähnel offer more affordable options – the Hähnel Combi TF costs around £50 and should meet the requirements of most enthusiast photographers.

☑ **Contacts**
Hähnel: www.hahnel.ie
Hama: www.hama.co.uk
Seculine: www.intro2020.com
Sekonic: www.sekonic.com

Studioflash: Why manual?

There is a good reason why we use manual mode when using studioflash. If you connect your camera to your studioflash heads with the DSLR set to shutter-priority (Tv) mode, the camera will try to select too wide of an aperture for you, resulting in a horrendously overexposed image with blown-out highlights. Similarly, if you select aperture-priority (Av) mode then you're likely to be rewarded with a blurry image as the camera automatically sets a long shutter speed based on the ambient light level. Only in manual mode can you control both settings to achieve a balanced exposure using flash.

Know your flash sync speed!

It's important to know your camera's flash sync speed (X-sync), because if you exceed it, you will be blighted by a black bar covering a portion of the image. This black bar is actually the camera's moving shutter curtain preventing the light from reaching the whole frame. Conversely, you can select a shutter speed that is slower than the maximum shutter speed without negative effects. Paul tends to keep his camera set at 1/125sec. Here are the typical shutter speeds for big-brand digital SLRs:
Canon: 1/200sec; **Nikon:** 1/250sec;
Sony: 1/250sec; **Pentax:** 1/180sec;
Olympus: 1/250sec.

Top techniques for metering studioflash

There are a number of ways you can make sure you get the exposure you want when using studioflash. Some take longer than others, some need a lightmeter, others not. Here are three to get you started…

IDEAL FOR BEGINNERS TO STUDIOFLASH LIGHTING

Technique one: Trial and error

The benefits of this method are that you don't need to buy a lightmeter, saving you money, and because you see the image on the LCD monitor immediately after firing the shutter, it's a very fast technique. If the image is overexposed, you need to lower the ISO and/or select a smaller aperture. If it's underexposed, you'll need to select a wider aperture and/or raise the ISO rating. You can also use the histogram to fine-tune the exposure. The main drawback of this technique is it's not as accurate as using a lightmeter and you're relying on the quality of the LCD monitor for accuracy. However, so long as you know how to read a histogram you'll get a good exposure. But when using two or more studioflash heads, you're not getting the benefits of metering each light separately.
1) I position my lights depending on the look I want to achieve. I then take an educated guess at the exposure settings – in this case 1/125sec at f/20 (ISO 160) – and take a test shot.
2) My camera's LCD screen allows me to review the image, which reveals it's underexposed and I need to open up the aperture.
3) I change my aperture to f/5.6, but it overexposes the image. You can see that highlights on the skin are what we call 'blown out'.
4) Finally, I change my settings to an aperture between the first two (f/11) and get a balanced exposure that is neither under or overexposed.

IDEAL FOR LESS EXPERIENCED PHOTOGRAPHERS

Technique two: Take a reading with all lights on

Most amateur photographers – and many pros, in fact – use this method to determine studioflash exposures. By taking a single exposure reading with the meter pointing away from the subject and towards the camera, you can quickly take a single meter reading that should give a correct exposure. It's a method that works really well, as you can view the result, then adjust the various power settings on each studioflash head, take another meter reading and set this new exposure setting. It's a less involved method but judging the lighting balance isn't as straightforward – it can also be difficult to judge how each light individually illuminates the subject. Paul shows us how it's done…

1) I make sure the camera is in manual mode and set my ISO (160) into the lightmeter so it can calculate an accurate reading.
2) I take a reading from Kate's face. The meter tells me I need an aperture of f/11 to get the correct exposure, so that's exactly what I do.
3) With the subject's exposure taken care of by the lightmeter, all I have to do is make the background darker or lighter is adjust the power setting on the studioflash pointed towards the background.
4) After balancing the background exposure by adjusting the power settings, I'm able to achieve a correctly exposed image of my model. After some cleaning up in post-production, the image is complete.

IDEAL FOR MORE EXPERIENCED PHOTOGRAPHERS

Technique three: Individual light readings

This is the method used by pros looking to get the best possible lighting effect. It involves using a lightmeter to take an individual exposure reading from each studioflash for very precise control of how each light falls on the subject to give the best possible effect. It's the most involved technique, so takes a little more time and effort, but if you want to master the craft of studioflash lighting, it's one you should keep practising at as it's the method used by most professionals.

1) With my lights set up and turned on, I'm ready to go. Note that I have put a diffuser in place to bounce light back onto Kate's face.
2) Input the ISO you're using into the lightmeter and make sure it's in flash mode – usually indicated with a little lightning symbol. By doing this, the lightmeter will wait until the studioflashes have been fired before telling you what aperture to set on your DSLR.
3) I then take a meter reading from my model's face so I know what aperture will correctly expose the skin. In this case, it's f/11.
4) I take a reading next to the background, which suggests I set f/16. This smaller aperture tells me that, using f/11, the background will be bright, and help me create a high-key effect with the backdrop.
5) By taking multiple readings, I'm able to control both the foreground and background exposures, resulting in a perfectly exposed final image.

Studio set-up: one light

Start learning studio lighting by mastering a series of techniques using simple one-light set-ups

IF YOU WANT TO LEARN how to control your lighting, you're best off starting with just one studioflash. One light is more than sufficient to produce some stunning results and many great photographers still use a single head for their work. After all, outdoors we only have a single light source – the sun. This set-up is very easy to control and the smallest adjustment to the light on your subject has a clear effect, forcing you to fine-tune the light's angle and method of diffusion. And while you'll only have one source of illumination, you can also use reflectors in your set-up to bounce light and fill in any shadows.

The set of images below shows what happens when you position your single light at different heights and angles. As you can see, it's crucial that you learn the dos and don'ts of how to set up your single studioflash head to avoid some of the unflattering results shown below.

As mentioned earlier, you need to set your camera to manual mode and set it to its flash sync speed (if you don't know it, use 1/125sec as a safe bet or refer to the user's manual). The aperture is determined by the meter reading you take, which is easy to do with a one-light set-up. With the sync lead from the light attached, hold the meter in front of the subject's face and press the button to fire the flash and take a reading. By adjusting the power setting on the flash head, you can effectively change the aperture you work with, too. Add power to set a smaller aperture and reduce power to use a wider aperture.

One light All you need to get started is your camera and a single flash head. With a bit of practice, you will soon find yourself getting great results!

1) Lit from above

With the light positioned high above the model's head the light looks natural but creates deep shadows under the eyes, nose and chin. For the best results, get the model to look towards the light. You could also ask her to hold a reflector on her lap to fill in the shadows.

2) Lit from below

Placing the light lower than the model's head, pointing upwards, eradicates any unsightly shadows under the nose and chin. For best results, get the model to look down towards the light, which, as you can see, also makes catchlights appear in the subject's eyes.

3) Lit from the side

Place the light to either the left or right side of your model's face for a strong, directional light, which will keep half of the face in shadow. To increase your chances of capturing catchlights in eyes, it is important to make sure the light is far enough forward.

4) One light & reflector

By holding a reflector close to the face, on the opposite side from the light, you will be able to reduce harsh shadows, much like using a second head. The closer you place it to the model, the stronger the reflection will be (though it helps to have an assistant!).

✓ **Tilt the head**
When shooting portraits, especially of females, try asking them to tilt their head slightly. This adds an air of friendliness to the shot, making the image look far more relaxed

5) Classic one-light set-up
This technique involves placing the studioflash slightly above and to one side of the model – approximately 45° to one side and down at 45°. The resulting lighting looks natural and provides well-placed catchlights for a really pleasing, flattering result.

Q&A: Studioflash

Q How much should I spend on a studioflash system?
A We'd recommend you start with a two-head system, with a softbox and umbrella. Tests by *Digital SLR Photography* found several to be excellent, including the Interfit EX150 Mk II and the Elinchrom D-Lite RX ONE twin-head kit.

Q What advantages do more expensive outfits offer?
A General build quality (and reliability) will be better, but the key benefits are power, features and performance. More power is useful as you can set the lights up further away from your subject, while relative light loss from attachments like softboxes is reduced. You'll find that more expensive heads allow more control over flash output and faster flash recycling times.

Q Are attachments from different systems compatible?
A In general, different brands have their own fittings so aren't compatible. However, Chimera makes speedrings for its softboxes that are compatible with just about any system. Visit: www.chimeralighting.com

Q How should I set up my camera to use studioflash?
A You will need to set it to manual mode, as the metering system will not work with studioflash. Set the shutter speed to the flash sync speed and aperture to the flashmeter reading.

Q How do I take an exposure reading with studioflash?
A Use a flashmeter connected to a light via a sync lead. Once you've set up the lights, hold the meter in front of the subject's face, take a reading and set the meter's recommended aperture on the camera. Don't forget that the flashmeter and camera both need to be set to the same ISO rating!

Q How do I connect my camera to my studioflash system?
A The plug at the end of the studioflash sync lead connects to your camera's PC socket. If your camera hasn't got a socket, buy an adaptor (around £10) that slots on your camera's hotshoe and connect the lead to this. A more expensive option is a wireless trigger that sits on your hotshoe and triggers a receiver on the flash head.

Studio set-up: Two lights

When you feel ready, extend your creative options by introducing a second studioflash head into the mix

MANY KITS COME WITH two heads, so once you've mastered lighting subjects with a single light, experiment with a second. Often when shooting with one light, a reflector is used to fill in the shadows and provide even lighting, but, without an assistant, they can be difficult to position. A second head can be used instead, with the benefit that you can control the power output and add attachments to diffuse or precisely focus the light. The second light, usually called the slave, is triggered when it detects the flash from the primary flash head. Using two lights gives you more scope for different scenarios: you can light the model from different angles, or aim one light at the model and the other at the background.

So how do you meter for two lights? The simplest way is to set up the lights how you would like them, then take a meter reading from the subject's face and take a test shot at the recommended aperture. Consider moving the lights' position, adjusting the light ratio between the two or changing the power. Whatever you decide, take another reading to see what aperture you need and fire another test shot. A more accurate way of taking a reading is to check the exposure of each light in turn (ie only one light on at a time) and adjust accordingly. This will allow you to control the balance of flash between the two lights more accurately, but is a more involved process, so we recommend using the simplest method first and try the second method once you have a bit of experience.

Two lights: This is a typical two-light set-up. The lights are fitted with a softbox and an umbrella to produce a diffused flattering light.

1) Lit from above & below
This is a typical headshot set-up, with the key light at 45° to the subject to give the most flattering light. The second light fills in the shadows under the chin. This technique works for almost any subject. Set the key light two stops brighter than the second light.

2) Lit from above & rim light
The key light is above and to the left of the model. The slave light is positioned behind the model, opposite the key light. This throws light over her shoulder, adding a touch of light to her cheek. It adds interest to the shot, and gives her face more of a three-dimensional feel.

3) Lit from back & front
Here, we have one light in front of the model to light her face, and another behind her to light her hair, adding a bit of shine to it. This works well if your model has silky or colourful hair, and is a technique commonly used for 'hair' shots used in magazine advertisements.

4) Butterfly lighting
This is an old-fashioned technique that is not used very much in contemporary photography. By placing both lights above the model, pointing down at a sharp angle, to cast the shadows on her face, you create an interesting 'butterfly' shape under the model's nose.

⊘ Brollies & softboxes
Brollies are included with most kits as a low-cost diffuser. They do a decent enough job, but it's worth investing in a softbox as soon as possible as they deliver very flattering light for portraits

5) Lit from both sides

Positioning both lights in front of the model, but off to the sides, is probably the most important two-light technique to learn. It helps to get rid of shadows and gives a very even light across the face. It's useful for eliminating wrinkles, so is commonly used for beauty and make-up shoots. This lighting technique works with just about any subject, and is seen as a 'safe bet' for studio portraiture.

Shoot bright and beautiful portraits

Professional photographer Paul Ward guides you through the simple steps to creating stunning high-key studio shots in a flash

Paul Ward: High-key portraits refer to shots that lean heavily towards the highlights, limiting any shadows for a bright, light-looking portrait. It's an extremely popular technique, which has been adopted by many high-street studios, possibly because it's so easy to shoot and post-process for polished, professional-looking results.

As a minimum, you'll need two light sources: one to illuminate the subject's face and another to overexpose the background. A home budget studio kit is perfect but, although it's a little trickier, you could try standing your subject in front of a sun-drenched window and illuminating the face with a flashgun. However, luckily for us, the price of studioflash has tumbled in recent years and it's now possible to buy a studioflash kit (with two flashes, brolly and softbox) for under £200 if you shop around. I used the Jessops Portaflash kit here, but you can see our other recommendations on p151.

The backdrop is also important to get right: ideally use a flat, white surface like a wall or a roll of background paper. You can get by using a white bedsheet, as long as it's pulled tight to reduce any shadows caused by wrinkles or creases. Finally, add a willing model into the mix and you have everything you need to produce a striking high-key image.

Time to reflect

As well as the studioflash kit, I also made use of a large reflector. If you don't have a reflector to hand, you can improvise by using a roll of tin foil, or if you're really stuck, a large mirror. That said, reflectors are so cheap now that you can pick one up for less than £20. Choose one that comes with a silver finish, or better still, one with a silver and gold reversible sleeve for extra lighting options.

1 Set up My first job was to arrange the lights around my model, Sophie. I used one studioflash and softbox to light the white wall. By overexposing the background, it prevents the light illuminating the subject from creating shadows on the wall. My second head, fitted with a brolly, was placed to the front right of Sophie. Finally, I rested a reflector on her knees to bounce light under her chin.

2 Test shot To start, you'll need to fire off a couple of test shots to fine-tune your settings. I opted to begin with an exposure of 1/125sec at f/11 (ISO 200), but my first attempt is a tad on the dark side, losing that bright high-key effect. This is due to the exposure, which I can correct easily by using a wider aperture.

3 Adjust settings I look again at my settings and this time select an aperture of f/8. Unfortunately, this setting means the image is too bright and the model's face has burnt out in places leading to unsightly white areas on her skin. I may be able to rescue some detail in Photoshop, but areas that are too white are beyond repair.

4 Next shot With a new aperture of f/9, I've finally got the right settings, but the reflector in front of Sophie has slipped and failed to bounce the light in the right direction. You can see from this image what a difference the reflector makes.

5 Different angles With the reflector correctly placed and the camera settings spot on, I'm at last happy with my lighting. While everything is working well, I ask Sophie to try out some different poses and angles.

6 Post-process With the correctly exposed image now uploaded onto my computer, I use the Levels slider to increase the brightness of the skin tone. Lastly, I adjust the Saturation slider to decrease the colour slightly before saving my file.

Final image
In under an hour you can produce a quality, high-key shot that brings striking impact to your portraits.

Create a graphic studio portrait

There's a secret to studio silhouettes – Caroline Wilkinson reveals all here…

Caroline Wilkinson: The simple lines and shapes of a silhouette are what makes them so appealing, but as simple as the images are and the technique may seem, getting a decent result is trickier than you might think. Aside from the lighting and exposure, as you're stripping the subject of character and features, the geometry of the pose and outline it creates has to be spot on to create any visual interest. Profile poses are a good place to start as they can accentuate curves, but also look for ways to stop your subject looking too static, such as adding movement and using dynamic shapes or graphic props. Finally, ask your subject to wear black clothing. And remember, if you don't have a studio, you can apply the same principles by shooting against a large window in direct sunlight.

Set-up Place two studioflash heads, set to a mid-power, pointing in either side of a Lastolite HiLite, and have the subject stand in front of the background. Simple. While a Lastolite HiLite is the ideal tool for the job, you can create a similar effect by placing two studio lights, set to full-power, behind and directed at a white paper or fabric backdrop. To avoid the light spilling on to the subject standing in front of the background, attach spills to the studioflash heads to contain the light and try to block any space around the background.

Pick the right power

The strength of the studioflash heads greatly influences the silhouette: too high and you'll get glare that illuminates the subject; too low and the background will be too dark.

Settings & technique

Set your camera to manual mode, its lowest ISO rating, Auto White Balance and image quality to Raw+JPEG. You'll need to dial in your camera's flash sync speed (in my case, that's 1/250sec). Set an aperture of f/11 or f/13 for optimum sharpness. Ask your subject to stand a couple of feet in front of the backdrop for a test shot. If they're illuminated, try turning the studioflash's power down or if the background is too dull, turn it up. Focusing can be a problem in low light, so place the autofocus point over an area of contrast, such as the edge of the body. Or, focus on the subject and switch from AF to manual to stop it hunting between shots. If your subject moves closer or further away from the camera, you may need to refocus.

1 Improve the contrast Even if your exposure is spot on, the background may look dull. Open the image in Adobe Camera Raw and push the *Brightness* and *Contrast* sliders between +80 and +100, with a small tweak to the Clarity for sharpness. Then, in Photoshop, improve the result by adjusting the contrast via *Layer>New Adjustment Layer>Levels*. Finally, crop and convert the image to black & white (*Layer> New Adjustment Layer>Black & White…*).

2 Extend the background If you used a Lastolite HiLite, you may find that you need to extend the background a little. In Photoshop, duplicate the image by dragging the layer down to the *Create a new layer* icon at the bottom of the Layers palette. Select the *Brush Tool* and hold down *alt* to change the cursor into an eyedropper: click on an area of white to take a colour sample, release *alt*, and 'paint' over the areas where the background's not in the frame.

Be inspired! Have fun with different poses: here's a few suggestions to get you started…

✔ **Add movement** If your subject has long hair, consider introducing a fan to add movement to the image. It immediately stops the shot from looking too static.

✔ **Strike a pose** Use repeated patterns and shapes to add interest. Try to contain the viewer's eye within the frame and subject by connecting lines.

✔ **Jump** Ask the subject to leap or jump for an energetic image: keep an eye on the pose to make sure that there's space around the limbs for a defined outline.

✔ **Be abstract** Concentrate on the composition and zoom in on the curved lines of the body or details like the feet for less conventional but alluring images.

Final image
Introducing props, like this
umbrella, can add extra visual
interest to a picture. Experiment
to see what effects you can get by
adding semi-transparent fabric
and/or a fan to your set-up, too.

Shoot Halloween portraits

If you should dare to venture out on All Hallows' Eve you might get a fright – and some fang-tastic spooky portraits if you're lucky!

Jordan Butters: Let's face it, Halloween is for kids. At what other time of year can they dress up in scary costumes and knock on neighbours' doors to demand free sweets and chocolate? On any other day they'd be shooed away, but All Hallows' Eve is different. Venture out into most suburban neighbourhoods on 31 October amidst the glowing pumpkins on doorsteps and you're likely to bump into all manner of sub-4ft ghouls, ghosts, goblins, witches and wizards. This makes Halloween a perfect time to capture some spooky portraits of the kids having fun in costume.

Preparation

We're aiming for a studio-esque, on-location portrait, so we need a backdrop and lighting set-up that can be moved around easily. The first variable to take care of is light. Halloween falls after the clocks go back in the UK, so by the time the trick or treaters are out, you'll be shooting in near darkness; therefore you'll need to use flash. Taking your flashgun off-camera will create a more dynamic light and this can be done using remote wireless triggers or a flash sync cable. Also, you'll need some form of modifier as the bare flash can create harsh shadows. Fitting a softbox and placing it close to your subject will give you nice, soft light that wraps around and allows you to control the spill of light, too. Failing that, use a photographic bounce umbrella, or 'brolly' – for light control similar to a softbox. Alternatively, use a reflector or white card to bounce the flash back on to your subject. You can use a light stand to position the flashgun or you can enrol the help of an assistant to hold the flash and modifier in position.

The second important consideration is the backdrop. You can, of course, use the neighbourhood as your background, but a plain backdrop creates a much cleaner image and removes any other distractions from your photographs. Black foam board is an excellent choice as its matt surface has a very slight reflective quality that you don't get with black fabric, which is perfect for separating your subject from the background. I couldn't source a single sheet of foam board large enough so I fixed four A1 sheets together using duct tape and wooden supports.

One final point: if you want colour images, be aware that street lights can create colour casts. When converting to b&w this isn't an issue, but they may still cast extra light on your subject, affecting the exposure.

Settings

With your camera in manual mode, choose the lowest ISO available. Set your WB to Auto or Flash and set the shutter speed to your camera's maximum sync speed, usually between 1/160sec and 1/250sec. Set your flash to manual and 1/8 power, positioning the softbox between 50cm to a metre from your subject, at just above their head height and to the left or right of camera. If you have a lightmeter, take a reading from your subject's face and dial in the corresponding aperture on your camera. If you don't have a lightmeter, a good starting aperture is f/5. Take a test shot and consult the LCD and histogram. If your subject is underexposed, increase the power of your flash or open up your aperture. If your subject is blown out and overexposed, decrease the flash output or shoot with a smaller aperture setting.

1 Prepare the shot Fix your background to a light stand, tripod or similar framework and weigh the stand down at the bottom to prevent wind toppling it over. As an alternative, you can get a friend or helper to hold the background in place. If you don't use a backdrop you could shoot against a plain or textured wall, but this will limit where you can move to and shoot from.

2 Position your subject Pose your subject approximately a foot in front of your backdrop and move your light into place. Crouch down and shoot from your subject's eye level. Use single-point autofocus to focus on your subject's eye closest to you. There should be enough ambient light around to help your camera autofocus but, if not, use a small torch or phone to illuminate your subject's face as this will help the AF to lock on.

3 Try different poses Try out a variety of different poses, but remember to wait for your flashgun to recharge between shots. Also experiment with lighting positions. Moving the light between frames will create different effects – lighting from beneath for a scary portrait is a great idea, for example. Remember to have fun and play up to the kids – ask the child to hold up their treat buckets towards the camera or to pull their scariest pose to try to make you jump!

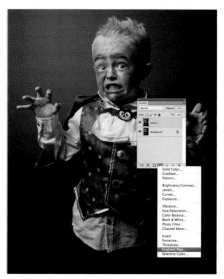

4 Post-processing Open your image and duplicate your main layer by going to *Layer>Duplicate Layer*. Use the *Spot Healing Brush Tool* to remove any visible joins in the background, switching to the *Clone Stamp Tool* for areas of detail near the edge of your subject. Convert to monochrome by pressing the *D* key to reset your colour palette before clicking on the *Add new fill or adjustment layer* button in the Layers palette and select *Gradient Map*.

Final image
To finish, I added an Unsharp Mask by selecting my image layer and going to *Filter>Sharpen>Unsharp Mask*. I used 100% as the Amount, set the Radius to 1.5 and the Threshold to 0.

Master the secrets of classic film noir lighting

Hollywood has given us many classics, not least its iconic lighting technique: a glamorous, low-key style that all portrait photographers can master using our expert advice

Bjorn Thomassen:
When photographers think of the 'Golden Age' of Hollywood, most recollect the likes of Rita Hayworth, Elizabeth Taylor and Vivien Leigh, not as on-screen sirens, but as iconic subjects of dramatic Hollywood portraits. The classic Hollywood portrait of the 1940s in particular was typified by its high contrast black & white images, created using strong directional light, with strategically placed shadows to add depth and drama. Today, Hollywood lighting is considered an art form that many still love to recreate – including us. While its style might be seen as dated, it's an immensely useful technique to learn.

Compared to the portraits we shoot today, posing is quite rigid and, as it's not the most flattering style of lighting, it's best suited to people with good skin. The slightest imperfection will be amplified. Being able to control and focus the light is key, as you need to be very targeted with where the light falls. Here, I've used a studioflash with a medium reflector dish and barndoors attached to direct the light, but taping thick black card to all four sides of your flash can work just as well. The hard light from the studioflash is then

tempered by the light bouncing off the reflector on the opposite side, before reaching the model. A second light is also used on the opposite side to accent the edges of the subject.

While most Hollywood portraits are against a plain black background, some images show texture in their backdrop, which is why we've chosen to use a carefully hung white background to show you how to create this effect should you want to use it. One of the reasons we're using barndoors, too, is to stop the spill of light on to the background, as without it the white backdrop will turn black, but still retain some tonal detail.

Original

Camera settings

Metering & exposure: The aperture you use depends on how much background detail you want in focus, how close the subject is to the backdrop and on the power of your lights. Here, the model is about a metre away, so f/5.6 provides enough depth-of-field to render her in focus but blur the backdrop. Hold the lightmeter by the face, but pointing towards the light source – not the camera – so it can accurately measure the amount of light falling on the subject. Now adjust the power of the studioflash until you get the aperture you want. With the camera in manual mode and the flash sync speed set, dial in your appropriate aperture and take your shot.

Lighting set-up

Place the main light close to the subject to have better control over the fall-off of the light: you want to avoid it illuminating the subject's lap. Position the main light 90° to the camera, pointing down 45° on the subject. Place the model in a 3/4 pose, so that the side of the face receiving the most light is turned away from the camera. By doing this, it casts a triangular shadow on the cheek closest to the camera, which is characteristic of the lighting style. The plane of the face needs to be relative to the main light for the shadow to be cast correctly. Every set-up is different, but when positioning the reflector to soften the main light and act as a fill-in, remember the law of reflection and avoid placing it too close to the model, as it may counteract the striking modelling and shadows you've created. Mine is placed approximately four feet away from the model. To add more dimensionality to the image, an accent light has been added three feet away from the subject and angled upwards at 30°, so light falls on to the opposite edges of the model. The set-up works on a lighting ratio of 3:1, as the accent light shouldn't overpower the main light.

Studioflash · Wireless trigger · Barndoors · Reflector dish · Reflector

Final image
Shot at 1/160sec at f/5.6,
this Hollywood portrait looks even
more striking with a soft sepia tone.
After some skin retouching and small
tonal adjustments using Levels, add
a duotone effect by going to
Image>Grayscale then *Image>*
Duotone, then choose *Sepia* style
from the *Preset* menu.

Photographing the female form

The female body must be up there as one of the planet's most photographed subjects – but it's notoriously difficult to get right. We show you the basics, from poses and lighting to all the equipment you need…

WHAT'S THE DIFFERENCE between an erotic image and a fine-art nude? Diverse tastes, tolerances and appreciation for the female form dictate the answer to this question, and it being so subjective means photographing intimate images of women can be both challenging and controversial. We hope, though, that this guide shows you how to create artistic portraits that tread that line between tasteful and tacky.

Photographs of semi- or fully-naked women should be a celebration of beauty and geometry, stirring an appreciation in the viewer rather than a sexual reaction. Fine-art images are produced for aesthetic or conceptual reasons rather than utility, and knowing this can help guide your imagery in the right direction.

The reaction of the viewer plays a strong role in the success of a fine-art nude, so having a clear idea of what you want to achieve and elicit from the viewer from the start makes it easier to get. There's a fine line between sexual and sensual imagery. A sensual image indulges the senses and emphasises beauty, but keeps the viewer on the outside as an observer by avoiding any sort of eye contact.

Once the subject looks into the camera, the subject is involving the viewer in what they're doing, heightening their engagement and running the risk of making the image sexual. Eye contact, however, isn't the only

contributing factor; the viewer's reaction is also influenced by the subject's expression, their pose, setting and the modesty of the model. Muted colours can also add to the artistic qualities of the image as it brings the shapes, composition, tonal range and lighting to the forefront.

There's no denying that the subject has a large role in the beauty of a picture, so picking a model with the right body for your concept can be one of the most important considerations when preparing for a shoot. Using regular women instead of professional models has its advantages if you want to portray 'real' women, but from a photographer's point of view, they'll be more nervous in front of the camera and need more direction. Whoever you decide to use, make sure you have them sign a model release form first.

Looking at the portfolios of other photographers' work is a good way to decide what it is that you like and dislike about certain styles of nudes and glamour photography. It's also an effective way to study the subtle differences but extremely different impacts of some images. The classic works of David Bailey, Ralph Gibson, Andreas Bitesnich and Ruth Bernhard are worth investigating. They're all different styles and modesty isn't always a consideration, but study the expressions and settings to see how they still make them work.

Part of the art of female photography is working well with shadow – it's just as important as light for giving depth and structure to your picture. They enable you to hide, shape and accentuate areas of the body as well as control the mood of an image. It's worth remembering that the transition from light to dark depends on the size of the light source relative to the subject. The smaller the light and further it is away, the crisper the shadows, and the opposite is true for a large light source that's close to a subject. So be careful when moving lights closer or further away to change their intensity as it can also change the shadow hardness. While shadows are ideal for disguising areas of the body, they can also make skin irregularities more pronounced, increasing your retouching work, so bear this in mind, too.

Learning how to work with shadows takes practice, but here are a couple of tips to get you started: if a shadow is too dense and you want to reveal some detail, use a fill light, whether it's from a reflector or a second light set several stops dimmer than the key light (main light source). But if you can't create deep enough shadows, it's probably because there's reflective light nearby, so use black cloth, panels of black foam core or the black side of a reflector as close to the areas you want in shadow as possible, without encroaching on the shot. »

Essential equipment

You don't need expensive or elaborate kit to take great portraits, but we do advise opting for the best lenses that you can afford. Fast prime or medium telephoto zooms such as the 24-70mm f/2.8, 24-105mm f/2.8, 50mm f/1.4 or 80mm f/1.4 are great options, but if you're tight on cash we recommend the 50mm f/1.8 – it's superb quality and can be bought for around £100. Opt for a longer lens like a 70-200mm f/2.8 if you want to put more distance between you and your subject. The shallow depth-of-field you get with fast lenses is invaluable with this type of photography as it softens skin, reduces the appearance of wrinkles and blurs the background and body beautifully. You can get by using only natural light, reflectors or a flashgun,

but invest in at least a basic studioflash set-up if you can afford it: Elinchrom and Bowens offer great selections of one- or two-head studioflash kits. Most of the lighting set-ups here can be done with one or two lights and reflectors – the difference is the light modifiers (see panel on page 99). To work with studioflash equipment, use a wireless flash trigger and a handheld flash meter. Using a light meter means you can measure the light falling on specific areas of the subject (known as incident light readings), allowing you to get accurate measurements and to work fast – important with nudes. We strongly suggest you avoid working out exposures by using the LCD monitor and trial and error as it's not accurate enough.

Top tip

There's a lot to learn when it comes to studio lighting, as you've probably gathered already from this section, so here's some helpful hints to hopefully make it easier for you to master. The 'inverse square law' is a useful principle to understand and basically dictates that an object that is twice the distance from a source of light receives a quarter of the illumination. For instance, if you move a light that's 6ft away from your subject 12ft away, doubling the distance, a quarter of the light's brightness will fall on the subject. This is incredibly important for creating mood in an image, as the further the light is from a subject, the wider the spread of light and more even the lighting. The closer the light is to the subject, the quicker the fall-off and the darker areas of the scene further away will become.

Strike a pose
Symmetry is highly important in nudes so ask your subject to adopt unusual and even poses. In this image, the arms and legs act as lead-in lines drawing the viewer's eyes around the body.

ISTOCK PHOTO

Use diffusing material

Give your silhouette a different twist by stretching some silk cloth or thin net curtain over a scrim frame between the subject and camera to soften the image. If you find the camera's autofocus struggles, switch to manual focusing.

As skin is primarily matte, it can help to create or enhance highlights by having the subject smooth oil or body lotion into their skin to reflect light, accentuating the body's contours and adding dimension. A shimmering body lotion, Johnson's Baby Oil Gel or Light Oil Mist are good options, but also try combining types on different areas of the body to add varying definition. You could even use water in a spray bottle, but be aware that this will be absorbed quickly under the heat of studio lights.

Next to lighting, posing is the most important feature and there are hundreds of permutations; which ones work depend on the shape and size of the subject. As a guideline, try to create 'C', 'D', and 'S' shapes to accentuate curves. Try to keep all lines connected and leading back to the face to contain the viewer's gaze and avoid straight limbs by bending them to form a triangle or curve. Complement the simplicity of the subject by picking compositions with balance and symmetry, too, and be aware of your camera angles. To render a body proportionally, shoot at eye level to avoid altering the perspective and have the subject turn slightly away from the camera for a very flattering angle.

Unless you hire a professional model, chances are your subject will be anxious about posing nude, so plan your poses and lighting set-ups as thoroughly as possible before the shoot to limit the time that they're exposed. Communicate exactly what you'll be doing before they undress and during the shoot to put them at ease, perhaps play some soft music, make sure the room is a comfortable temperature and that there's a robe handy for in between set-ups. Whether you're male or female, respect the subject's boundaries: don't touch them, instead demonstrate the pose first, show them example pictures and even turn away while they get into position if it makes them more comfortable. It can often make the shoot more relaxed by having a third party present, too, be it their partner, a friend, make-up artist or stylist. If you're a male photographer, it helps if that person is female. It's a good idea to have the subject leave some loose clothing on while you practise poses, but ask them to go without a bra or elasticated socks at least two hours before the shoot to allow for strap marks to disappear. This gives you the basics to start with, now go ahead and try some of our lighting set-ups. Good luck!

Graphic nudes

The outline of a curvaceous woman is simple and soft, and isolating these lines can make for graphic imagery. The best way to capture the outline is to backlight the subject, either by using a white background to create a silhouette or rim-lighting the curvatures against a black background. For the silhouette, choose a graphic pose and point one or two naked studioflashes, set to full power, at the white background, being careful not to allow too much light to fall on the subject. Meter for the background to silhouette the body. Rim lighting is slightly more sophisticated as you need to control the light to place a highlight along the body's edge to pick it out from the background, but without it spilling on to the front or the backdrop. Use a striplight placed 45° behind the subject, as close as you can without it encroaching on the frame, to control the fall-off. Place the light and model at least four feet from the background to stop it illuminating the backdrop, set the studioflash to its lowest power and select f/5.6; narrow or widen the aperture to control the highlight.

Lighting modifiers

 Softbox: Typically shaped like a rectangle or octagon, a softbox provides soft light that wraps around the subject, replicating the qualities of natural window light, but offering more control. The bigger the softbox, the larger the light source, giving less contrast and smoother tones.

 Beauty dish: A large dish-shaped modifier that reflects light from the flash head on to the subject. Available in white or silver finishes – we recommend white for a soft, crisp light.

 Striplight: A tall, narrow softbox that creates a soft but defined highlight; it works well as a rim light and when you need to restrict the fall-off of light on to a backdrop.

 Snoot: It attaches to a flash head's silver dish to restrict the spill of light into a narrow beam.

 Barn doors: Another modifier that shapes the spill of light, barn doors have four panels of metal that can be moved to control the beam of light, restricting it to areas of the body.

 **Honeycomb grids:** Works by concentrating the light so that only the centre beam reaches the subject with a smooth fall-off at the edges. It's a similar but more efficient modifier than the snoot, which can waste a lot of light, but is often a lot less expensive. There are also soft grids available that can be attached to softboxes for similar effects.

Umbrella: The quality of light brollies produce is very similar to a softbox, but they are much more portable, making them ideal for on-location shoots. A brolly acts like a large reflector, delivering a wide and soft spread of light. Reflective umbrellas come in opaque, white, silver and gold finishes for varying light intensities. There are also shoot-through transparent brollies that diffuse the flash output.

 Reflectors: Able to bounce and direct light as a main light source or to fill in shadows, a reflector is an invaluable accessory. Available in various sizes, styles and colours – gold, silver and white, with varying combinations of all three. The light bounced off a gold reflector is warm and strong, a silver's is cool and harsh, and white reflectors produce subtle and softer results. Some have a black side, too, for shielding light.

Top tips: Golden guidelines for post-production

If you get the image right in-camera, there should be very little to do in post-production. However, unless you're opting for a raw finish for artistic reasons, there is some basic but essential editing to be done. The first thing is to make sure your computer screen is correctly calibrated, then address…

■ **White Balance** If you're processing your image in colour, skin tones require some delicate care and attention. When there's too much magenta in the image, usually from mixed lighting, skin can look too red, while cool window light can make it blue and pale. Use a grey card to ascertain the correct White Balance or shoot in Raw and adjust the colour temperature later in post-production. Overexposing an image can also produce an orange and magenta cast, especially in warm light, which is why using a light meter to take an exposure reading from the skin is so important. Using Raw conversion software can help recover overexposed areas. Be watchful of your environment, too, as you may find that certain materials – grass, for instance – tints the light that reflects off the surface and onto the subject.

■ **Retouching** Blemishes, cellulite and uneven skin tone are a few things to look out for if you want to sensitively retouch a portrait. Lighting can disguise areas your subject would rather

not reveal and reduce imperfections, but you can help it in post-production, too. Brightening the eyes and smoothing the skin are two basic techniques, as well as emphasising the highlights. See the portrait retouching feature on page 132 for the best ways to do this.

■ **Exposure control** If you've shot in Raw, which we recommend you do, you can make global tonal adjustments using the Exposure, Recovery and Fill Light tools in Adobe Camera Raw. After you have got your base exposure, we suggest opening the image in Photoshop, creating a duplicate layer and using the Dodge or Burn Tool, set to a low Exposure, to brighten or darken areas of the image, accentuating highlights and darkening areas that need more concealment. Be careful not to lose too much tonal or skin detail, though.

■ **Black & white** Toned or simple black & white conversions are often what elevate a nude to its artistic status. It's an effective way of detaching the image from reality, forcing the viewer to consider its artistic properties: its tonal balance, lighting, composition and elegance, rather than just the nudity. We recommend investing in Nik Software's Silver Efex Pro 2 plug-in (www.niksoftware.com) as it's packed with fantastic presets and adjustable settings that make strong and artistic conversions as

complicated or as simple as you want to make them. Alternatively, use a Black & White or Channels adjustment layer in Photoshop.

■ **Sharpening** A little bit of sharpening goes a long way. Convert your image into a fully editable Smart Filter (*Filter>Smart Filter*) and then apply Unsharp Mask (*Filter>Sharpen> Unsharp Mask*), increasing the Amount slightly to draw out detail. The Clarity slider in ACR is also useful. A fundamental step for skin softening.

■ **Vignetting** By darkening the edges of an image, it draws the focus to the subject. There are several ways to do this – see the January 2012 issue of *Digital SLR Photography* for a couple of them – or try this method: use the *Lasso Tool*, with a *Feather* of *50-100px*, to create a frame within the image, then go to *Select>Inverse*. Add a Curves adjustment layer (*Layer>New Adjustment Layer…*) and move the sliders to darken the edges. If the vignette encroaches on the subject too much, use the *Brush Tool* with *Black* paint on the adjustment layer's Layer Mask to reduce its effect.

■ **Paper and inks** Don't skimp in this area after all your hard work: opt for the best fine-art paper you can afford and quality inks. Look at brands including Hahnemühle Fine Art, Innova, PermaJet, Canon and Epson.

Bodyscapes

When shooting nudes, don't be limited to full-length portraits. Focusing on the geometry of small areas creates striking bodyscapes. Draw your attention to specific parts of the body and their lines: the curves of the back, the buttocks, the slope of the chest, nape of the neck,

muscles of the abdomen or creases in bent and crossed limbs. Any area can create an interesting abstract if lit and composed well, with a strong tonal range. Get up close and use a wide aperture for a soft fall-off in focus and carefully place shadows and highlights to emphasise

depth, lines and to create interest. Part of the art of abstracts is evoking a mystery about the subject, so choose a balanced or frame-filling composition that makes the viewer look twice to figure out what it is. Converting to black & white can complement the simplicity of the shots.

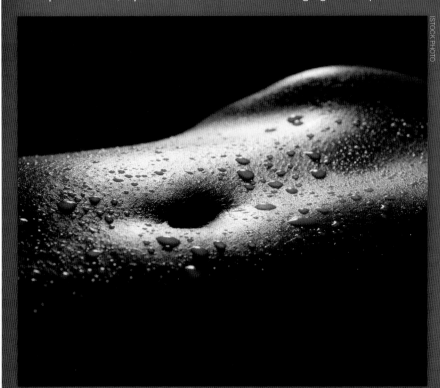

ISTOCK PHOTO

Give your nudes a different look

There are many set-ups and poses you can try, but here are three of our favourites...

No eyes

Classical nude photography is rooted in the principles of Greek and Roman sculpture, where the artist emphasises form, line, simplicity, balance and technique, rather than emotive content. By framing this picture from the neck down, the viewer has no eyes or expression to connect with, so is forced to study the nude's form, shape and lighting rather than as a person, developing a distance between the viewer and the image. You can create a similar effect by photographing a person from behind or having their hair obscure their face, like in our opening shot. While it's an effective and classic approach to nudes, it's also a good pose if your subject would rather keep their identity hidden. This image is very simply lit using one Bowens Gemini 400W flash head and a 140x100cm softbox, approximately five feet high and away from the subject, so it's aimed straight at her back. The distance of the light to her and the background means the light spills on to the backdrop and illuminates it, but casts her torso into shadow. The top of her back was metered for f/8 and the image was processed using Nik Software's Silver Efex Pro and its 'Antique Plate 1' preset. The vignette was also added to darken the edges and her legs, to draw the focus to the sculpting of her back. To see more of Jan Doef's work, visit: www.jandoef.nl

Averted eye contact

Sometimes the simplest set-ups are the best. This image was shot against a white wall using two 130x50cm Elinchrom Rotalux Rectangular striplights fitted to Elinchrom heads. The key light is approximately six feet away from the subject to our left and a fill light is placed six feet in front of her at 45°, next to the camera. As she's angled towards the key light, a meter reading of f/8 was taken from her forehead, with a second reading from her knee to make sure that it didn't burn out as it's closer to the light. Working by a lighting ratio of 3:1, the key light was 1.5 stops brighter than the fill light and turned 10-15° away from the background so the main thrust of the light passes her and doesn't overexpose the wall. A household fan was set on the ground to the left of her to add lift to her hair. The beauty of this shot is in the model and how the lighting accentuates her curves and bone structure. Notice how the averted eye contact makes the image sensual as the viewer is still an observer and the tasteful pose doesn't show too much, while highlighting what makes her form photogenic. The impact of the image and viewer's reaction would be different if she was looking at the camera. To see more of Bjorn Thomassen's fine-art nudes or to contact him about training courses, visit: www.bjornofinspire.com

Direct eye contact

Less is often more and this portrait arguably wouldn't be as elegant or alluring if more of her body was revealed. Similarly, it's the eye contact that makes this shot so impactful as it engages the viewer, but it's the pose that retains the interest by containing the viewer's gaze through the connected limbs: there's a continuous line running through the pose that keeps the viewer returning to the subject's eye contact. When working with nudes, it's best to work with low light so it's softer and easier to control. Umbrellas deliver a very wide, and therefore soft, spread of light that's typically low in contrast, especially with an opaque umbrella. To recreate this shot, position an opaque umbrella 20° to the right of the subject and the camera, at a height that's level with the crouching/sitting model. Meter the face for f/11 to get sufficient depth-of-field and adjust the flash head's power accordingly. The studioflash should be as near to the subject as possible, without encroaching on the shot, to control the fall-off of light. The light should fall softly on the subject so as to illuminate her front; if it's too strong, the light will fill the shadow that's wrapped around her. It can help, however, to deliberately overexpose the image to expand the tonal range and then use Levels or Curves to draw the exposure back to get a more gentle graduation of tones.

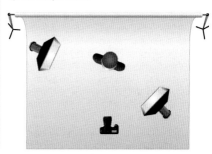

Master boudoir photography

The art of boudoir is not that different from nudes, but with a shifted emphasis on to the subject's sexuality

MORE AND MORE women want boudoir photographs, either nude or in lingerie – not just for their partners, but for themselves. Unlike nudes, boudoir images are meant to be alluring and connect with the viewer, but they're also different from erotic imagery in that they emphasise the aesthetic qualities of the subject and the photography over their sexually stimulating nature.

In many ways, you should handle a boudoir shoot the same as a nude, with taste, dignity and photographic prowess. The same lighting principles apply, depending on the mood you want to create, but a lot more consideration needs to be given to the styling of an image – hair, make-up and lingerie – as well as how you might use props and furniture.

Unless you have a studio with various set-ups, most boudoir sessions are done on location, such as at the subject's home or in a hotel room, giving you lots of options for posing them in different scenes and set-ups. While shooting nudes is a lot about the photographer's vision, boudoir-style imagery is often shot for the subject, who will want to look the best they can. And besides the correct posing, well-chosen lingerie, lighting and props can cover flaws and pronounce your subject's strengths.

We asked award-winning professional boudoir photographer Emma Jones about the way she works, the secrets behind her most popular lighting set-ups and the common errors novices make. "If you're starting out, research what works for various body shapes and sizes, and test them out to build up a

mental library of poses," says Emma. "If you want a delicate and feminine result, avoid a black backdrop, strong lighting that creates harsh shadows and bold colours. Opt for a soft, even spread of light that can be gained with softboxes and reflectors. For glamour images with more sass, opt for a large beauty dish or parabolic umbrella for sleek highlights and strong shadows. Use a reflector to avoid shadows underneath the eyes and a second light to pick the body out from a dark background. Get your client laughing to relax them as an uncomfortable client will ruin a photo. And steer clear of feather boas and cowboy hats. It depends on your tastes but I think they potentially turn great pictures into cheesy photos." To hire or see more of Emma's work, visit www.missboudoir.com.

Natural daylight

If your studio has a window, use it. Depending on the time of day, size of the window and the direction it faces in relation to the sun, the light can cast harsh shadows and produce vibrant colours or have soft qualities with flattering, barely-there shadows. Diffused daylight through a small window is very directional with soft-edged shadows, while a large window like the ones used here work like giant softboxes with light that wraps around the subject. Regardless of the type of light, the challenge is photographing the subject against the window as they will be backlit, so you need to bounce as much available light back onto the subject's body as possible. In the above picture, a large rectangular floor-standing silver reflector is positioned to the left of the window about 6ft away and tilted upwards to reflect light back onto the subject. A silver Lastolite TriFlector in front evens out the light.

Exposure: 1/125sec at f/2.8 (ISO 1000).

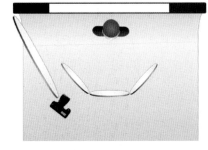

Fill light versus reflector

The point of this set-up is to create a sensual and softly-lit setting to flatter all body shapes. The background is made up of unobtrusive damask wallpaper and a variety of soft netting over a satin base. Mixed in are a few petals to break up the colours. The set-up consists of a main light fitted with an octagonal softbox and a diffuser grid metered from the subject's torso at f/4. The light is placed directly to the left of the model, 6ft away and 5ft off the ground, pointing down at 45°. This lights the top-left side of the model, creating curvaceous shadows to the right.

In the left picture, a fill light metered at f/2.8 is placed high above the model, off to the right, pointing down to ease the shadows created by the main light. It is fitted with a silver Spill Kill and covered with softbox fabric to take off a little of the sharpness. You can use a softbox or brolly for this if you'd prefer the light to be very soft.

The same set-up can be very easily adjusted to add more atmosphere by simply replacing the fill light with a large silver reflector to the right of the model (right image). In doing so, the light from the octagonal softbox is bounced back onto the wall, adding depth to the shot and highlighting the wallpaper's shimmery surface. Because there is no fill light, the shadows on the body are deeper, making the curvature more pronounced. If you'd prefer to bounce the light onto the model instead of the background, simply angle the reflector accordingly. Both these shots use Bowens Gemini 500W studioflash heads.

Left: Exposure: 1/30sec at f/2.8 (ISO 100).
Right: Exposure: 1/125sec at f/3.5 (ISO 100).

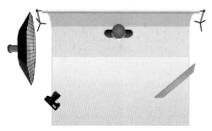

Chaise longue

When using furniture you need to consider how best to light your subject so she has the freedom to move into a variety of poses while remaining well-lit. As the wallpaper and the chaise longue are ivory,

I wanted to make sure the lighting and shadows are very soft and the highlights don't bleach out. The studioflash is fitted with a horizontal striplight along the main length of the chaise, creating darkened vignetted edges. It is placed 6ft away from the chaise, 5ft up and slightly angled downwards. A honeycomb grid is used to further soften the light.

Exposure: 1/125sec at f/2.8 (ISO 100).

Beanbag

Here, the subject is laying on a satin-covered beanbag, backed by a black curtain. Her head is tipped back towards the camera, ensuring her face is well-lit. The main light, metered from the

face at f/4.5, is fitted with a vertical striplight and honeycomb grid, placed 5ft away from the subject and 4ft high, with a downwards angle. A snoot is placed at the bottom right, 6ft away, 9ft high and angled downward. Metered at f/3.5, this adds a little bit of light onto the bottom of the fabric and legs. A reflector bounces light onto the left side of the subject.

Exposure: 1/125sec at f/4.5 (ISO 100).

A three-light set-up

This is the perfect lighting to accentuate curves: it provides deep shadows and gorgeous smooth highlights on the skin. Again, we are using a black curtain backdrop and want to limit the amount of light reaching it, so a vertical striplight with a honeycomb grid is used. It's placed 5-6ft away from the model, 5ft high, with a slight downward angle and metered at f/4.5 from the torso. A snoot is placed high up behind the subject, slightly off to the left, 7-8ft away and metered at f/3.5 to catch the hair and shoulders, picking the model out from the dark background. On the opposite side to the softbox, a 70cm silver beauty dish with honeycomb grid is placed 6ft away and metered at f/3.5 to add a strong and smooth highlight to the left side of the model. If there are any unwanted shadows, use a reflector. **Exposure: 1/125sec at f/4.5 (ISO 100).**

SIGMA

PHOTOGRAPH © BILL SULLIVAN

2013
Amateur
Photographer
AWARD
WINNER

SIGMA 3
3 YEAR UK WARRANTY
For registration and conditions log on to
www.sigma-imaging-uk.com/warranty

SIGMA
105mm
F2.8
EX DG OS HSM Macro

For Sigma. Canon, Nikon, Sony and Pentax
Supplied with fitted padded case,
lens hood and APS-C lens hood adapter.

Fast aperture medium telephoto macro lens with a 1:1 maximum magnification also allowing a generous working distance.

Sigma's Optical Stabilisation allows the use of shutter speeds approximately 4 stops slower than would otherwise be possible. As the stabilisation effect is visible through the viewfinder, it aids composition and accurate focusing. SLD glass provides excellent control of aberrations and the floating inner focus system ensures high rendering throughout the focusing range. HSM provides quiet, high speed autofocus and allows full-time manual focus, even if the lens is set to the AF position. This lens has a rounded 9 blade diaphragm which creates an attractive blur to the out of focus areas. This also creates smooth, rounded out of focus highlights. The lens is compatible with Sigma's APO Tele converters allowing an even greater working distance or closer than 1:1 magnification.

DIGITAL TECHNIQUES

GET TO GRIPS WITH POST-PRODUCTION TO PRODUCE EVEN BETTER IMAGES

CREATIVE TREATMENTS

CONVERT TO BLACK & WHITE

FINISHING TOUCHES

Convert images to black & white

Sometimes images need help to convert well to mono – adjusting tones separately will often give a better result than a simple straight conversion

Caroline Wilkinson: The strength of a monochromatic portrait depends largely on its tonal range, form and composition. If you're stripping an image of colour, you need to ensure that these raw components are strong enough to give the picture impact. If the other factors are taken care of, once you start to recognise the greyscale shades of different colours, it can be fairly easy to assess the potential for a strong black & white conversion. For instance, yellows are highlights, while deep reds and purples shadows, and greens and certain shades of blue often render as mid-tones. You need a complete range of these tones to create good contrast and to stop the viewer's eye from lingering too long on heavy dark and light areas. Imagining a colour image in black & white is one way to do it, another is to do a quick temporary conversion using Photoshop by desaturating the image (see below) to assess potential.

Look for images with strong tonal separation between the background and subject – for instance, if your subject is wearing a blue coat against a green bush, you know there will be limited tonal separation between these two mid-tones, making the image look flat. However, if you've got a dark colour against a bright blue sky, you've probably got something to work with. The same goes for the model: if you've a mid-toned background, opt for a blonde model rather than a brunette for that tonal distinction, and visa versa.

There are lots of ways to convert an image to black & white in Photoshop, not to mention creative plug-ins like Nik Software's Silver Efex Pro 2 or Power Retouche's Black & White Studio. But for this tutorial we're using the lesser known, but highly effective, Gradient Map adjustment layer. I've also included a brief outline of three other popular ways to convert images to black & white below.

Original

Three other ways to convert to black & white using Photoshop

Black & White adjustment layer Go to *Layer>New adjustment layer>Black and white*. The image instantly turns mono and you can adjust the coloured sliders to darken or lighten the different tones for exquisite contrast control.

Channel Mixer Choose *Image>Adjustments> Channel Mixer* and tick the *Monochrome* box. Now use the colour channel sliders: *Red*, *Green* and *Blue* to adjust contrast, making sure they all amount to *100%*.

Desaturate You can do this either via *Image> Adjustments>Desaturate* or using a *Hue/ Saturation* adjustment layer and dragging the *Saturation* slider to *0*. It offers no control over contrast, but you could use *Levels* afterwards.

1 Open your colour image With your image open, make sure the Layers palette is visible (*Window>Layers*) and then click on the *Add new adjustment or fill layer* button at the bottom of the Layers palette and select *Gradient Map*.

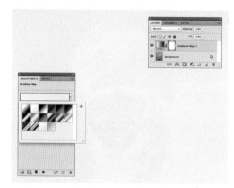
2 Add a Gradient Map With the Gradient Map accessed, you'll notice the colours might not be black & white yet. Click on the gradient in the adjustment panel to access the *Gradient Map Editor* and select *Black to White*.

3 Edit the contrast With the Gradient Map Editor open, you can use the sliders under *Gradient Type* to set the black and white point in your image. This can give your picture beautiful deep blacks and really bright whites.

4 Adjust the transition To control the gradient transitions between the two stops, move the *Color Midpoint*, as circled in the palette above, to steepen the transition towards the nearest colour stop.

5 Add a stop or two You can edit as intricately as you want by creating new colour stops and transitions by clicking where you want them within the gradient. If you get stuck, click *alt* to turn the *Cancel* button to *Reset* or delete to remove the stop.

6 Add colour By adding a stop and changing its colour via the *Color* box, you can create some interesting effects, like this silvery conversion, or even a sepia effect by selecting a deep orange. Have a play to see what works.

Final image
By carefully editing the tonality of an image you can transform a black & white portrait from bland to beautiful.

Add colour to mono images

Dust off your colouring book skills to transform black & white images

Jordan Butters: Most of us are not strangers to converting images to monochrome. The process can be completed in a matter of seconds with just a few clicks of your mouse. Performing the conversion in the opposite direction is not quite as straightforward, unfortunately, but it is still easily achievable. The main issue is that the colour information is no longer present in the image and therefore the only way to achieve this is to reintroduce the colours manually into areas of the image. This may sound a complicated process, but don't worry – you don't have to be Van Gogh to make this technique work, thanks to the different Blend Modes in Photoshop and Elements. The colouring process can be done in a few simple steps – however, the more care taken, the more convincing the final effect will be. You can apply this technique to images that were shot on black & white film, too – just scan in the photo and use the Dust & Scratches filter and the Healing Brush Tool to tidy up any marks first. As you'll discover, there's something enchanting about seeing an old image converted to colour and given a new lease of life.

Original

Top tip

Blend Modes
Your choice of Blend Mode will affect how each layer of colour is applied to your image. The most useful Blend Modes for this technique are Soft Light and Color. Some experimentation is often required when it comes to applying Blend Modes, as no two modes will offer exactly the same effect when applied.

1 Create a new layer To begin, click on the *Create new layer* button in the Layers palette. This layer will contain the base colour for our subject's skin tone. Click on the *Foreground color* icon in the toolbar and use the colour map to choose a suitable skin tone.

2 Add skin colour Select the *Brush Tool* and, in the brush options at the top, set the *Hardness* to *50%* and pick an appropriate brush *Size*. Begin painting over your subject's skin. Do not worry if you go outside of the edges or over facial features as we will correct this later.

Final image
Adding different hues can make an image feel incredibly fresh and vibrant.

3 Change Blend Mode In the Layers palette, change the *Blend Mode* to *Color*. If the skin tone doesn't look realistic, adjust the *Opacity* slider in the Layers palette to desaturate the tone slightly. If this doesn't correct it, try a different foreground colour and repeat the previous step.

4 Add a Layer Mask Create a Layer Mask by clicking on the *Add layer mask* button and make sure that your *Foreground color* is set to *Black*. Use the *Brush Tool* on the Layer Mask to paint over any areas where you have coloured outside of the lines, including the eyes and mouth.

5 Paint in hair colour Click on *Create a new layer* again in the Layers palette and choose a *Foreground color* to suit your subject's hair. Once again, use the *Brush Tool* to paint the hair colour onto your image, again not worrying too much about going outside of the edges.

6 Change Blend Mode In the Layers palette, change the *Blend Mode* of this layer. The Blend Mode will depend on the colour of your subject's hair. It's worth trying both *Color* and *Soft Light* to see which produces the nicest effect, again adjusting *Opacity* if needed.

7 Add a Layer Mask Add a *Layer Mask* to the same layer and brush out any areas of overspill. Repeat these steps for each section of colour, starting on a new layer each time and experimenting with the *Blend Mode* and *Opacity* for each layer until you're happy with the finish.

8 Experiment with colour Don't be afraid to have fun with the colours that you choose. Obviously certain things have to be the correct colour to look right, but there's no reason why you can't spice things up by experimenting with different background or clothing colours.

Create sepia images

Give your images a nostalgic twist with this easy way to sepia tone

Jordan Butters: Sepia toning has been around since the early days of film photography. Its original purpose being to prolong the lifespan of the print, as images that weren't treated with sepia tended to fade and degrade more quickly.

Today, sepia toning is still one of the most popular and long-standing photographic effects. Now used for purely aesthetic rather than archival reasons, sepia-toning can add a romantic bygone feel to an image. It has power to add drama and atmosphere in much the same way as black & white photography, while retaining a warmth rarely present in the cold tones of a greyscale image.

For this reason, sepia is suited to portrait and wedding photography. There are several ways to sepia-tone images and each gives slightly different results. Sepia has no defined shade or hue as it is simply a warm brown tint applied to a mono image, so look to create your own favourite shades.

I've added a twist in the final two steps by reintroducing a little of the original colour – if you prefer a traditional sepia image, save your work after the fourth step.

Sepia in Lightroom 4

Thanks to the various presets available in Adobe Lightroom 4, users of this software can also apply this effect in a few easy steps. With your image loaded into the *Develop* module, click on the *Presets tab* on the left-hand side and then, under Lightroom *B&W Toned Presets*, select *Sepia Tone*. To bring a hint of colour back into your image, click on *Treatment: Color* at the top of the *Basic* tab on the right and drag the *Saturation* slider down until you reach the desired effect. You can also adjust the *Vibrance* slider to affect how much colour shows through. Have a play around until you find a result you're happy with.

Final image
A sepia tint with a hint of colour suits this romantic shot perfectly.

Original

ISTOCK PHOTO

1 Create a duplicate Work nondestructively by opening your image and clicking on *Layer>Duplicate Layer* to create a copy of your main image layer. In doing so, if you make a mistake or want to start over, your original image remains intact.

2 Convert to monochrome In the Layers palette click on the *Create new fill or adjustment layer* button and select *Black & White*. In the Adjustments palette, tweak the respective colour sliders to tune the effect and suit your image.

3 Add the sepia Create another Adjustment Layer, this time selecting *Photo Filter*. In the Adjustment palette make sure that *Preserve Luminosity* is checked and select the *Sepia* filter. Use the *Density* slider to adjust the effect's strength; I chose 55%.

4 Boost contrast Create another Adjustment Layer and select *Brightness/Contrast*. Use the sliders to fine-tune the contrast of your image. You can either stop here and save your image or continue to bring back a hint of colour to your image with the following two steps.

5 Group the layers Group your Adjustment Layers together by right-clicking on one of your Adjustment Layers in the Layers palette and choosing *Select similar layers*. Then go to *Layer>Group Layers* to put them into a Group folder.

6 Bring back some colour Click on the *Add layer mask* button before going to *Image>Apply Image*. In the dialogue box that appears you can check or uncheck the *Invert* box to alter the effect as well as change the *Blend Mode* and *Opacity*.

Composite subjects with fine hair

Wispy strands of hair are a headache to select even for the seasoned Photoshop user, but this simple step-by-step technique should make the process a lot smoother and give a really good result

Luke Marsh: If you've ever tried to composite a person on to a different background, then you'll know that the hair can be the hardest area to select. Extracting the fine, flyaway strands can be frustrating and time-consuming, but crucial if you want your composite to look seamless and not like a hard-edged helmet.

The success of this technique depends on the type of background you're extracting from and it's a lot easier if the subject is against a grey or white backdrop, or one that's uniform and light in tone. If it's not uniform, you could use the Brush Tool to paint the background white.

1 Duplicate layer Create a copy of your image layer (*Layer>New>Layer via Copy*), then go to *Image>Adjustments>Desaturate* to remove the colour from this new layer. Next, go to *Image> Adjustments>Levels...* and move the black slider right to no more than *100* for lighter hair or no more than *50* for dark or black hair. This process is to darken the hair significantly – the hair strands don't need to be perfectly black at this stage.

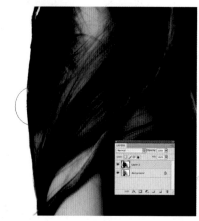

2 Brush the edges Select the *Brush Tool* set to *Black*, with a medium-sized, soft edge and with the *Mode* set to *Overlay* in the Options bar. Now, brush around the edge of the model to darken areas missed by Levels. The brush will darken areas of the subject while the white background will remain unaffected. Don't go over any areas of fine hair yet as this is best done gradually with reduced opacity to avoid problems.

Workflow tools

■ Different backgrounds
Creating a Layer Mask that works well with fine hair can be time-consuming, but once it's done, pretty much any background can be dropped in without the need for further editing. Simply reveal the silhouette layer hidden in step seven by clicking on the eye icon, then repeat the instructions from step five to step eight, using your replacement background accordingly.

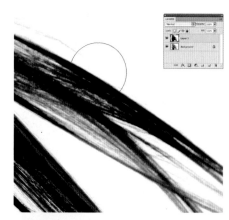

3 Darken the fine hair Reduce the brush *Opacity* to *50%* in the Options bar then, using the same principle as before, work over the hair strands to darken them. The reduced opacity will help to build up the effect, especially on very fine hair strands. Don't attempt to get the strands completely black at this stage as this can thicken them irreversibly. Once the background is added, final tweaks can be made to perfect the strands.

4 Fill the gaps Now the edges of the image have been darkened, it's time to fill in detail in the centre. Change the brush's *Mode* to *Normal* and *Opacity* to *100%*, and begin to fill any areas of detail that remain. As the brush is now set to Normal, be sure to work at the centre of the subject, and prevent your strokes from overlapping into the white areas of the image. You should now have a perfect silhouette of your hair image.

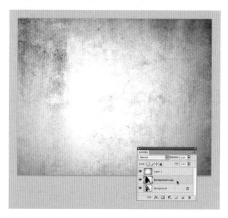

5 Add a background Open your background file and go to *Select>All* then *Edit>Cut* to copy the image. Go back to your hair file and click *Edit>Paste* to place the background image at the top of the Layers palette and resize the image if necessary. Click on the hair silhouette layer beneath, go to *Select>All* and then *Edit>Copy* to place the silhouette on to the pasteboard. Now click back on the background image layer above.

Final image
A perfect process that will take you one step closer to creating elaborate composites.

6 **Add a Layer Mask** Add a Layer Mask to the background image by going to *Layer>New Layer Mask>Reveal All* – the Layer Mask will appear next to the image thumbnail in the Layers palette. Hold the *Alt* key and click on the *Layer Mask*: the screen will go blank to show that the content of the mask is empty. Now go to *Edit>Paste* to place the hair silhouette into the Layer Mask. It will also appear on the blank screen.

7 **View the effect** The original silhouette layer has served its purpose so hide it by clicking on its eye icon in the Layers palette. Hold down *Alt* and click on the *Layer Mask* attached to the background layer to hide the preview. You will now see a rough composite of the hair and background image. The hair at this stage is looking good but by no means perfect. Change the *Blend Mode* to *Multiply* to improve the composite further.

8 **Final tweaks** With the Layer Mask active, open *Image>Adjustments>Levels...* and move the grey slider left while previewing the results on the image. Stop when you feel the hair strands are almost perfect without any halos appearing around them. Finally, using the *Brush Tool*, with the *Mode* set to *Overlay* and the colour to *Black*, work over any remaining imperfections, which tend to be in areas of very fine hair.

Bokeh panorama

Favour shallow depth-of-field, but limited by your lenses and sensor size? Learn the secrets of the amazing 'bokeh panorama' technique and you'll transform your images and the way you work

Caroline Wilkinson: Us APS-C users gaze at full-frame and medium-format photographers with envy. Paired with fast glass, their camera's bokeh is far superior to ours and image quality frankly surpasses anything we could muster – until now. Using this technique, coined the 'Brenizer method' (after being popularised by photographer Ryan Brenizer), we can expand the size of our sensor by stitching multiple images, thus creating a level of shallow depth-of-field that rivals a full-frame camera, and even approach the realms of medium-format, depending on how many images you take and stitch.

Long before the dawn of digital, landscape photographers have created panoramas by joining lots of images together to exceed the field-of-view of their camera format. A bokeh panorama is a similar technique, but instead of joining images to create an ultra-wide image, you're combining them to create a shallower depth-of-field than your camera would normally allow – in effect, extending the size of your camera's sensor. If you try this technique with a full-frame DSLR and fast telephoto lens you'll get a depth-of-field that surpasses the capabilities of any DSLR. Focal lengths between 85mm and 200mm are ideal, but the humble 50mm f/1.8 can do the job well enough too.

IMAGE: SYLVAIN LATOUCHE

Achieving bokeh panorama

The success of this method relies on your technique. You must ensure that your focus, exposure and position do not change while shooting the frames, as you'll encounter difficulties when aligning the images. It's up to you the number of frames you shoot, but the more you do, the more pronounced the effect. Aim for at least four images shot on an APS-C camera to mimic a full-frame bokeh, but bear in mind that the more frames you use, the smaller your subject will be in the final image as the field-of-view increases. I shot this using 12 frames: one for the subject, and the rest of the images overlapping around the main frame to capture the out-of-focus areas. When shooting, mimic the action of a pan & tilt tripod head and tilt the camera while keeping it anchored in the same spot, rather than moving your arms to take the surrounding images. If you want to know what equivalent lens and aperture you've mimicked in your final image, Google-search 'Brenizer Method Calculator', input the data and be amazed.

■ **comparison shot** To highlight the difference in depth-of-field, this single shot of similar framing was also taken at f/2.5.

1 Lock focus and exposure First things first, half-press your camera's shutter button to lock focus on your subject. Press and hold the Autoexposure Lock/Autofocus Lock button and then shoot your main frame. Compose the main shot so that none of your subject's features are cropped; be wary of any movement as it can cause ghosting when images are stitched together later.

2 Shoot the surrounding frames Lock your elbows into your sides to ensure that the camera's position doesn't change between frames, only the angle that the camera is facing should change between shots. If you struggle shooting handheld, try using a tripod with a pan & tilt head. There needs to be a slight overlap between each frame to ensure there are no gaps when the final image is merged.

Continuity is crucial

Every image you take has to retain the same exposure and focus for this technique to work. The easiest way to do this is to set everything to manual: manual exposure mode and manual focusing, using the main area you want in focus as the benchmark. You could also use your camera's AE-L/AF-L button to lock exposure and focus if your camera has one (check your manual for details). Use this function by taking a shot while pressing the AE-L/AF-L button on the back of the camera and keeping it depressed for subsequent shots. Also bear in mind White Balance. If you use the Auto White Balance setting, you run the risk of colour shifts between frames. Your best bet is to select a preset appropriate to the shooting conditions, eg Shade.

Finishing in Photoshop

3 Import the images Open up your editing software – I've used Photoshop CS5 – and go to *File>Automate>Photomerge*. Select *Reposition* and check *Blend Images Together*. Click on the *Browse* button and locate the files on your computer. Once located, click *OK* to start the merging process.

4 Crop your image The Photomerge process may take a while, depending on how many images you are asking the software to combine. Once it has completed, you'll be left with an image that has jagged edges and a lot of layers. Go to *Layer>Flatten Image* and use the *Crop Tool* to remove any empty space.

5 To compose your image well, you may have to include some empty space in the crop. Use the *Clone Stamp Tool* to fill it in; press *Alt/Option* to select a source area from the background close to the area you want to fill. Don't worry about any white lines – these won't show up in the final image.

Final image

Consisting of 12 separate images, taken using a 50mm f/1.8 lens set at f/2.5, this final image gives a depth-of-field only possible from a digital SLR shot at 35mm at f/1.6. A quick conversion to mono and it's finished!

Do a double take

Merge two images into one to create a fantastic abstract portrait that places one subject within another for striking results

Jordan Butters: Double exposures originate from the days of film photography whereby the photographer would expose a scene and then take another exposure without winding the film on to the next frame, therefore exposing the same frame of film twice.

Fast-forward to the digital SLRs that we use today and multiple exposures is still a commonly used technique, although you might not realise it. High Dynamic Range (HDR) images are a classic example of combining multiple exposures. It can also be used to combine two or more short exposures of a moving object to create the effect of a single long exposure to emphasise the motion in the scene.

Aside from these practical uses, the technique can also great for artistic effect, like combining a classic high-key portrait with an everyday shape or texture to create an abstract image. Here, I used an image depicting an element of the natural world as my fill image for a thought-provoking link between humans and nature.

To achieve the effect digitally you'll need to use Photoshop or a similar image-editing package, but if you have a Nikon DSLR, it can be done in-camera (see panel). Before we get to the editing part, capture the images; you'll need at least two pictures to work with but there's no reason why you can't merge three, four or even more exposures once you know the basic technique. Strictly speaking, you can

merge any images together – skip straight to the Photoshop part of the guide for this, but follow the full step-by-step to learn how to create a similar abstract portrait for yourself.

Exposures with Nikon

Nikon digital SLRs allow you to perform double exposures in-camera. Press the Menu button on the back of the camera and select the Shooting Menu. Scroll down until Multiple exposure is highlighted and press OK. Pick the number of shots – start with two while you familiarise yourself with the technique. For this style of portrait, set Auto Gain to Off before highlighting Done and press OK. Now simply take your shots. Note that if you take your first shot and take no action for 30 seconds, the camera will end multiple exposure mode. After each multiple exposure, you'll need to head back into the menu and enable the function each time.

1 Set up With your camera in aperture-priority mode, select spot metering; this will ensure your subject is exposed correctly. Dial in positive exposure compensation to ensure the camera overexposes the sky. Select an ISO of 100 and an aperture of around f/5.6 – you may need to go wider if the scene isn't bright enough.

2 Position your subject Position your subject against a bright background, such as the sky on a bright day. A profile shot works better than face-on as the shape of your subject's face will be more identifiable. Avoid any scenery creeping into the background, too. If the background isn't bright enough, add more exposure compensation.

3 Shoot your second subject Choose an evenly lit scene and take your second shot. Consider the placement of your first subject in the frame and compose the shot with this in mind. This picture will effectively fill the silhouette in the first image so choose a scene containing interesting shapes or textures.

Finishing in Photoshop

4 Import Open your fill image in Photoshop and go to *Select>All* and *Edit>Copy*. Open the portrait shot and go to *Edit>Paste* to drop one image on top of the other. In the Layers palette, select the top layer and change the *Blend Mode* to *Screen*. Any overexposed areas will be blown out to white when combined.

5 Adjust the fill image With the fill layer selected, use the *Move Tool* to position the fill image. You can also use the Transform tools by going to *Edit>Transform* to scale, rotate and flip your fill image. I also used the Flip Horizontal command in the *Edit>Transform* menu to get the best position for my fill image.

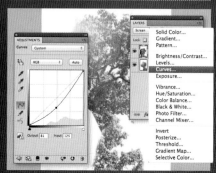

6 Adjust the curves To bring out the details, add a Curves adjustment layer by clicking on the *Add new fill or adjustment layer* button in the Layers palette and selecting *Curves* from the menu. In the Adjustments palette, drag the middle of the curve downwards to bring out detail in the mid-tones.

Final image
The result is an unusual double-exposure portrait that wouldn't look amiss hanging in a fine-art gallery.

Add a creative lens flare effect

What's your average summer portrait lacking? See how adding faux lens flare in Photoshop can give that extra interest to your images

Jordan Butters: Lens flare is caused by harsh light entering your lens and bouncing between the lens elements. The results vary from colourful circles of light scattered across your image to reduced contrast, overexposed areas and colour casts. On the surface they all sound like the kind of thing we strive to avoid in our photographs, but half the fun of photography is in breaking the rules.

Lens flare is great for adding atmosphere and a summery feel to an image. Capturing flare intentionally in-camera is relatively simple – however, controlling flare so that it doesn't detract from your image is another matter altogether. Thankfully, lens flare is relatively straightforward to recreate using Photoshop.

Lens flare is one of those elements that very much depends on the type of image it is being applied to; it certainly won't work for all pictures. It is a warm, soft effect so tends to suit outdoor portraits of women and children very well. It's also an effect that has to be applied with caution, as incorrect placement

of the flare can completely spoil an image. It works best when applied to photographs whereby your light source is above and behind your subject – for example, when the sun is low in the sky, such as during early morning or late afternoon. If you apply lens flare to an image in which the sun is directly overhead, the direction of the shadows in the image will contradict the direction that the flare is coming from, instantly discrediting the effect. Therefore, before you start editing your image, the most important step is to identify the direction that the light is coming from. Look at the direction of any shadows for clues or for areas of light and dark on your subject. Always apply the flare to complement the direction of the natural light.

Furthermore, this is one of those effects that should be applied with restraint. The temptation is always there to crank the sliders all the way across for the most dramatic effect, but the further you push the parameters, the less realistic the effect will appear. If done right, the viewer shouldn't be able to tell that the flare isn't all natural.

Original

1 Create a layer for the flare Create a blank new layer for your flare by going to *Layer>New>Layer*. In the New Layer dialogue box that opens, change the *Blend Mode* to *Screen* and tick the *Fill with Screen-neutral colour* (black) checkbox. Click *OK* to create the layer.

2 Add the flare Go to *Filter>Render>Lens Flare* to open the Lens Flare dialogue box. Click on the black thumbnail window to set the position of the flare in relation to your image and select your choice of flare and *Brightness*, I have chosen 50-300mm Zoom at 165%. Click *OK*.

3 Create an Adjustment Layer In the Layers palette, click on the *Add new fill or adjustment layer* button and select *Hue/Saturation*. Go to *Layer>Create Clipping Mask* to clip the Adjustment Layer to the lens flare layer only.

Final image
Tweak the effect by adjusting the *Opacity* slider of the flare layer in the Layers palette.

4 Adjust the Hue In the Adjustments palette, click the *Colorize* check box and change the *Hue* and the *Saturation*. I found setting the Hue to around 45 and Saturation to around 60 gives the flare a warmer, more realistic cast.

5 Add a Layer Mask If any flare artefacts are distracting or cover important areas of your image, click on the flare layer in the Layers palette before clicking on the *Add layer mask* button. Select the *Brush Tool* and adjust the *Opacity* to *50%* at the top menu bar.

6 Remove distractions Make sure that your *Foreground color* is set to *Black* and paint over any areas of flare that you wish to remove from the image. If you go a step too far, switch your *Foreground color* to *White* and brush back over.

Create a rainy-day portrait

Today we forecast a heavy downpour! Give your images the
illusion of rain with a few tweaks using Noise and Motion Blur...

Luke Marsh: For most photographers, shooting in the rain isn't their favourite pastime, but it can add a different dimension to your pictures. So how can you create the appearance of rain without having to actually get you or your camera gear wet? Easy – follow this technique!

Its success lies in trying to make the scene look authentic, so if your starting image is of a street scene, make sure it was taken just after it's rained when the ground is still wet. Similarly, have your subject/s hold an umbrella for the same reasons – if it's pouring with rain, they'd be soaking wet without one. An umbrella is the perfect cover-up, quite literally.

Original

Let it snow, let it snow!

You can also adapt this rain technique to create a great snow effect! In step five, when using Motion Blur, reduce the *Distance* down to less than *10* pixels to give the appearance of drifting snow, as opposed to heavy rain. Also, having different sized flakes adds extra dimension to the scene, so go to *Layer>New>Layer via Copy* to duplicate the layer. Then *Edit>Transform>Scale* to increase the size of the new snow layer by holding *Shift* and dragging a corner widget.

ISTOCK PHOTO

1 Open your image Create a new layer above the original by going to *Layer>New Layer...* and clicking *OK* in the pop-up window. To be able to affect this layer, you need to put content into it. For this, go to *Edit>Fill...* and, under *Contents*, change *Use* to *Black* and ensure *Mode* is *Normal* and *Opacity* is *100* under the *Blending Options*.

2 Add some noise Now add noise to the new black layer by going to *Filter>Noise>Add noise...* Select *Gaussian* under *Distribution*, and ensure that *Monochromatic* is ticked. The *Amount* of noise you need to enter will depend on the image's resolution. For large files, you will need to enter the maximum amount of *400%*.

3 Scale the noise Even though the maximum amount of noise was used, the noise 'dots' need to be bigger (the higher the image resolution and size, the more this will be the case). Go to *Edit>Transform>Scale*, enter *400%* in the horizontal scale field and click the *link* icon to scale in proportion. Double-click to apply.

Final image
Adding rain is a simple
technique, and one that
adds life and movement
to your images.

4 **Create raindrops** Now change the noise layer's *Blend Mode* to *Screen*, making the image beneath visible. The noise needs editing to create fine raindrops, so go to *Image> Adjustments>Levels…* and drag the *black slider* all the way to the right, making the drops smaller and allowing a better interaction with the image.

5 **Blur the raindrops** Use *Filter>Blur>Motion Blur…* to add the effect of moving rain. In the control panel, enter an *Angle* that suits your particular image. Here, 60° was used to reflect the position the little girl holds her umbrella. Then enter a *Distance* that gives intermittent streaks rather than solid lines running across the image.

6 **Perfect the storm** The final tweaks are done using Levels (*Image>Adjustments> Levels…*). Move the *black* and *white sliders* to change the rain's appearance depending on your image. The black slider reduces the appearance of rain from sheets to drizzle, whereas the white slider improves the contrast of the rain.

Create 'golden hour' light

A balmy summer's evening can give a supremely flattering glow to your subject. Recreate the look using Curves and the Burn Tool

Luke Marsh: There's nothing quite like a glorious summer sunset to add ambience and colour to your portrait images. However, capturing such a backlit effect can be technically challenging with tricky metering and flare posing problems, but with this simple step-by-step you can transform daytime portraits with minimal effort.

You can try this technique on any outdoor portrait, but the effect will be more dramatic the cooler the original image tones are. You rarely see clouds when there's a burning sunset so pick an image with a generous expanse of clear blue sky in a summery location such as a flower-filled field or one with plenty of lush greenery. An image with shallow depth-of-field can also enhance the final hazy warmth of the image, though it's not essential.

Getting the Photoshop effect correct relies on you working well with Layer Masks, but the beauty of them is that they're fully editable so you can refine and retry the technique without damaging your original image. Use Black paint and a soft brush on a Layer Mask to hide effects and White paint to reveal them again, altering the Opacity for better control.

Quick find

Layer Masks
Click the *Layer Mask icon* at the bottom of the Layers palette. A thumbnail appears on the active layer in the palette.

Adjustment Layers
Click and hold on the *New Adjustment Layer* icon at the bottom of the Layers palette, then scroll down to select the adjustment.

Original

ISTOCKPHOTO

1 Create the sun First, add the sun. To do this, create a duplicate of the original image: go to *Layer>New>Layer via Copy*, then open *Filter>Render>Lens Flare...* Select *105mm Prime* from *Lens Type* and position the small cross hairs on the thumbnail preview. Finally, enter an appropriate *Brightness* amount for the image.

2 Improve the face The flare strength means the subject's face appears very burnt out. To solve this, add a *Layer Mask* by clicking the icon in the Layers palette. Select a soft-edged brush, set to *Black*, with an *Opacity* of around *20%*, and paint over the subject to reduce the effects of the flare, without removing it completely.

3 Sunset gradient In the toolbar, make sure the *Background Color* is *White*, then click on the *Foreground Color* icon. In the *Color Picker*, change to a sunset colour. Now click on the *Add new adjustment layer* icon in the Layers palette and select *Gradient...* Set *Style* to *Linear* and tick *Reverse*, so the gradient runs from top to bottom.

Final image
Give your images the Midas touch by adding a gorgeous sunset to your shots.

4 Tweak the gradient Change the *Blend Mode* to *Color*. To reduce the colour tint on the subject, use a *Layer Mask*, as in step two. A Gradient adjustment layer has a Layer Mask by default, so click on it in the Layers palette, select a medium soft-edged brush, set to *Black*, with *Opacity* at *20%*, and begin work on the subject.

5 Use Curves Click the *Add new adjustment layer* icon and choose *Curves*... Now you can create an 'S' curve or choose *Strong Contrast* from the *Preset* menu and click *OK*. The effect can be harsh on the subject's face, so add a *Layer Mask* and reduce the effects by using the *Brush Tool* set to *Black*, as in the previous step.

6 Burn the foreground To finish, click on the duplicate image layer that holds the flare, ensuring the image thumbnail is active and not the Layer Mask. Select the *Burn Tool* and, using a large soft-edged brush with *Opacity* set to about *20%*, begin to work around the foreground of the image to darken it off, adding depth to the image.

Create a photo mosaic

Photo mosaics are often time-consuming to put together but five minutes is all you need when you follow our simple guide…

Jordan Butters: A mosaic is an image made up of lots of smaller images. A true mosaic image is created by matching the colours of hundreds or thousands of smaller pictures to the tones of the final image. It's a complicated process that requires you to possess a huge library of pictures to pull from. Thanks to Photoshop's Blend Modes, however, creating a mosaic effect couldn't be easier and you only need a small selection of images to choose from. You can apply this effect using just a single image, but the effect tends to look more pleasing the more you use. You might find it easier if you put them all in one folder to keep everything organised.

Mosaic software

There are various standalone photo mosaic software options available online – ideal if you are planning on putting mosaics together regularly. Two popular software packages are Mosaic Creator and AndreaMosaic. Mosaic Creator is available as a 30-day trial with the full version starting from around £20. Visit www. aolej.com to download. AndreaMosaic is available to download as freeware at www.andreaplanet.com/andreamosaic.

Original

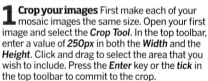

1 Crop your images First make each of your mosaic images the same size. Open your first image and select the *Crop Tool*. In the top toolbar, enter a value of *250px* in both the *Width* and the *Height*. Click and drag to select the area that you wish to include. Press the *Enter* key or the *tick* in the top toolbar to commit to the crop.

2 Paste in your images Go to *Select>All* and *Edit>Copy*. Go to *File>New* to create a blank document. Set both the *Width* and *Height* to *1,000* pixels and click *OK*. In the *View* menu, ensure *Snap* is turned on, then click on *Edit>Paste* to paste in your image. Using the *Move Tool*, lock the image in the top-left corner.

3 Repeat and arrange Repeat the first two steps for each of your images, cropping, resizing and copying before pasting them into the new document. Use the *Move Tool* to lock each image into place alongside the previous image. If you have any gaps you may need to duplicate some images to fill the page.

4 Create a pattern Once complete, go to *Layer>Flatten Image* to combine all of your images in to a single layer. Go to *Edit>Define Pattern*, name your pattern *Mosaic* and click *OK*. Your pattern is now saved for future use. Close your image without saving and open the file that you wish to use as your final image.

5 Insert your pattern Click on the *Create new layer* button in the Layers palette. Select the *Paint Bucket Tool* and in the top toolbar click on the *Foreground* menu and select *Pattern*. Click on the thumbnail to the right and select your new *Mosaic* pattern. Insert the pattern onto the image by clicking anywhere on the picture.

6 Change the Blend Mode In the Layers palette, change the *Blend Mode* to *Hard Light*. Use the *Opacity* slider to reduce the opacity of the mosaic layer. The final opacity depends on how clear you want the original image to show through – I found around 60% was the perfect amount for this image.

Final image
A quick and easy mosaic. This effect works great with kids' portraits, but experiment with different themes and see what you can come up with.

Six steps to better portraits

Find out how being smart with your portrait retouching in Photoshop Elements 10 can make your editing easier than ever

Caroline Wilkinson: Retouching portraits is usually the one editing tutorial photographers yearn to know more about. With mountains of megapixels in our modern DSLRs, the detail they capture is incredible and somewhat unforgiving. Unless you're photographing one of the rare few with a flawless complexion, every portrait you shoot will need some degree of retouching if you want a flattering, more attractive image. Faces wear the sins of our night-before antics, hectic schedules and junk-food diets, but with a little Photoshop help you can make your subject look the glossy and healthier version of themselves, and give you a more pleasing image.

Elements 10 has really made portrait retouching easy for you. Its Smart Brush and Detail Smart Brush Tools offer you several actions that can make editing simple. It's worth exploring these tools to see what features they offer to benefit your other images, too, but for the sake of this article we'll concentrate on the Portrait presets.

Useful tools

■ Quick access
Coloured icons appear on your image when you make a new edit. If you click on one it will navigate you to the corresponding layer and Layer Mask – it's a really useful tool if you end up with dozens of layers.

Personally, I prefer the Detail Smart Brush as you can paint the adjustment on to the face, whereas the Smart Brush Tool creates a selection. Try both to see which you prefer. When you make an adjustment with these tools, it automatically creates an Adjustment Layer and Layer Mask, which means any edits you make don't affect the original image and are fully editable at any point during the process. The Smart Brush Tools are divided into three: New Selection, Add Selection and Subtract from Selection. As default, it will be set to Add Selection, but if you wish to undo one of your edits, simply switch to Subtract

Original

from Selection in the top toolbar and brush back over the area. Before you start any retouching, though, apply exposure or contrast adjustments to create a solid base image. Now off you go…

1 Access the tools Use the *Spot Healing Brush Tool* to remove any obvious blemishes from the skin. Now click on the *Smart Brush Tool* in the toolbar and select the *Detail Smart Brush Tool* underneath. In the far right of the top toolbar, click on the white picker arrow (by the picture box) to access features. Click the *All Purpose* drop-down menu and select *Portrait*.

2 Adjust skin tone To apply a healthy glow to the skin, select *Spray Tan*. As you hover over the face you'll see a small cursor appear to brush the effect over the skin. Use *Size* in the top toolbar to adjust the size of your brush. As default, the effect is set to *50% Opacity*. To strengthen or weaken the effect, drag the layer's *Opacity* slider higher or lower respectively.

3 Smooth skin Before you apply the next adjustment, click on the *Background layer* in the Layers palette to deselect the previous adjustment. If you don't, you'll override the Spray Tan adjustment. This time select *Soft Focus* and brush over the skin to soften it, trying to avoid features like eyes, eyebrows and lips. Adjust *Opacity* to control the effect's strength.

4 Brighten eyes & teeth Click the *Background layer*. Now select *Pearly Whites* from the drop-down menu and brush over the teeth: adjust the layer's *Opacity* to control the effect. Deselect the adjustment and pick *Brighten Eyes*. Zoom into the eyes and brush in the adjustment. Refine with the *Subtract from Selection* brush and set *Opacity* lower than *40%*.

5 Add shine to the hair Deselect the adjustment and then pick *Lighten Skin Tones*. Avoiding the skin, brush over the hair to enhance the highlights and shine. You may find going over other areas of the image can help improve the impact, too, like I've done here to brighten the background as well as her hat. To exaggerate the shine, repeat this step again.

6 Enhance details For your next adjustment, click *Detail*; this works in a similar way to sharpening, allowing you to increase the clarity of certain areas. Use this feature on the eyes, teeth, hair and eyebrows, but stay clear of the skin; you don't want to undo all that flattering skin softening. Now save your image as a TIFF file to keep the layers.

Final image
With a few subtle changes you can make your portrait picture perfect.

Learn how to retouch your portraits like a pro

Always wanted to create polished portraits like the professionals? Well, now's your chance. The best-kept secrets of retouching are disclosed in this guide from some of the world's leading retouchers – read on to find out how to enhance the natural beauty of your subjects with expert tutorials and advice

OFTEN THE DIFFERENCE between average portraits and the polished images that you see by high-end pros or in glossy magazines is not only photographic prowess, but the skill of the retoucher. In many respects, the taking of a portrait is just one step towards a finished picture, but great lighting and photography are fundamental as Photoshop is not a miracle worker: it's an enhancement tool – and a powerful one at that. It can transform good photos into great images with impact, but you need a quality picture to begin with to get the most from post-production.

While how you originally lit the subject doesn't affect retouching, the lighting should be as close as you can get it to the finished look and your exposure needs to be spot on: if you can get the skin looking light and bright, rather than a muddy tone, retouching is going to be a lot easier. If you have to lighten up pixels, you'll have noise issues, the colour won't be as good and it'll take a lot longer to get a half-decent result. Some photographers mistakenly start with a bad image, thinking they can transform it in Photoshop, but apply so much manipulation that the picture loses any sense of realism.

There are some other things you can do to make retouching easier. Make sure you shoot in Raw rather than JPEG. Make-up is helpful, too: apply foundation that's the right tone for the skin to avoid any lines between the face and neck, as well as a light dusting of powder to get rid of shine caused by the heat of the studio lights. Lipstick should be applied perfectly: make sure the lips are sculpted properly and there's no bleeding over the edges of the mouth and the eye make-up shapes the eyes. Lighting and smoothing are essential for beautiful hair. Split ends are a nightmare to retouch, so try to make sure the hair is in good condition before you start and preferably lit well to create highlights. The more highlights there are to begin with, the easier they will be to draw out during editing.

Before you start retouching, you need to calibrate your monitor (we'd recommend X-Rite's i1Match, Datacolor's Spyder3 Elite or Pantone hueyPRO for easy-to-use calibration devices). Skipping this step could mean your printed image looks nothing like it did on screen and those hours of colour refinement and tonal tweaks were wasted. Then plan what you want to do to the image – it should stop you from over- or under-processing areas – make yourself a coffee and be prepared for a long time in front of your monitor. The most polished and subtle retouching takes an abundance of time, an eye for detail and plenty of patience to ensure natural-looking results. Retouching is not about changing a model beyond recognition or transforming them into a Barbie doll; you should be trying to enhance features and work with the person's natural beauty so the portrait presents the very best version of them and improves the overall image impact.

Start by assessing the overall quality of the skin: blemishes, under-eye 'bags', how even the colour is, the cleanliness of the make-up,

Original

deep-set wrinkles, crow's feet and unwanted highlights created by shiny skin. Next, address the features: do the eyebrows need to be neatened? Can the shape be improved or stray hairs eliminated? Could the eyes be brightened and the colour intensified? Is the nose too wide or the teeth a little stained? There is so much that can be refined that even small tweaks make a huge improvement.

For the final image to look great, you need to work on the details, and that means zooming in and working on areas of pixels close up. Use lots of layers, but keep them organised and remember to save, save, save: it's easy to get engrossed and forget. Once you're finished, save the layered image as a .PSD file in case you want to come back to it, but also flatten the layers (**Image>Flatten Image**) and save the image as a TIFF to compress the enormous file size for print. *This article was produced with the advice and insight of professional retouchers Fay Bacon, Amy Dresser and Chanelle Segerius-Bruce.*

Retouching software

While manually retouching portraits offers unlimited control, there are a few automated software packages and plug-ins for Adobe products dedicated to retouching. If you're wanting one-click wonders with automated results, then check out these three: they're not cheap additions to your arsenal, so we'd advise giving each of them a trial run first in combination with these Photoshop techniques to see which ones you prefer.

■ **Portrait Professional 10**
Free trial / starting from £64.95
www.portraitprofessional.com

■ **Portraiture 2**
Free 15-day trial / $199.95
www.imagenomic.com

■ **Perfect Portrait 1**
Free 30-day trial / $99.95
www.ononesoftware.com

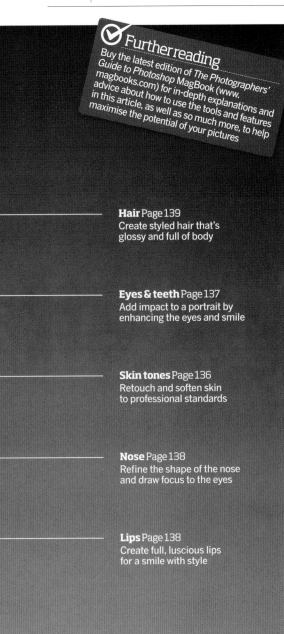

Photoshop fundamentals

This entire guide is based on techniques that you can do in Photoshop CS3, 4, 5 and, in some cases, Elements 10, but it's also been written for Macintosh users, so a few of the shortcuts might be different for PC users. As some of the tutorials are already quite detailed, we've kept them as concise as possible by avoiding explanations of the tools and features. If you're unsure of how to access or use a feature, refer back to this list.

■ **Organisation:** Amy Dresser groups her layers into folders; she does this to aid organisation. If you want to do the same thing, click on the **Create New Group** icon at the bottom of the Layers palette (looks like a folder), give the folder a name and then click and drag the appropriate layers into the folder. You can hide the layers in the folder by clicking on the arrow next to the group layer. Re. Mac v PC: Substitute **Cmd** (Mac) for **Ctrl** (PC) and **Option** (Mac) for **Alt** (PC).

■ **Layers:** Layers are at the heart of successful retouching as they allow you to apply edits to separate layers so that you can return and edit them at any stage. There are three types of layers: a new layer (**Layer>New**), which is empty; an Adjustment Layer (see below) that enables you to apply non-destructive edits to your image, like contrast and colour adjustments; and duplicate layers (**Layer>Duplicate**), which allow you to create an identical copy of a layer and its contents.

■ **Layer Mask:** Use this to edit adjustments on a layer. Use the **Brush Tool** with **Black** paint to brush over areas to hide or minimise the adjustment and White paint to reveal it again. Vary the opacity of the brush to adjust the strength of the edit. You can add a Layer Mask to a layer by clicking on the **Add New Layer Mask** icon at the bottom of the Layers palette or going to (**Layer>Layer Mask> Reveal all/Hide all**). By default, the Layer Mask should be white, so you should use **Black** paint to hide the adjustment on areas of the image. You can also invert the Layer Mask (**Command & I**) to fill it with Black to hide the entire adjustment and then use **White** paint to selectively reveal adjusted areas in the image you want to show. To delete a Layer Mask, click on the link symbol to disconnect it from the layer and drag to the trash.

■ **New Adjustment Layer:** As your image editing should be carried out in stages and be non-destructive (never irrevocably affecting the original image in case you need to use it again), Adjustment Layers are fundamental to your workflow. You can access them either via **Layer>New Adjustment Layer** or by clicking on the **Add New Adjustment Layer** icon at the bottom of the Layers palette. Each Adjustment Layer has a Layer Mask attached, allowing you to use the **Brush Tool** to edit the adjustment on areas of the image.

■ **Blend Modes:** Accessible via the **Blend Mode** menu at the top of the Layers palette, these modes dictate how the layer it's applied to 'blends' with the layer below it.

■ **Clone Stamp Tool:** One of the most used tools in Photoshop when it comes to retouching, the Clone Stamp copies pixels from one area of an image and replaces them in another. It works by pressing **Alt** on the area you want to copy from and then clicking on the area you want to replace, like a spot or blemish. We'd advise picking a 'source' area close to the area you want to replace for similar skin tones. Once you've selected this tool from the toolbar, you can adjust the size of the **Clone Stamp Tool** and its **Opacity** from the Options bar. We suggest, unless you're working on hairs where 100% opacity and a hard edge is necessary, set the **Opacity** slider to around **20%** with **0% Hardness** and gradually build up the effect for smoother and more forgiving results.

■ **Liquify:** Useful for sculpting the face, body and hair, Liquify can be a tricky tool to control, so use it carefully and as described in this guide, or see the *The Photographers' Guide to Photoshop* 4th Edition MagBook (www.magbooks.com) for an in-depth look at how to use it. To use it, go to **Filter>Liquify**.

■ **Smart Object:** If you're opening a file you've edited in Adobe Camera Raw (ACR), we'd suggest opening it as a Smart Object by holding down **Shift** to change the **Open** button to **Open Object**. At any point now, you can re-edit the Raw file by double-clicking on the image layer in Photoshop.

Using a graphics tablet & stylus

Making selections can be made much easier with a pressure-sensitive graphics tablet such as Wacom's Bamboo or Intuos4 (the latter is for the advanced users in need of more control over their editing). With practice, they're easier and more versatile than a mouse as they're ergonomically better for drawing. You can also assign shortcuts to different pressure points on the pen, such as brush Size and Feather. For details, visit: www.wacom.com

Skin

Learn the techniques that help
the professionals to get portraits
with picture-perfect skin

THE CLASSIC MISTAKE when retouching is to
over-process the skin, hiding the natural
pores, hair and texture. Applying Gaussian
blur to soften the skin is a popular technique
with amateur photographers as it's quick and
easy to do, but it's also easy to 'overdo',
causing you to lose the sculpting and fine
details on the face that make it look natural.

We advise spending as much time as
possible retouching the skin for the best
results and there are several techniques to try,
depending on how much time you've got and
how dramatic you want the finish to be. In this
section, we concentrate on simple steps in
Photoshop but if you want to know more, we
suggest buying *The Photographers' Guide to
Photoshop* MagBook 4th edition as it features
a comprehensive workflow tutorial by Annie
Leibovitz's retoucher, Amy Dresser, so you can
learn how to retouch images from Raw. Amy
focuses on small, selective tonal and colour
adjustments that even out the skin tone for
flawless results. It's an advanced technique
that takes practice to perfect, but the simpler
steps here will get you started and can
dramatically improve your portraits.

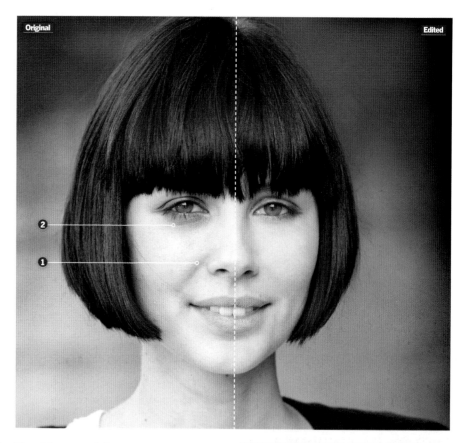

Original / Edited

Pro tip: Fay Bacon

■ **Patch Tool and Clone Stamp Tool**
First, use the *Patch Tool* to remove
large blemishes and lines. Duplicate
the image layer and then 'patch' away
any lines. Add a Layer Mask and 'paint'
over the areas you've 'patched' with a
low opacity brush and *Black* paint to
bring back some of the texture, lines
and wrinkles to a level that you want
them visible. When it comes to reducing dark
under-eye circles, use the *Clone Stamp Tool* with
the *Opacity* set to around *20%* and lightly blend
in the new skin. You can go over it more until you
get your desired coverage and use a Layer Mask
to reveal details if you overdo it. To apply the skin
to an empty layer from the image layer, make
sure *Sample* is set to *All Layers*.

Rapid retouching

1) Blemishes and wrinkles: Use the *Healing
Brush* and *Clone Stamp Tool* (set to a large,
soft brush with low opacity) to reduce the
appearance of wrinkles and blemishes. Click
the *Fade* command (*Edit>Fade*) after each
adjustment to bring texture back, gradually
building up coverage. The Healing Brush Tool
is very good at covering wrinkles and if you set
the Clone Stamp Tool's *Blend Mode* to *Lighten*,
it works well to brighten as well as soften the
skin. Make sure you work on a new layer for each
major adjustment, so you can adjust or delete
stages with ease.

2) Dark under-eye circles: Apply a *Curves*
or *Levels* adjustment layer and brighten the
image, focusing on the under-eye area. Invert
the attached Layer Mask to hide the adjustment
and use the *Brush Tool* with *White* paint to reveal
the under-eye areas. You can then reduce the
Opacity of that layer if the under-eyes look too
bright compared to the rest of the face.

Airbrush with Gaussian blur

1) Remove blemishes
Use the *Patch Tool* on a
duplicate layer and then
create another new layer
and use the *Clone Stamp
Tool* to remove obvious
marks, reduce wrinkles
and smooth out the skin.

1) Adjust colour
Use the *Lasso Tool* with
a generous *Feather* to
select sections of the skin
where the colour needs
to be adjusted using the
Channels in a *Curves*
adjustment layer.

1) Apply blur
Select all your layers and
click *Command+Alt+Shift
+E* to create a combined
copy of all the layers. Go to
Filter>Blur>Gaussian Blur
and set a blur of between
20 and *30*.

1) Reveal details
Add a Layer Mask and
invert it, then use the
Brush Tool with an
Opacity of *20%* to brush
over the skin to smooth it.
Avoid areas like the eyes,
mouth and nostrils.

**Top tip: Enhance the
highlights to add sheen**
Create a duplicate layer
and use the *Dodge Tool*, set
to a low *Exposure* (2-3%)
and a soft, medium-sized
brush to enhance what
natural highlights there
are. Gradually build up the
effect, varying the *Range*
between *Highlights* and
Midtones to brighten areas
of the face and to create
highlights where there
might not be any to sculpt
the face. Remember to
work on a duplicate layer,
in case you need to revert
back to the original image
or reduce the opacity of the
layer to control the effect.

Features

Enhance your subject's facial features with these simple yet very effective steps

THE EYES, TEETH, lips and nose all require similar amounts of attention, and are just as important as the skin when it comes to trying to make a portrait more beautiful. Here are a few pro techniques to try:

Eyes & teeth

Original

Edited

IMAGES ISTOCK PHOTO

1) Use the Dodge Tool: Duplicate the image layer so you're not working on the original image's pixels. Select a brush *Size* a little smaller than the whites of the eyes, set the *Range* to *Midtones* and the *Exposure* to around *2-3%*, then 'brush' over the whites of the eyes and teeth. You only want to go a couple of shades brighter, so be careful as they can quickly look unnatural.

2) Use Hue/Saturation: Apply a *Hue/Saturation* adjustment layer and reduce the *Reds* and *Yellows*, then use the Layer Mask to hide the adjustment, just revealing the eyes and teeth. Next, select the eyes with the *Lasso Tool* and a *Feather* of *3px* or *4px*. Then apply a *Curves* adjustment layer and create an 'S' curve to boost the contrast in the eye.

3) Use Selective Color: Select the eye or the teeth with the *Lasso Tool* and apply a small *Feather* of *10px* to soften the edges. Then add a *Selective Color* adjustment layer and click on the drop-down menu at the top of the dialogue box, select *Neutral* and adjust the sliders until you see the area/s selected gradually whiten. Do the same with *Whites*.

Pro tip:
Chanelle Segerius-Bruce

■ Add a soft catchlight
As some eyes are quite deep-set, they often need a bit of brightening and life added. One way is to use a *Curves* adjustment layer to lighten the eye, then invert the Layer Mask and use the *Brush Tool* to paint in a half-moon shape, using *White* paint underneath the pupil to create a highlight similar to what you'd get if you'd used a reflector.

Change eye colour

Use the *Lasso Tool* to draw around the iris and set a small *Feather* to soften the edges. Add a *Selective Color* adjustment layer and then adjust the sliders via the colours/tones offered in the drop-down menu to alter the colour of the eye to suit your subject or image. Select the eye again in the same way, but this time apply a *Hue/Saturation* adjustment layer and make small tweaks to the intensity of the colour. Finally, add a *Curves* adjustment layer, if necessary, to boost contrast and enhance that twinkle!

Reshape the nose

1) Slimming a nose: The nose can be a very prominent feature and while we don't suggest you completely reconstruct someone's nose as it's a key aspect of their face, you can minimise its distraction from the eyes with a few simple tricks. Access Liquify (*Filter>Liquify*) and select the *Forward Warp Tool*, set a low *Density* and *Pressure* and a brush *Size* appropriate for the size of the nose, and carefully push in the side of the nose and nostrils.

Editing lips

2) Make fuller lips: Once again access *Liquify*, but this time select the *Bloat Tool* with a low *Rate* and *Pressure*, then make small clicks along the inside of the lips to make them 'bloat'. Remember: less is more, so don't attempt to make it look like bad collagen injections – it won't flatter any subject!

3) Enrich the natural colour: Create a new layer and paint *Black* on top of your model's lips using the *Brush Tool* (you can use any colour here, but Black is good for enriching the natural lip colour of your model). Next, click *Filter>Blur>Gaussian Blur* and set it to *4px* to smooth the edges. Change the layer's *Blend Mode* to *Soft Light* and reduce the *Opacity*, if necessary. Now use the *Dodge Tool* on the image layer, with its *Range* set to *Highlights*, and brush over the top of the lips to improve the highlights and give them a glossy appearance.

Original

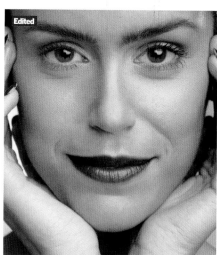
Edited

1

2

3

How to apply make-up

Ideally, make-up should be applied correctly before taking a picture. If not, a digital makeover can enhance features.

Original | Edited

1) Create the base Do what skin retouching you need to. Here, the model's lips are quite chapped, so we've zoomed in close and used the Clone Stamp Tool to smooth out the area, and then enhanced the colour. We used a different image layer for every adjustment in case we needed to go back to edit later.

2) Eyeliner Create a new layer and zoom into the first eye so it fills the screen, select a small brush with *Black* paint and draw around the edge of the eye to add definition. Change the layer's *Blend Mode* to *Soft Light* and reduce its *Opacity*, if necessary. You can use the same technique to draw in eyelashes, too.

3) Eyeshadow Create another new layer and, using a larger, soft brush, 'paint' over the eyelid and slightly under the eye with your chosen *Foreground Color*. Then change the *Blend Mode* to *Soft Light* or *Color Burn*, reducing the *Opacity* of the layer to suit. Use *Hue/Saturation* to adjust colour.

4) Enhance the eyes Give the eye more impact by selecting the iris with the *Lasso Tool* and then add a *Selective Color* adjustment layer and adjust the sliders to suit the subject. Brighten the whites using the *Dodge Tool* as previously explained or by using a *Curves* adjustment layer.

5) Blush Pick your colour for the cheeks and, using a soft, large brush, 'paint' over the cheekbone area onto a new layer. Next, go to *Filter>Blur>Gaussian Blur* and set a *Radius* of *40px* to drastically soften the edges. Click *OK*. Change the layer's *Blend Mode* to *Color Burn* or *Linear Burn*.

6) Skin tone To warm up a cool skin tone, apply a *Photo Filter* adjustment layer and set *Warming Filter*, adjusting the *Density* slider to control intensity. Invert the *Layer Mask* and reveal the areas of skin you want affected by the adjustment, reducing the layer's *Opacity*.

Hair

Get glossy, healthy hair with this tutorial

YOU'D BE AMAZED at the time it takes to retouch hair at a professional standard; we're talking days or weeks for those retouchers preparing a picture for a shampoo commercial or competition. For straight hair, they would literally have to clone each stray hair so it was straight using a very hard 2px brush set to 100% opacity. You also have to reduce the amount of flyaway hairs to smooth out the surface, but if you eliminate too many, the hair can end up looking like a helmet.

To make the hair look fuller and thicker, some retouchers may even composite hair from various different shots into the picture and morph them together using layers and Layer Masks. It can be a huge amount of work, which is why we've picked up a few tips from our professional contributors, including retoucher Chanelle Segerius-Bruce (www.retouchme.co.uk), who has retouched images for Pantene campaigns and The Body Shop.

Neatening up hair

To reduce those niggly little flyaway strands and smooth out the surface of the hair, start by adding an empty new layer and set the layer's **Blend Mode** to **Darken**. Now select the **Clone Stamp Tool**, set the **Hardness** to **100%**, **Opacity** to **100%** and the **Blend Mode** to **Darken**, too. Use a small brush, big enough to cover the strand of hair, and take a sample from the area just next to it and clone over the strand. While the **Darken** blending mode works on light, flyaway hairs, if the strands are dark, set the **Blend Mode** for the layer and brush to **Lighten** instead. To get rid of hairs entirely, use the same technique by setting the **Blend Mode** to **Normal**.

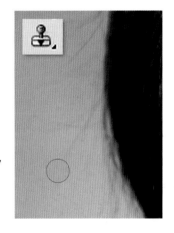

Change hair colour

Only alter colour a few shades from the original: dramatic changes make it difficult to target flyaway hairs

1) The easiest way to select the hair is to use Quick Mask Mode (**Select>Edit in Quick Mask Mode**) and 'paint' over the hair area. When you're done, click **Select>Edit in Quick Mask Mode** again to remove the red mask and reveal the selection.

2) Create a new layer and use the **Brush Tool** loaded with your choice of colour. 'Paint' over the selection onto the empty new layer and change the **Blend Mode** to **Soft Light** to merge the colour with the texture and natural colour of the hair.

3) The tricky part is when it comes to targeting missed stray hairs of the original colour. Zoom in close and use a small brush to edit the obvious hairs and then use a **Layer Mask** to remove colour where needed.

Want shampoo commercial-worthy hair? Then follow these few easy steps...

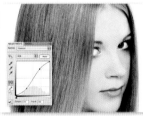

1) Boost contrast Add a **Curves** adjustment layer and boost the contrast (concentrating on bringing out the natural highlights in the hair), click **OK**. Now invert the attached Layer Mask (**command & I**) to fill it with **Black**, hiding the adjustment.

2) Refine Using the **Brush Tool** on the Layer Mask, 'paint' over the natural highlights to strengthen them. Reduce the **Opacity** of the adjustment layer if needed and switch the layer's visibility on and off to see the effects and to help judge where the highlights are.

3) Dodge Next, duplicate the image layer and select the **Dodge Tool**. With a large brush, target the highlights with an **Exposure** of **10-15%**, varying the **Range** between **Midtones** and **Highlights**. Reduce the layer's **Opacity** if you overdo it slightly.

4) Sharpen Duplicate the layer again and apply a High Pass filter (**Filter>High Pass**) set to **5px** and change the layer's **Blend Mode** to **Soft Light**. As High Pass can be a little harsh on skin, add a Layer Mask and hide the skin, leaving only the hair looking crisper.

Advanced retouching skills

Want professional retouching results? This tutorial may take time and an eye for detail, but your portraits will reap the rewards

Caroline Wilkinson: It's easy to cake a face in blur or paint over skin for a porcelain finish; the difficulty comes when you want to keep the natural texture but even out and improve the tone. Portrait professionals do it with ease and keep their methods close to their chest, but we have a few secret techniques that we're more than willing to share. Some of you will probably already use quick-fix techniques to smooth skin and reduce imperfections, and it will be all you need for a while, but more seasoned Photoshoppers might be ready to move on to this more thorough and advanced technique. Yes, dedicated software helps you get flawless results, but why spend the money when you already have Photoshop? Layers, Adjustment Layers and Layer Masks are essential here, so make sure you understand how they work as we're skipping the basics. Be prepared for lots of layers, lots of selections and employ your eye for detail, as you'll have

to target specific areas – no one-stop-shop global adjustments here! So grab a cuppa, your latest portrait and get ready for a couple of hours' work – the aim is amazing but undetectable editing. Here we go…

1 Cover up dark circles Under-eye shadows can make a subject look unduly tired. The easiest way to brighten a complexion is to minimise these shadows and even out the skin tone. Duplicate your image layer (*Layer> Duplicate Layer*) and select the *Clone Stamp Tool*, set its *Opacity* to around *20%* and lightly blend in the new skin. Be careful not to hide all the shadow as you can make the subject look unnatural. If you go too far, use a Layer Mask to pull back the effect (see box out above).

2 Remove blemishes Duplicate your new layer by dragging it down to the *Add new layer mask* icon at the bottom of the Layers palette and name it 'Blemishes'. Select the *Patch Tool* from the toolbar and select *Source* in the top toolbar. Now draw around a blemish and then click and drag that selection to an area of skin that you want to replace it with. As you release the mouse/stylus, the selection will blend with the pixels, hiding the blemish. Repeat for all spots, scars and wrinkles.

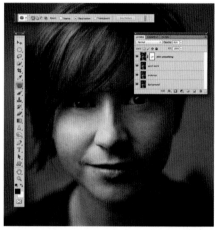

3 Smooth the skin Duplicate the 'Blemishes' layer and name it 'Skin Smoothing'. Use the *Patch Tool* again, but this time change *Source* to *Destination* in the top toolbar. Now select an area of skin that's of even tone and smooth texture, then click and drag that selection on top of areas that show visible pores and redness. If the result looks patchy – try reducing the layer's *Opacity* slider to around *85%* and use a Layer Mask with a very low opacity brush to smooth the skin's surface.

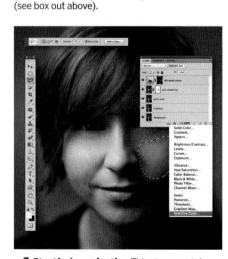

4 Start being selective This stage can take many Adjustment Layers, so try to keep organised by naming the various layers if necessary. On your last image layer, select the *Lasso Tool* and set the *Feather* to *150px* and loosely select an area of skin of similar tone. Go to *Layer>New Adjustment Layer>Selective Color* to create an Adjustment Layer to target that selection. Assess your image and decide what colours are affecting the skin – is it slightly too dark, light, magenta, red or yellow?

5 Target specific areas In the *Adjustments* panel, select the appropriate colour to target from the *Color* menu, using the sliders to adjust that colour and even out the skin tone. Repeat the process for different areas of the face, using the *Lasso Tool* to create new selections and adding new *Selective Color* adjustment layers. As my model's skin had a red tinge, I mainly focused on the Red and White to reduce redness using the Black slider. Also try *Curves* adjustment layers to adjust local contrast.

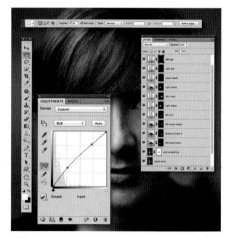

6 Finishing touch Don't rush steps four and five: be prepared to take time over perfecting the colour to ensure all areas match. Some colours will suit different areas better than others, so experiment – you can always return the sliders to 0 if needed. Once you're done, use the *Elliptical Marquee Tool* with its *Feather* set to *40px* and select the inner eye. Next add a *Curves* adjustment layer and create a soft 'S' shape with the line to pump up the contrast. Repeat for the opposite eye.

Final image
A degree of patience is required
for subtle retouching, but your
time is rewarded with
natural-looking results.

PORTRAIT KIT

FIND OUT ABOUT THE EQUIPMENT YOU NEED TO GET THE BEST SHOTS OF YOUR MOST ACCESSIBLE SUBJECTS – FRIENDS AND FAMILY – WITH THIS COMPREHENSIVE GEAR GUIDE FOR PORTRAITS

CONTEMPORARY PORTRAITURE has moved on from the days of sitting in front of a mottled brown background in a stuffy studio and smiling politely for the camera. As you'll have seen in this guide, portraits need to exude fun, energy, laughter and capture something of the subject's character. Known more as 'lifestyle' photography, these new style of portraits show a person living their life and doing the things they love. There's a massive market for this style of photography, so whether you just want to capture some great shots of the kids to put up on your wall, or you have more ambitious plans to earn some cash from portraiture, there are plenty of willing subjects around. What's more, you don't need to hire a studio and know how to operate studioflash – it's much better to get out and about, visit your subjects at home or shoot them in a location that's personal to them. This brings its own photographic challenges, however, and without the right equipment you run the risk of your portraits turning out like a snapshot.

So, in the first section of this gear guide, we walk you through the equipment you need to surmount the challenges location portraiture present. As well as cameras themselves, we'll look at the best lenses for portraiture and which ones will help you take pictures that stand out from the crowd. You'll also need some lighting to give your shots the wow factor no matter what the weather, but don't panic if you're daunted by flash: we've picked out flashguns that aren't complicated to use. For the more confident photographers, we'll show you the advanced off-camera flash systems top lifestyle photographers use and there's advice on accessories and gadget bags, not forgetting the props, too! So, what are you waiting for? Dive in and start finding out about the gear you need to shoot cracking portraits.

Key contacts

Arctic Butterfly
www.visibledust.com

Canon
www.canon.co.uk

Cokin
www.intro2020.com

Gitzo
www.gitzo.co.uk

Giottos
www.daymen.co.uk

Green Clean
www.flaghead.co.uk

Hähnel
www.hahnel.ie

Hitech
www.formatt.co.uk

Hoodman
www.newprouk.co.uk

Lowepro
www.daymen.co.uk

Kenko
www.intro2020.com

LaCie
www.lacie.com

Lastolite
www.lastolite.com

Lexar
www.lexar.com

Lowepro
www.lexar.com

Manfrotto
www.manfrotto.co.uk

Nikon
www.nikon.co.uk

Op/Tech
www.newprouk.co.uk

Panasonic
www.panasonic.co.uk

Peak Design
www.peakdesignltd.com

Rogue
www.daymen.co.uk

Samsung
www.samsung.co.uk

SanDisk
www.sandisk.co.uk

Sigma
www.sigma-imaging-uk.com

Slik
www.intro2020.com

Tamrac
www.intro2020.com

Tamron
www.intro2020.com

Velbon
www.intro2020.com

The novice lifestyle portrait photographer

When starting out, an entry-level camera, affordable lenses, a simple flash and a few accessories are all you need as you begin to shape your craft. There's really no need to rush out and spend a fortune at this stage – better to find your feet and make sure it's the style of photography you intend to pursue before making a serious investment. So, if you're buying your first 'proper' camera kit, take a look at our suggestions below…

Flash modifier

Flashguns at this end of the market don't offer manual control to reduce the flash power, so accessories to modify and diffuse the flash can really help. The £17 Sto-Fen Omni-bounce simply slips over your flashgun to diffuse the light, or for more creative effects, such as a spotlight, Rogue offers three sizes of its FlashBender accessory, ranging from £24-£30.

Basic flashgun

Your camera's pop-up flash produces a burst of light that's too harsh for portraits, making images look more like a quick snap. But if you use a dedicated flashgun attached to the hotshoe, you can direct the flash away from your subject for a more subtle effect. They also boast more power than your pop-up unit, so when your subject is a bit further away, you'll still be able to light them properly. Look out for flashguns with the swivel and bounce facility, as well as TTL metering, such as the £75 Nissin Di466 or £55 Metz 24 AF-1.

Entry-level camera

You don't need a pro camera to take great lifestyle portraits; an entry-level DSLR or Compact System Camera (CSC) with a kit lens is fine to start off with. The advantage of CSCs is that they're smaller and easier to carry, so you're more likely to have one to hand to grab those candid portraits. The range of CSC lenses and other accessories is limited compared to DSLRs, however, so if you want more versatility and flexibility, the latter is the way to go. For a CSC, check out the Olympus E-PM2 with 14-42mm kit lens for £475 or the Panasonic Lumix GF5 with 14-42mm kit lens for £375. If you decide to go the DSLR route then look out for the £500 Pentax K-30 with 18-55mm lens, £360 Canon EOS 1100D with 18-55mm or the £450 Nikon D3200 with 18-55mm VR lens.

Fast standard prime

A standard prime is a very popular lens for portraits and for good reason. Taking account of the APS-C crop factor, the 50mm focal length converts to around 75mm, depending on the camera you use, which is a great focal length of portraits. These lenses also boast a 'fast' f/1.8 aperture, so you can easily throw the background out of focus. They're cheap, too. All the major manufacturers have an own-brand model for around £100, like the £84 Canon 50mm f/1.8 II or £140 Sony 50mm f/1.8 SAM.

Small gadget bag

As your portrait kit begins to expand, you'll need a solution for both transporting it and keeping it safe at home. The £28 Lowepro Nova 140AW shoulder bag provides room for a DSLR, flash and 50mm standard prime, but if you're thinking of carrying a superzoom and reflector, too, then check out the larger £60 Tamrac Aero 60.

Belt clip

If you want to keep a second body within easy reach, clip it to your belt using a dedicated accessory. Peak Design's £70 Capture Camera Clip fits over your belt and features a quick release plate and a tough aluminium body. Also available is the £40 b-grip, which is a larger belt-mounted camera holder.

Superzoom

If you're looking for an affordable and versatile second lens for portraits, a superzoom is a good option. With focal lengths ranging from wide-angle through to telephoto, you can shoot wide group shots and tighter head and shoulder portraits without having to change lens. Superzooms at this end of the market use a 'slow' variable aperture, however, so shallow depth-of-field effects can be a bit of a challenge. Sigma offers an 18-200mm f/3.5-5.6 II DC OS HSM lens for £280 or, if you want more zoom, take a look at the £380 Tamron 18-270mm f/3.5-6.3 Di II VC PZD.

5-in-1 reflector

Whether you're working with natural light or flash, a reflector is an essential part of any portrait photographer's kit. Reflecting light that initially missed your subject back onto their face helps fill in the darker shadows for a more balanced portrait. There's a vast range of reflectors available, but we'd recommend the 5-in-1 varieties that offer translucent, black, white, gold and silver surfaces for different effects. Interfit do a 32-inch 5-in-1 reflector for £32.

The enthusiast lifestyle portrait photographer

You're starting to shoot friends, colleagues and even people you don't know, so you need more sophisticated kit to improve results. You'll want 'fast' aperture lenses to isolate your subjects from a background, manual control of your flashgun for subtle lighting effects and gear to take your flash off camera. When you're shooting outdoors, you'll also need some filters to control bright light, not to mention a gadget bag to keep it all in.

Mid-range flashgun

As you get more confident with flash, a mid-range flashgun will help you experiment more. As well as TTL, they boast manual functions so you can reduce the power output for a more subtle effect when working close up. They also boast wireless capabilities for taking your flashgun off-camera and placing it to the side or behind your model for more impressive lighting. Models like the £190 Canon Speedlite 320EXII, £229 Nikon Speedlight SB-700 or £200 Metz 52 AF-1 have a slave function, which means they can be triggered by a burst of flash from your camera's pop-up unit. You can also control the output of each flash source in your camera's menu system to achieve the desired effect.

Mid-range DSLR

As you start to take your portraiture more seriously, you'll no doubt consider upgrading your camera. Generally speaking, mid-range DSLRs offer improved build quality over their entry-level counterparts, so they're equipped to handle a bit more hammer. They also boast higher resolutions for sharper images using low ISO speeds and they boast advanced features like wireless flash control: although some entry-level cameras feature this now, too. If you've already started investing in lenses from one brand, you'll probably want to stick with that manufacturer when you upgrade your camera body, but if you've not committed yet, the latest £530 Canon EOS 650D or £700 Nikon D5200 should go straight to the top of your list.

Fast standard zoom

Kit lenses are fine when you're starting out, but their general build quality and optical construction leaves much to be desired. When you're looking for a step up in quality, fast standard zooms are the way to go. They only cover the same focal length as your kit lens, but the fixed f/2.8 aperture at 50mm is perfect for portraits on an APS-C sensor and you'll appreciate the smoother zoom action and metal lens mount. Own-brand options can be expensive, but there's a range of third-party ones, too, like the £370 Tamron 17-50mm f/2.8 XR Di II VC or £450 Sigma 17-70mm f/2.8-4 OS HSM. Be prepared for some extra weight to carry, however, as the improved build and extra glass in these lenses makes them much heavier than your kit lens.

Fast-access camera bag

Lifestyle portraits involve grabbing those split-second moments, so you need to work quickly. Therefore, when you want to change lenses or swap memory cards, having a bag quite literally at your side is a real bonus. The £95 Speed Freak is the mid-sized bag in Think Tank's Speed convertible range, and allows you very fast access and lots of storage. It's an alternative to using a belt with separate pouches, such as the Tamrac Modular System or Lowepro's Street & Field series, both from around £10-£15.

Very 'fast' standard prime

The f/1.4 aperture of these lenses lets in twice as much as a f/1.8 lens, which is great when shooting in low light. Not only that, but the maximum aperture allows you to throw most of the image out of focus, just keeping small details like the lips and eyes in focus. For a more regular portrait, though, stopping down the aperture to f/2.8 provides cracking corner-to-corner sharpness. For around £300, Canon and Nikon have their own versions and third-party options include the £370 Sigma 50mm f/1.4 EX DG HSM or the £300 Tamron 60mm f/2 SP Di II, which, although not as 'fast', doubles up as a 1:1 macro lens, too.

Lighting stand, flash bracket and umbrella

Once you start taking your flashgun off-camera, a whole host of creative possibilities open up. One of the most basic and classic approaches is to place your flashgun at 45° to your subject and use a reflective or shoot-through umbrella to soften the light. To do this, you'll not only need the umbrella itself, but also a flashgun bracket to attach your flashgun and umbrella to, as well as a stand so you can position it securely without having to hold it. Westcott do a collapsible umbrella flash kit that includes a stand, umbrella and flashgun bracket for £65.

Wireless flash triggers

Using a lighting stand and umbrella can have its problems if you're using your camera's pop-up unit to fire the flash. The sensor on the flashgun needs to receive the flash in order to fire and if you position the flashgun where your umbrella blocks the line of sight from your pop-up unit, the off-camera flash won't fire. This is where wireless radio triggers – which send a radio signal from your camera to your flashgun – come into play. With one transmitter connected to your camera's hotshoe and one receiver on the flashgun, you can place your flashgun out of direct line of sight and it'll still fire. Hähnel's £50 Combi RF is a brilliant buy.

Reflector on stand kit

Unless you've an assistant or a willing volunteer to handhold your reflector in the right place, operating your camera at the same time can be a challenge. A good solution is the Interfit Flat Panel Reflector & Stand package for £90 that features a 35x75in reflector, making it suitable for close-up or full-length shots.

Grip reflector

A reflector is an invaluable lighting aid, but can be difficult to position when you have no one around to hold it for you. The £55 Lastolite TriGrip gets around this problem by boasting a solid handle that you can grip with one hand while shooting with the other.

Wide-angle zoom lens

It's not a traditional portrait lens, as the distortion associated with wide-angles will stretch the proportions of your subject's face. That said, a wide-angle lens will give you another option in your armoury, allowing you to capture more of the surroundings and get shots others won't. They're also essential if you find yourself in a small or enclosed space where you can't get far enough back from your model. Again, own-brand options are available, or take a look at the highly recommended £455 Sigma 10-20mm f/3.5 EX or £515 Tokina AT-X DX 11-16mm f/2.8 Pro.

In the bag

Flash gels
Coloured gels slotted over your flashgun can produce colourful and fun creative flash effects. Try the £20 Honl HP-Filter 3 Colour Effects Kit.

Back-up body
A second DSLR body means you can have a telezoom attached to one camera and fast prime or wide-angle on the other, giving you multiple options without the inconvenience of having to keep changing lens.

White Balance aid
With most lifestyle portraits, you'll be mixing ambient and flash light sources, which makes it tricky for the camera to get the White Balance right. Shooting in Raw and taking a quick shot of a grey card at the start of the shoot will help make sure the White Balance can be quickly and easily corrected across all your shots later in software. Check out the £16 Lastolite 30cm Ezybalance Grey Card.

Lightmeter
These aren't essential and many digital photographers get by without one, but when you start using off-camera flash and manual controls, they can be useful for getting your exposures spot-on. The Sekonic Flashmate L-308S offers a digital display, incident and reflected readings and four different modes for £140.

Filters
Many filter effects can be achieved in Photoshop – however, some can't, and for these you'll need to use filters. Polarising filters are great for adding more punch to your shots when shooting portraits in bright conditions as they reduce lens flare, cut out reflections and help darken down the blues in the sky. Check the diameter of your lens to get the right size filter, but, for an example, the Tiffen 72mm Circular Polarising Filter costs £60. ND grads also allow you to balance the exposure between a bright sky and darker foreground when taking wide-angle portraits. Screw-on ND filters are available, but a filter holder system gives you more flexibility as you can use it across all your lenses. The Cokin Z-Pro ND kit costs £144.

Tripod
A tripod is an unlikely bit of kit for a lifestyle portrait photographer as you'll usually need to change shooting position quickly as your subject, particularly younger ones, move around. There are lots of tripods available, including ones that let you shoot very low to the ground, but a good model to start with is the £120 Manfrotto 055XPROB. As an alternative, you might also want to look at monopods for flexibility.

Remote release
For a more relaxed or spontaneous moment, a remote release allows you to set a shot up and then move away from the camera to interact with the subject. One of the best budget buys is the £20 Hähnel RC280 Remote Release.

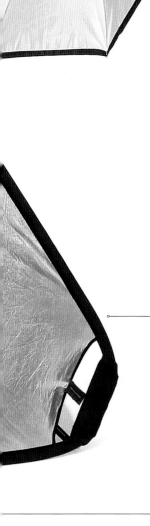

The semi-pro lifestyle portrait photographer

Having cut your teeth in lifestyle portraiture, you now want to make some money doing it part-time. It's a competitive market, though, and with dozens of pros looking for the same customers, you need the best equipment to compete. The big question is whether you're going to upgrade to full-frame with all the extra investment in new glass involved, and you'll want to look at multiple flash set-ups and top-end reflectors, too.

Semi-pro DSLR

If you already own a suite of lenses designed for the smaller APS-C sensor, then it'll be a hard decision and large investment to upgrade to full-frame. If you stick to APS-C, but want the best available, then top-of-the-range models offer superb build and handling (making them more comfortable to use), more AF points, faster focusing and a faster continuous shooting. The £800 16.2-megapixel Nikon D7000 performs well in low light, but if you're after more resolution and full HD video, check out the £1,100 Canon EOS 7D. The advantage of going full-frame is that the larger image sensor gives each pixel a little more space to breathe and improves the overall picture quality – particularly at high ISOs. The £1,500 24.3-megapixel Nikon D600 produces incredible results using ISO speeds up to ISO 3200, as does the £1,600 20.2-megapixel Canon EOS 6D.

Fast standard zoom

If you need new glass for a full-frame camera, then you can thankfully forget about all that confusing crop-factor stuff. Fast standard zooms offer a versatile focal length from wide-angle to short telephoto, and that fixed f/2.8 maximum aperture is great for creating a shallow depth-of-field and isolating your subjects from the background. The full-frame game is not cheap, though, and you'll need £1,800 for a Canon EF 24-70mm f/2.8L USM or £1,300 for the Nikon AF-S 24-70mm f/2.8G.

'Fast' telephoto zoom

When you need to crop in tighter for a head and shoulders portrait, a fast telezoom is perfect. Pro lenses have a fixed f/2.8, so shallow depth-of-field isn't a problem, and the optics deliver incredibly sharp results. The most recent releases also feature image stabilisation (Canon IS or Nikon VR), which reduces camera shake when using longer focal lengths and slow shutter speeds. The Nikon 70-200mm f/2.8 ED VR II costs £1,600 or £1,800 for the Canon 70-200mm f/2.8L IS II USM. Also consider the capable but slower (and more affordable) £900 Canon EF 70-200mm f/4L IS USM.

Wide-angle zoom

In reality, the 24mm wide-angle focal length on your standard zoom should be wide enough for all but a very few portraits. That said, a wide-angle zoom will generally perform better at 24mm, giving less distortion or chromatic aberrations than your standard zoom, and you can go wider should you want to. The Nikon 16-35 f/4G ED costs £850, while the Canon 16-35mm f/2.8L II USM is £1,100.

Very 'fast' telephoto prime

The 85mm f/1.4 is the ideal portrait lens, flattering facial features while slightly compressing perspective to isolate your subjects from the background. They are incredibly sharp, too, but expensive. The Sigma 85mm f/1.4 EX DG is great value at £669, especially when you consider the Nikon 85mm f/1.4G is £1,200 and Canon 85mm f/1.2L II USM is £1,649.

Camera bag

With two or three larger lenses, filters, flash, radio triggers and other essentials like batteries and memory cards, that small gadget bag isn't going to cut the mustard. The £120 Lowepro Magnum 200AW is very large, has all-weather covers and lots of dividers to keep your gear safe. If you're after a bag that doubles up as both a shoulder bag and a waist belt for quick access to your kit, then check out the £120 Think Tank Speed Freak v2.0.

Softbox kit

Softboxes are another method of diffusing flashlight – only until fairly recently have they been the preserve of the studio photographer. Smaller softboxes that attach to standard flashguns are now available, making them convenient on location. They offer an advantage over brollies, too, as the four sides of the softbox direct the light better, giving you more control over where it'll fall. You need to check the compatibility of any kit with your flashgun, but look at the £115 Westcott 70cm Apollo kit or £103 Lastolite 54cm Ezybox.

Wireless flash trigger

If you're planning on using multiple flash set-ups, look for wireless trigger sets that use additional receivers. The £90 Interfit Titan Pro system is superb value, while the most popular model with pros is the £269 PocketWizard Plus II set.

Framed reflector

If you're shooting without assistance, consider investing in a framed reflector, which is sturdier and easier to handle than a traditional type. The best are by California Sunbounce, which makes them in four sizes and various effects. Prices start at around £1,110 for the 60x90cm Micro-mini reflector.

In the bag

Skylight Diffuser Panel
It might seem an odd statement, but when shooting lifestyle portraits on location, the sun can be a real pain. Not only will your models often squint, but the deep shadows and bright highlights make controlling your exposure a big challenge. You can always seek out some light shade, but that can also present problems with messy backgrounds or dappled light, so many pros use a large sunscreen instead. In effect, it's a large stretched piece of fabric in a frame and, using a pole or stand, it's positioned above your subject's head to cast a light shadow over them while you shoot. The £289 California Sunbounce Pro Sunswatter comes as a complete kit and is like a giant fly squatter, so you'll need an assistant to hold it. The Lastolite Skylight system can be free-standing using standard light stands. There's no kit available, though, so you'll need to buy the fabric, frame and two grip heads separately, which will set you back around £255.

Second flashgun
Creative lifestyle portraits are often produced using several light sources. You might like to invest in a second flashgun so that you can light your subjects from the side and back at the same time for an attractive rim light or hairlight effect. Top-end models also kick out more power (look out for Flash Guide Numbers: the higher the number, the greater the power), which is important when using umbrellas or softboxes as they reduce the amount of flashlight reaching your subject. Try Nikon or Canon models: £340 for the Nikon Speedlight SB-910 or £430 for the Canon Speedlite 430EX II. Remember you may need a wireless trigger too.

Post-production

The gear you'll need for top-end lifestyle portraits isn't just the hardware. Just take a look at your local portrait studio's website and you'll see the funky colour splash, cross-process or high-saturation effects that can only be achieved using software.

Image enhancement
For general image organisation and enhancement, including good basic portrait retouching tools like Red Eye Removal and Teeth Whitening, Photoshop Elements 11 at £60 will suffice for the novice or enthusiast portrait photographer.

Image management
If you start taking on a lot of commissions, shoot Raw and need to turn shots around quickly or upload easily to bespoke web galleries, the advanced features and functionality of packages like Adobe's £100 Lightroom 4 or Apple's £140 Aperture 3 are worth their weight in gold.

Advanced retouching
Pro portrait lenses like 85mm f/1.4 are so sharp, they're pretty unforgiving and will show up spots and blemishes, even on the smoothest of complexions. For advanced and quick retouching, Portrait Professional offers a whole series of adjustments, including removing blemishes, lighting eyes, adjusting hair tone and even reshaping facial features, all automatically. It's better suited for classic head and shoulder portraits than family or group portraiture, but as it's now available for around £30, it's a bit of a steal.

Creative effects
With Photoshop Elements loaded, a whole host of creative effects are available if you have the skill and time. If not, OnOne's Perfect Photo Suite 7 (prices start at £80) offers a range of effects at the touch of a button. There are five plug-ins in all, but look out for Perfect Effects 2 for creative effects, Perfect Portrait 2 for retouching, Perfect B&W for amazing mono results and Focal Point 2 for instant bokeh.

Printers
With your lifestyle portraits shot, organised and enhanced, the final and often most rewarding stage is sharing your work with family, friends or clients. Digital distribution has its place and reaches lots of people quickly, but there's nothing better than a framed print on the wall to enjoy day after day. Affordable A3+ is the way to go, so consider the £310 Epson Stylus Photo 1500W or £165 Canon PIXMA IX6550. It's the next best thing to having a printing company produce your professional prints.

Accessory belts and pouches

If you do shoot portraits on location with a lot of pro kit, you're either going to have a very heavy bag on your shoulder or a rucksack that spreads the weight. Either way it's difficult to get to your gear quickly. Another solution, however, is a belt that allows you to carry cameras, lenses and accessories around your waist for easy access. They're usually modular systems, so you can configure the number and size of the pouches attached to the belt to suit your kit. The Lowepro S+F Deluxe Technical belt costs £40, but remember to budget extra for the pouches you need, or the £70 Lowepro Outback 200 beltpack includes pouches for one camera with lens attached and two extra lenses to boot.

Portable studioflash kit

If you're serious about flash, invest in a studioflash kit. Cheap entry-level kits are available for a few hundred pounds, but they require mains power, which isn't always available on location and they're pretty cumbersome, too. A portable kit gives you the same amount of power using a battery pack, so you could shoot a lifestyle portrait on top of Mount Snowdon if you wanted, and they come in smaller cases, making them easier to carry. The £1,549 Elinchrom Ranger Quadra RX 2 Head kit is the popular choice with pros, while the £780 Lencarta Safari Classic Battery & 2 Heads kit is great value.

The best lenses for portraits

The standard kit zoom supplied with your camera is a good general-purpose lens for shooting satisfactory portraits, but we'd recommend you consider one of these two types of optics for far better quality results

The 'standard' 50mm f/1.8

IN THE DAYS OF 35MM film SLRs, you'd invariably find a 50mm f/1.8 prime lens attached to the front of almost every SLR, and it remained popular until the late '80s. It was around this time that standard zooms started to appear. With their variable focal lengths ranging from wide-angle to short-telephoto, the 28-70mm (and similar) lens represented a step forward in terms of flexibility and sadly it led to the demise of the 50mm as the standard lens of choice. However, its popularity has recently seen a resurgence for a number of reasons.

The first is that it's a very inexpensive lens to get hold of. With 50mm lenses from the likes of Canon, Nikon and Sony costing just over £100 new, and used versions available for a little over half that, they're an affordable choice for most of us. To add further credence to the value-for-money argument, consider this fact. The lens of choice for many portrait pros has long been the 85mm telephoto, which for an f/1.8 version will set you back around £300. If your DSLR uses an APS-C sensor, as most do, a 50mm that costs you £100 equates to a 75mm f/1.8 (or 80mm f/1.8 if you use Canon) – but with an effective saving of around £200!

Also, if you don't mind buying a used manual-focus lens, you can pick one up for around £25. So for the price of a decent memory card, you can get a high-quality piece of glass that may be a few decades old and lack AF, but won't leave you wanting in the optical department. So, there's no denying a 50mm lens is affordable, but what else does it

offer? Well, the biggest selling point must surely be its maximum aperture of f/1.8. Having a lens with such a fast maximum aperture offers stacks of potential. With your average 18-55mm having a maximum aperture of f/3.5-5.6, the 50mm is two to three stops faster, giving a brighter viewfinder image and allowing you to shoot handheld in low light, while using lower ISO ratings than you would normally get away with.

The most remarkable benefit of the wide maximum aperture is the extremely shallow depth-of-field when you shoot wide open, which helps isolate the main subject from its surroundings. This single feature provides significant creative opportunities, especially in the field of portraiture. The 50mm lens also scores better than virtually any other lens in the size and weight department. Weighing around 150g and measuring about 5cm in length, it's the perfect optic to keep with you, especially when you're travelling and when storage is at a premium.

The final benefit is possibly the most important – image quality. As with the majority of prime lenses, the optical quality from the humble 50mm lens is arguably better than all but the high-end zooms and, in terms of sharpness, is superior to a standard zoom. For sharpness, distortion, light fall-off and contrast, and even when used wide open, you'll have little to complain about. So, there you have it: a small, lightweight and affordable lens with a super-fast aperture and razor-sharp optics. Is it not time you bought one?

AF 50mm f/1.8 lenses

You'll find that brands with full-frame DSLRs in their range have retained 50mm lenses in their line-up. If you're on a budget, avoid the faster f/1.4 and f/1.2 variants aimed at pros, as they're larger and cost far more. The Canon and Nikon lenses have been around for years, so look for mint-condition used lenses!

Canon EF 50mm f/1.8 II
Guide Price: £130
Street Price: £100
Dimensions (WxL): 68.2x41mm
Weight: 130g
The Mk II lens is virtually identical to the original – both are well worth buying.

Nikon 50mm f/1.8D
Guide Price: £135
Street Price: £110
Dimensions (WxL): 63x39mm
Weight: 160g
Small, light and very sharp. Look for the 'D' tag to avoid buying an older series lens.

Sony DT 50mm f/1.8 SAM
Guide Price: £160
Street Price: £150
Dimensions (WxL): 70x45mm
Weight: 170g
A great lens but not so easy to find. Remember, Minolta Dynax lenses fit too!

What's the big deal about the 50mm's f/1.8 aperture?

You have to experience a lens as fast as the 50mm to really understand and appreciate its benefits but, trust us, once you've tried you'll be hooked. The 50mm's f/1.8 aperture enables you to throw the background completely out of focus and isolate the main subject from its setting. This set of images shows the changes in depth-of-field at various apertures from f/1.8 to f/22.

Telephoto zooms

IN THE LATTER YEARS of the film era, the 70-300mm was the most popular choice of telezoom due to the versatility of its focal lengths. For most digital SLR users, the 55-200mm covers a similar zoom range, thanks to the 1.5x effective increase in focal length associated with the smaller sensor size. That's great news, as a 55-200mm lens is smaller and lighter than a 70-300mm lens and it's also far more affordable.

The 55-200mm zoom is suitable for a wide variety of subjects. At its widest end, it's perfect for general portraiture, while zooming to the telephoto end is ideal if your subject is further away or you are shooting candids. There is a wide number of 55-200mm zooms available and all perform well and produce decent results. We've offered you a closer look at the Nikon and Tamron models as we feel that they offer

particularly good value for money. Most 55-200mm lenses are budget zooms, offering good enough quality for general-purpose photography, but if you're intending to produce large prints, you should look at upgrading to a mid-range zoom with a faster maximum aperture and better optics. For this reason, we've included Canon's 70-200mm f/4L USM as it's one of the best in its class.

You may find stores try selling you a 70-300mm, which effectively behaves as a 105-450mm. While a great choice for digital SLRs with a full-frame sensor, we'd not recommend the 70-300mm for use with cameras using the APS-C sensor due to problems associated with the increased focal length, such as camera shake and its restrictive angle-of-view at close range.

Canon EF 70-200mm f/4L USM

Guide price: £790	
Street price: £550	
www.canon.co.uk	
Lens optics: 16 elements in 13 groups	
Lens mount: Metal	
Maximum aperture: f/4	
Minimum aperture: f/32	
Minimum focus: 1.2m	
Filter thread: 67mm	
Weight: 705g	
Supplied accessories: None	
Dimensions: 76x172mm	
Compatibility: All Canon EOS models	

Canon has a number of budget zooms and also a couple of pro-spec f/2.8 options. This is one of two mid-range f/4 lenses (the other offers an image stabiliser) and arguably the best value of Canon's four 70-200mm zooms. It boasts an f/4 maximum aperture throughout its focal length range and these faster optics result in it being a longer and heavier lens than budget alternatives. However, this drawback is soon forgotten once you start using it – the autofocus is whisper-quiet and very accurate, while the image quality is far superior compared to cheaper zooms, with less distortion, a lot more detail and better contrast. Unless you're a pro requiring the f/2.8 maximum aperture, this lens (or the more expensive IS version) is good enough for all your needs. Well worth checking out.

Verdict

It costs far more than budget zooms but optical quality is far superior and worth the extra.

Handling	★★★★★
Features	★★★★★
Autofocus	★★★★★
Image quality	★★★★★
Value for money	★★★★☆

OVERALL ★★★★★

Nikon AF-S VR DX 55-200mm f/4-5.6G ED

Guide price: £320	
Street price: £210	
www.nikon.co.uk	
Lens optics: 15 elements in 11 groups	
Lens mount: Plastic	
Maximum aperture: f/4-5.6	
Minimum aperture: f/22-32	
Minimum focus: 1.1m	
Filter thread: 52mm	
Weight: 335g	
Supplied accessories: Case and hood	
Dimensions: 73x99.5mm	
Compatibility: APS-C Nikon	

This version sits alongside the original Nikon DX 55-200mm G ED Nikkor lens but boasts a VR (Vibration Reduction) facility. The result is a slight increase in the size and weight, but more importantly, improved performance in low light and at the telephoto end due to shake being minimised. The Nikon boasts a very wide zoom ring but the slim manual focusing ring at the end of the barrel could do with more width. The autofocus is quick, quiet and responsive, even in low light, and is one of the better lenses in terms of sharpness. As with other zooms of this type, images at the wide to mid-focal lengths are better than at 200mm. At its maximum aperture, sharpness is satisfactory and improves significantly as soon as the lens is stopped down, proving best at f/8-13.

Verdict

A great telezoom thanks to decent all-round performance and the VR facility.

Handling	★★★★☆
Features	★★★★☆
Autofocus	★★★★☆
Image quality	★★★★☆
Value for money	★★★★☆

OVERALL ★★★★☆

Tamron AF 55-200mm f/4-5.6 LD Di II

Guide price: £160	
Street price: £120	
www.intro2020.co.uk	
Lens optics: 13 elements in nine groups	
Lens mount: Plastic	
Maximum aperture: f/4-5.6	
Minimum aperture: f/32	
Minimum focus: 0.95m	
Filter thread: 52mm	
Weight: 300g	
Supplied accessories: Hood	
Dimensions: 71.6x83mm	
Compatibility: APS-C (various fittings)	

This zoom has proven extremely popular thanks to a combination of low price, decent build quality and good all-round performance. The wide zoom ring is very easy to grip and has a smooth action, but as with the Nikon, the manual focusing ring is thin and not the easiest to use. The autofocus turns in a good performance – it's not the quickest or quietest, but it is accurate and performs better than expected in low light. As with most 55-200mm zooms, it performs best at the shorter end, but quality through the range is good, especially once the aperture is stopped down, with f/8-11 giving the sharpest results. Please note this lens is designed for use with APS-C sensors only and isn't compatible with larger sensor sizes. It is available in Canon, Nikon and Sony fittings.

Verdict

A budget zoom lens that turns in a better performance than you expect for the price.

Handling	★★★★☆
Features	★★★★☆
Autofocus	★★★☆☆
Image quality	★★★★☆
Value for money	★★★★☆

OVERALL ★★★★☆

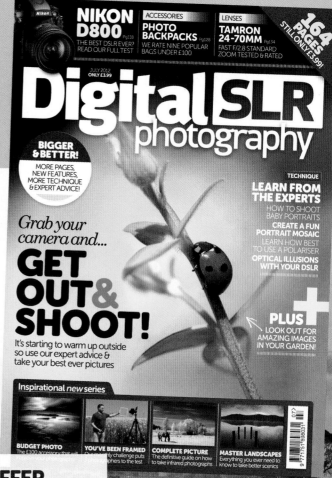

Top picks: Flashguns and studioflash kits

Photography is simply the manipulation of light. But, sometimes, natural light doesn't provide the effect you want, so we've selected our top flashguns and studio kits to help shed light on products that offer great value

Nissin Speedlite Di622 II

www.kenro.co.uk; 01793 615836

MAIN SPECIFICATIONS
Guide Price: £150
Street Price: £115
Guide Number: 44-62 (ISO 100, m)
Flash coverage: 16-70mm (24-105mm)
Recycling time: four to six seconds
Bounce facility: Yes (0 to 90°)
Swivel facility: Yes (0 to 270°)
TTL: Yes
AF assist beam: Yes
Strobe flash: No
Wireless flash: Yes

The Nissin Di622 has excellent build quality for a flash unit that costs less than £150; it's as good as models costing twice its price. This flashgun also has some rewarding features that set it apart from many other flashguns in this price range. These include second-curtain sync, slave flash and a standby mode that kicks in after two minutes of non-use to save your battery power. It also includes a flash stand, a diffuser for coverage as wide as 16mm and a fill-in reflector. There is no LCD panel on the rear; instead, a series of LEDs indicate power and a single button handles the modes. The Nissin Di622 Mk II flashgun is available for Canon, Nikon and Sony DSLR cameras and, considering the quality of features and the reasonable price, offers a decent cut-price alternative to branded models.

Sigma EF-610 DG Super

www.sigma-imaging-uk.com; 01707 329999

MAIN SPECIFICATIONS
Guide Price: £260
Street Price: £180
Guide Number: 34-61 (ISO 100, m)
Flash coverage: 17-105mm
Recycling time: Five to seven seconds
Bounce facility: Yes (0-90°)
Swivel facility: Yes (0-180°)
TTL: Yes
AF assist beam: Yes
Strobe flash: Yes
Wireless flash: Yes

Sigma not only makes great value lenses, it also boasts a couple of excellent flashguns, with this being its top model. The EF-610 DG Super is available in Canon, Nikon, Pentax, Sigma and Sony versions, and has stacks of features. In fact, it will take you quite a while to read the EF-610's instruction manual to get to grips with them all! One interesting feature is the high-speed sync, which allows you to fire the unit at shutter speeds above your camera's usual flash sync speed. The unit can also be used as a master or a slave unit, and offers a wide-angle flash diffuser panel. The unit is also easy to use with the buttons spaced out, and a bright and clear LCD monitor. As well as the sophisticated range of TTL facilities, it also offers various manual power settings too. The Sigma is an excellent flashgun that we highly recommend.

Interfit EX150 MK II outfit

www.interfitphotographic.com; 0121 522 4800

MAIN SPECIFICATIONS
Guide Price: £250
Street Price: £220
No. of heads: 2x 150Ws
Power: 19-150Ws
Guide number (ISO 100, m): 22
Modelling lamp: Full (100W)/Off
Fitting: EX type
Trigger Voltage: 5v

KIT INCLUDES
2x flash heads, 2x stands, 2x sync leads, 2x power leads, 1x white brolly, 2x spill kills, 1x softbox, 1x DVD

Replacing the successful EX150 kit, the Mk II version has brought some impressive new features to the table. The heads are a decent size, with a strong polycarbonate build, and are compatible with the full Interfit range of accessories. Though there is no storage bag with this kit, the box it comes in is sturdy and adequate for holding it. The modelling lamps give a useful amount of light and the flash power (1/8 to full-power) is very respectable and, when channelled by the spill kills, can add 50% to the Guide Number. Light temperature is a little on the cool side, so using Raw or a manual WB setting is advised. This is a great kit for the money and a good choice for the amateur. It may not be as extensive as some others out there, but the build quality of the equipment more than makes up for it.

Elinchrom D-Lite 4 IT outfit

www.flashcentre.com; 020 7837 5649

MAIN SPECIFICATIONS
Guide Price: £730
Street Price: £550
No. of heads: 2x 400Ws
Power: 25-400Ws
Modelling lamp: Full (100W)/ proportional/Low/Off
Fitting: EX type
Trigger Voltage: 5v

KIT INCLUDES
2x flash heads, 2x stands, 2x power leads, 2x softboxes (one medium, one small), 1x light bag, 1x stand bag

This update of the original D-Lite system is one of the best kits out there for beginners. The heads are compact but sturdy, and feature an integral Skyport wireless trigger. The heads are available in 200- and 400-Watt versions (D-Lite 2 IT & D-Lite 4 IT respectively) and, if possible, we recommend you buy the 400-Watt heads as the extra power is very useful. The control panel couldn't be easier to use. An LED shows the current power setting with two large buttons beneath allowing it to be changed. Other controls allow you to set the modelling light to be on at minimum or full power, off, or proportional to the power setting, which is set in 1/10th increments. There is also a button to switch the audible ready 'beep' on or off. The D-Lite kit has everything you need to get started and is worthy of a Best Buy tag.

Ringflash adaptors

We test two 'budget' adaptors designed to mimic the flattering
and funky effect produced by a ringflash. Find out how they did…

MANY PROFESSIONAL fashion and portrait photographers love using a ringflash to capture
images with a distinctive shadowless lighting effect. With a basic ringflash kit costing several
hundred pounds, a number of manufacturers have produced adaptors that, when fitted over
the head of a standard flashgun, aim to mimic a ringflash effect. We test the two most
popular models from Orbis and RayFlash.

Orbis

The Orbis is made from tough ABS plastic,
which is able to withstand heavy general
usage and seems durable enough to survive a
drop, although we've not tested that fact! At
20cm diameter, the ring area is larger than the
RayFlash (although the 86mm tunnel for the
lens is smaller), and at 500 grams, it's also
slightly heavier. The standard way to use the
Orbis is to slip the flashgun into the housing
and handhold the flash with your left hand,
resting your thumb and forefinger on the
grooved surface of the Orbis. The housing has
a flexible grip that holds a variety of flash
heads, so if you've a well-known brand of
flash, it will most likely fit. With the lens poking
through the tunnel, the set-up works well, but
does become uncomfortable if you're
shooting for a prolonged period of time. In this
instance, we'd recommend the optional Orbis
arm, an adjustable aluminium bracket that
fixes to the flashgun's hotshoe and the
camera's tripod bush. The £50 arm was
unavailable for this test, but you should
consider it if you plan to use the Orbis for
extended periods of time.

The output from the flash travels straight up
and around the ring, which has a diffuser
around the entire front surface. Within the
Orbis ring, the light is distributed to provide an
even effect and to limit light loss.

Because the flashgun is handheld, flash
exposures aren't straightforward. You can use
Canon's infrared flash trigger or Nikon's CLS
flash system for TTL flash, or independent
dedicated off-camera cords. This has the
advantage of providing more accurate flash
exposures. If you use a third-party flash
trigger, such as a Pocket Wizard, Hahnel
Combi RF or Seculine TwinLink (used for this
test), TTL flash information isn't
communicated to the camera, so you need to
set your flash to manual power settings. This
involves taking test shots at 1/2 power, 1/4
power etc and adjusting power until you have
a decent exposure. It's also worth noting that
because it's handheld, you can position the
Orbis to shoot from an angle, much as you
would a softbox or beauty light.

It took a fair bit of effort to fit our Canon
Speedlite 580EX II into the Orbis housing, but
once in, the grip was tight and secure. Our
Canon 28-70mm f/2.8 lens fitted snugly
through the tunnel, but occasionally we found
the AF/M switch had been moved to manual
by contact with the Orbis tunnel, so do ensure
you keep an eye on this.

The output from the Orbis was excellent
and it allows enough flash output through to
illuminate subjects a few feet away.

Catchlights
The Orbis delivers
a prominent
catchlight and even
spread of light.

Price: £200 (Guide)/ £185 (Street)
Supplied accessories: Case, strap,
self-adhesive pad
WEBSITE: www.orbisflash.com

Orbis users should buy the £50 Orbis Arm for
better handling. It can be tripod-mounted too.

Verdict

Having to handhold the Orbis
means it's more of an effort to
use than the RayFlash, but it is
versatile as you can position it at
any angle. However, we'd suggest
you buy the optional arm to improve handling.
Ideally, use a dedicated off-camera lead for TTL
compatibility, but even if using manual flash, you
should be able to produce flattering portraits.

 Like Well made, beautiful lighting effect,
near-universal compatibility

 Dislike Handheld without optional arm. No
TTL flash without dedicated accessories

OVERALL ★★★★☆

RayFlash

The RayFlash is a less chunky and lighter unit than the Orbis but just as well made, and has a considerably different design. The ringflash diffuser is smaller and thinner, although the tunnel through which the lens sits is wider. The RayFlash is designed to be used with the flashgun mounted on the hotshoe. Because it's so light, the flashgun's head supports its weight, so there's little undue pressure on the hotshoe. The end that attaches to the flashgun is angled so that the flashgun's head faces forward when fitted. This has the advantage of the ringflash adaptor being positioned securely around the lens and, unlike the Orbis, negates the need for the photographer to handhold the unit. The other major benefit is that because the flashgun sits on the hotshoe, it retains TTL flash functions, meaning you don't have to invest in an off-camera cord or worry about having to calculate the exposure. These two factors mean that the RayFlash handles better than the Orbis, but more importantly for beginners is far easier to use. It's also worth noting that you have the option of fitting a remote trigger/off-camera lead to the RayFlash and use the flashgun away from the camera much as you can with the Orbis.

When fired, the flash output travels through a series of prisms and reflectors that, like the Orbis, aims to distribute the light evenly around the ring. The output from the flash travels up and around the ring, which has a diffuser around the entire front surface. Within the RayFlash ring, the light is distributed to provide an even effect and to limit light loss. Where the flashgun's head fits is smaller than that of the Orbis and designed to fit particular models of flashgun. Therefore, you need to buy the correct RayFlash model for your flashgun, which is easy to do by referring to the table on the distributor's website.

The adaptor's flash housing has a locking pin that holds the flash head securely, but take care when tightening it as our sample cracked a little when we twisted it too far. Once the RayFlash is fitted, you can start taking pictures straight away with the comfort of knowing that the camera is taking care of the exposures. You should, however, regularly check the LCD monitor to ensure images are not over or underexposed. If you're not happy with the results, you can boost or reduce power using flash exposure compensation.

The RayFlash is easier to use than the Orbis thanks to it retaining TTL. However, you do need to keep an eye on exposures as getting too close will lead to overexposure. While the RayFlash is efficient, don't stray more than a couple of metres from your subject as you'll quickly lose its effect. Its output is very similar to that created by the Orbis.

Top tips for using adaptors

- Zoom the flashgun's head to its maximum setting to help increase the flash's range
- Regularly review images and the histogram to ensure good exposures, in particular when you have moved closer or further away from the subject
- Fit a colour gel to your flashgun's head if you want to change the colour temperature of the flash output
- Write down your exposure settings for later reference

Fun flash
The RayFlash is very easy to use and delivers great results.

Price: £170 (Guide)/ £160 (Street)
Supplied accessories: Case, strap, self-adhesive pad
Website: www.flaghead.co.uk

Verdict

The design of the RayFlash gives it a couple of distinct advantages over the Orbis. Its lighter weight means it is easier to use and the advantage of TTL flash will prove a major benefit to those inexperienced with flash photography or wanting to work quickly. For these reasons, the RayFlash is a better overall choice to the Orbis.

 Like Nice design, retains TTL functions, nice effect

 Dislike Design of holding clamp; not as universal as Orbis

OVERALL ★★★★★

Test conclusion

We were a little sceptical about ringflash adaptors before this test. Can a piece of plastic with a ring-shaped diffuser really match the performance of a proper 'pro' ringflash? Well, we found they can't, but they do a very good job nonetheless at getting close to replicating the effect. Sure, neither can match a true ringflash, but they do come near in some respects, delivering an effect that is sure to suit those who can't afford the high price of a ringflash but wish to capture images that reproduce its lighting effect. There is little doubt that a ringflash is easier and more enjoyable to use, but let's be honest, it's an accessory very few of us can afford to buy, especially as it's something that won't be used on a regular basis. The Orbis and RayFlash both offer a very good buy for those looking to add a modern, funky fashion feel to their portraits. Both deliver great results, but the RayFlash is the better buy thanks to its neater design, which offers TTL flash photography without the need for a dedicated off-camera lead.

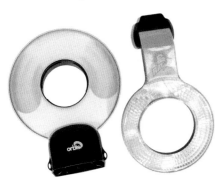

Buyers' guide: Lighting aids

Whether working with ambient light or shooting in a studio with flash, reflectors and diffusers are an inexpensive and versatile aid to help manipulate light. We show you the main types to consider

THERE IS A COMMON misconception that you need expensive equipment to get professional-looking portraits. While a better camera and superior optics do make a difference, there are many affordable bits of kit that can lead to far better pictures if used correctly. Lighting aids – in other words, reflectors and diffusers – are two such items, proving useful whether you're using daylight, studioflash or any other form of lighting.

The various technique articles featured earlier in this guide provide some perfect examples of how and when to use lighting aids

with daylight, but it's worth remembering that they're also suitable for use with any subject that requires lighting control, so are great for still-lifes or close-ups. And, of course, they can be used in the studio, too: a reflector, for instance, is often used to bounce light from the key light source to fill in shadows on the subject, negating the need for a second flash head.

There are several different types of lighting aids available in different sizes, shapes and colours, from small handheld options to those that require a stand or assistant to hold them. For the majority of amateurs and enthusiasts, a

small handheld option is suitable for most needs, while for the more avid photographers who like to dabble in money-making photography, larger reflectors and diffusers prove far more effective, especially when shooting on location.

Our buyers' guide covers a range of products from all the popular brands that are worth considering for everyday use, but check their websites for more specialist products, too. We've also a comparison test of a number of 5-in-1 reflector kits, which will help you make the right choice and save you money, too.

Reflector size guide	
30cm	12in
50cm	20in
56cm	22in
81cm	32in
95cm	37in
107cm	42in
120cm	47in
70x110cm	28x44in
90x120cm	36x48in
100x165cm	40x66in
60x90cm	24x36in
90x125cm	36x50in
100x150cm	39x59in
130x190cm	52x76in
180x245cm	72x98in

California Sunbounce

www.theflashcentre.com

The California Sunbounce range of reflectors is a favourite with professionals thanks to their stability, build quality and light weight. The reflector panels are fitted to aluminium frames that come in various sizes and are quick and easy to assemble, disassemble and pack up for storage and transportation. There is a good choice of reflective panels available, although not every colour is suitable for every frame, but you still have several options open to you (the downloadable PDF catalogue has a very useful easy-reference table).

While you can buy extra panels to use with a frame, the difference in price for complete kits and individual panels isn't that wide, so it's often worth buying the complete outfit to save you having to swap panels while on location. As with other brands, there are silver/white and gold/white reflector options, but you'll find that there are other reflective finishes, eg zebra/white (zebra is a mix of gold and silver), as well as a number of translucent diffuser options.

As they're made for professional use, you'll find that they're relatively expensive, but they are made to last for years of professional use and are produced from the

best possible materials. The Sunbounce system is extensive, so contact importers The Flash Centre if you require further details, or download the catalogue at: www.sunbounce.com.

Because the number of options is huge, we've listed the different reflector ranges below and stated the price of the two most popular reflective colours. While a number of sizes are available, we'd recommend the Mini or Pro as your first choice, and the Mega (stated as Big in the catalogue) if you're a very keen enthusiast. Here are the main options:

Micro-mini: (60x90cm)
Silver/white: £101; Zebra/white: £125
Mini: (90x125cm)
Silver/white: £156; Zebra/white: £190
Pro: (130x190cm)
Silver/white: £235; Zebra/white: £275
Big: (180x245cm)
Silver/white: £370; Zebra/white: £430

While a couple of translucent panels are available for the Pro and Mega panels, for diffusing purposes we'd recommend you check out the Sun Swatter. This is a large diffuser that is ideal for outdoor use as it can be held by a boon over the subject and outside of the image area. It's easy to assemble and designed to be used in windy conditions. There are two sizes available and a number of options for the light-reducing value of the translucent material (1/3, 2/3 or one-stop light diffusion). We'd recommend the smaller Sun Swatter with the 1/3 or 2/3-stop diffuser as a good first option.

Other specialist reflectors in the range include the Sun-Mover, which allows for additional control of the spread of light and the Sun Cage – a purpose-made mobile studio for location shooting.
Sun Swatter (130x190cm)
1/3-stop complete £230
Sun Swatter (130x190cm)
2/3-stop complete £240
Sun Swatter Giant (180x245cm)
1/3-stop complete £385
Sun Swatter Giant (180x245cm)
2/3-stop complete £400

Kenro

www.kenro.co.uk

Kenro produces a circular and a rectangular 5-in-1 kit. The circular reflectors measure 12in, 22in, 32in and 42in, and cost £16, £30, £55 and £68 respectively. The rectangular kits measure 28x44in, 36x48in and 40x66in, and cost £56, £75 and £99 respectively. All the kits are supplied in a bag with a translucent panel and a reversible gold, silver, white and black cover.

Kenro also offers a range of reflectors and diffusers with handles called Easy Grips. It has three 60x90cm (24x36in) models in the

range: the £41 translucent and the £45 silver/white and sunlight/white variants. Each 5-in-1 reflector kit features a translucent panel over which a reversible gold, silver, white or black cover can be attached. It folds down into a handy round zip bag when not in use.

Calumet

www.calumetphoto.co.uk

Calumet is a major photo retailer and has an extensive number of own-brand photo accessories, including its ZipDisc range of collapsible reflectors. These include two colour reflectors, translucent panels and four-colour sleeves (gold/silver/white/black). The ZipDisc kits are as follows:

■ **Translucent white ZipDisc panel**
The circular diffuser at the heart of its 5-in-1 kit is available on its own, too.
56cm £15; 81cm £26;
107cm £37; 130cm £46

■ **Zigzag gold-silver/white ZipDisc**
The gold-silver side combines gold and silver for added warmth to the subject.
56cm £15; 81cm £26; 107cm £37

■ **Silver/white ZipDisc**
The classic hand-held reflector. Supplied with a zip case.
56cm £15; 81cm £26; 107cm £37

■ **ZipDisc four-colour cover**
This four-colour (gold, white, silver and black) sleeve cover can be used on any round or oval reflector.
56cm (22in) ZipDisc reversible: £13
81cm (32in) ZipDisc reversible: £15
107cm (42in) ZipDisc reversible: £16

■ **5-in-1 kit**
This is a combination of the ZipDisc translucent panel and the four-colour sleeve. We've tested the 81cm 5-in-1 in our comparison test.
56cm £21; 81cm £34; 107cm £41

Please note that if you visit Calumet's website, you may get a little confused about the product descriptions, so if you've any queries, phone the customer service line on 08706 030303.

Elemental

www.studio-flash.com

Budget studioflash specialists Elemental currently only has two collapsible reflectors in its range, but we've included them in this guide as they represent excellent value for money. Both the 80cm and 107cm 5-in-1 kits comprise a white diffuser with an interchangeable gold, silver and white reflector cover, all supplied in a black bag. The 80cm costs £25, while the 107cm is £35. Elemental also has a reflector arm available for £25.

Interfit

www.interfitphotographic.com

Interfit is one of the UK's leading brands of studio equipment and has an extensive range of reflectors, from handhelds to larger stand-supported types, so you've plenty of choice!

■ Soft sun/white; silver/white and silver/gold

Round, collapsible reflectors available in three finishes and four sizes.
30cm £10.50; 56cm £16.50; 82cm £27.60; 107cm £39

■ 5-in-1 kits

These feature a translucent reflector, with a four-colour overlay sleeve (gold, silver, black and white), supplied in a zip-up bag. They are available in three sizes, as follows:
56cm £26.50; 82cm £37; 107cm £44

■ Easy Grip

Interfit's Easy Grip reflector has a thick handle for one-handed use and measures 90x60cm (36x24in). It is available in the following colours: sunlight/white; gold/silver; silver/white and 1/2-stop translucent and costs £40.

■ Portrait Reflector Kit

Interfit's Portrait Reflector Kit is essentially three reflector panels attached to a frame that fits easily on a lighting stand. Each 90x60cm (36x24in) panel can be individually positioned for improved lighting control. The kit is supplied with one silver/gold panel and two sunlight/silver panels, and costs £100.

■ The Large Flat Panel Reflector

Studio-based photographers may be interested in these large reflector panels, made for full-length portraits and fashion shoots. The Large Flat Panel Reflector measures 89x178cm (35x70in) and is supplied complete with a stand and a rotating/tilting bracket for using the panel vertically or horizontally. Silver/gold and white/black versions are available for £82.

■ Flexi-lite 5-in-1

This stand-mounted panel reflector is aimed at pros and can be used handheld or on location. The aluminium frame has a boon arm that can be positioned at any angle. Various kits are available in medium (100x150cm) or large (150x200cm). The INT303 has a gold/silver/black/white cover and costs £306.

Lastolite

www.lastolite.com

Lastolite is one of the world's leading studio accessory brands and is particularly renowned for its lighting aids, so it's no surprise to discover it has an extensive range of products. Many are designed for specific pro uses, so due to space constraints, we've selected the products most suitable for general portrait photography. A comprehensive brochure PDF can be downloaded from Lastolite's website if you'd like to check out the entire range.

■ Collapsible reflectors:

When it comes to collapsible reflectors, no brand has as many options as Lastolite. Its round reflectors are available in 30cm, 50cm, 76cm, 95cm and 120cm diameters and there is a huge 1.8x1.2m rectangular option, too. All of these are available in the following finishes: silver/white; Sunfire/white, silver/gold, Sunfire/silver; gold/white and Sunlite/soft silver. A two-stop diffuser is also available in all sizes from 50cm upwards. Guide prices for silver/white are as follows:
30cm £13; 50cm £24; 75cm £35; 95cm £58; 120cm £75; 1.8x1.2m £91

■ Bottletops 5-in-1 kit:

This includes a diffuser panel with elasticated covers. The kit comprises the diffuser panel and a gold/white and Sunfire/silver cover and comes in four sizes: 50cm (£41), 75cm (£47), 95cm (£57) and 120cm (£85).

■ TriGrip:

The original TriGrip was the first collapsible reflector to feature a handle and proved extremely popular. The design has been updated, with a new moulded handle improving handling and there are now three sizes in the range: the £47 Mini TriGrip (45cm); £62 TriGrip (75cm) and £77 Large TriGrip (1.2m). For each size, you can choose reflectors in silver/white, gold/white, Sunfire/silver and Sunlite/soft silver finishes, as well as a one-stop or two-stop diffuser. Accessories for the TriGrip include a support bracket and the TriFlip, a set of seven reflector covers that can be placed over a TriGrip to offer the ultimate in versatility. You can also buy a £185 TriFlip 8:1 kit that supplies a two-stop diffuser (Mini TriGrip or TriGrip) with seven colour sleeves.

■ Triflector:

The Mk II kit consists of a support frame with three collapsible panels, all easily packed away in a case weighing a total of only 1.2kg. The panels are available in the following reflective finishes: Sunfire/silver, silver/white, gold/white and a 1.2-stop diffuser. A kit is £123; extra sets of panels range from £33-£45.

■ UpLite 4:1:

A set of self-supporting 120x90cm reflector panels for use by photographers working on their own, who need to bounce light at an angle from the floor. The angle can be adjusted from 30-80° and the two panels can also be separated for handheld use. The UpLite comes in two versions: the Cool Tone has sunlite/soft silver and silver/white reflective surfaces; while the Warm Tone has gold/white and Sunfire/silver reflective surfaces. It comes supplied with a waterproof shower cap and a carry case, and costs £120.

■ Skylite:

Best suited for serious photographers looking for a lightweight, durable and large diffuser that can also double up as a reflector. The rigid, hollow aluminium frame supports a diffuser (0.75 or 1.25 stop) or reflector (gold/silver, silver/white, black/white or Sunfire/white) via secure Velcro fastenings. The Skylite can be bought in a number of kit forms and three sizes are available as follows: small 1.1x1.1m (1.3kg); medium 1x2m (2kg) and large 2x2m (2.3kg). The standard kit includes the frame, silver/white and translucent fabrics and carry bag, and are priced at around £138, £180 and £260 for the small, medium and large respectively.

The Royal Photographic Society

Patron: Her Majesty The Queen.   Incorporated by Royal Charter

SPECIAL OFFER
20% OFF
RPS MEMBERSHIP

Only applies when paying by Direct Debit

IMAGE: TIM RUDMAN FRPS Kirkjufell

MEMBERSHIP SUBSCRIPTION RATES (tick as appropriate)

Standard £111 **Now £88.80** ☐

Family £162 **Now £129.60** ☐

Overseas under 65s £99 **Now £79.20** ☐

65 and over (enclose proof of age) £82.20 **Now £65.76** ☐

25 and under (enclose proof of age) £52.80 **Now £42.24** ☐

Student ☐   Disabled ☐
(enclose proof of status)
£52.80 **Now £42.24**

APPLICATION FOR MEMBERSHIP

Please complete this form and return to:
**THE ROYAL PHOTOGRAPHIC SOCIETY,
Fenton House, 122 Wells Road, Bath, BA2 3AH.**

Mr/Dr/Mrs/Miss/Ms First name(s):

Surname:

Address:

Postcode:

Email Address:

Tel: Date of Birth:

Which do you consider yourself? Professional ☐ Amateur ☐ Semi professional ☐

Are you happy to receive emails from The Society? Yes ☐ No ☐

If you are a student, is your course either Full time ☐ Part time ☐

gift aid it

Tick the box to make every £1 of your gift worth 28p more for FREE. ☐

I am a UK taxpayer and would like all donations I have made over the past four years and those I make from the date of this declaration until I notify you otherwise, to be treated as Gift Aid donations.

Remember you should be paying income tax or capital gains tax equal to the amount The Society can reclaim on your donations in any particular year.

I would like to pay by Direct Debit   Annually ☐   **Monthly** ☐

INSTRUCTION TO YOUR BANK OR BUILDING SOCIETY TO PAY BY DIRECT DEBIT

DIRECT Debit

Service User Number 940467

Reference number (for office use only) [   ]

Name and full postal address of your bank or building society:

Account name:

Name and address of Bank:

Postcode:

Bank account number ☐☐☐☐☐☐☐☐

Branch sort code ☐☐ – ☐☐ – ☐☐

Instructions to your bank or building society
Please pay The Royal Photographic Society Direct Debits from the account detailed in this Instruction subject to the safeguards assured by the Direct Debit Guarantee. I understand that this Instruction may remain with The Royal Photographic Society and, if so, details will be passed electronically to my bank/building society.

Signature:

Date:

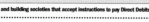

This Guarantee is offered by all banks and building societies that accept instructions to pay Direct Debits

DIRECT Debit

THE DIRECT DEBIT GUARANTEE
- This Guarantee is offered by all banks and building societies that accept instructions to pay Direct Debits
- If there are any changes to the amount, date or frequency of your Direct Debit The Royal Photographic Society will notify you ten working days in advance of your account being debited or as otherwise agreed. If you request The Royal Photographic Society to collect a payment, confirmation of the amount and date will be given to you at the time of the request
- If an error is made in the payment of your Direct Debit, by The Royal Photographic Society or your bank or building society, you are entitled to a full and immediate refund of the amount paid from your bank or building society – If you receive a refund you are not entitled to, you must pay it back when The Royal Photographic Society asks you to
- You can cancel a Direct Debit at any time by simply contacting your bank or building society. Written confirmation may be required. Please also notify us.

DISCOVER
THE ROYAL PHOTOGRAPHIC SOCIETY

MEMBERSHIP BENEFITS

ENJOY The Society's acclaimed journal (10 issues per year) packed with news, reviews, in-depth articles and inspirational photography

ACHIEVE a Society Distinction. Improve your skills and demonstrate your photographic ability

PROGRESS with your photography by receiving expert advice and guidance from our panel members, whilst working towards a Distinction

PARTICIPATE in local meetings and events run by your region

BELONG to one or more of the 14 Special Interest Groups and discover different areas of photography. Each group produces their own newsletter and holds regular events and meetings

PROMOTE yourself with exclusive use of The Society's crest on your website

CREATE a portfolio of your work on The Society's website, along with a brief biography and a link to your website

SHARE your photographs with other members by entering the free monthly online competition

DEVELOP your photography skills by taking advantage of the members discount on our practical workshops

SAVE on entry to Society competitions and events, product discounts from our corporate patrons and other associated offers

EXHIBIT your work internationally and online in Society exhibitions

Full details on all the above can be found on our website www.rps.org

5-in-1 reflector kits

If you're looking to buy your first lighting aid, make it one of these 5-in-1 kits. They offer silver, white, gold and (rarely used) black finishes to suit a variety of shooting situations. The translucent panel, which these reflective sleeves wrap around, can be used as a soft white reflector, although its efficiency is poor. You can also use it to shade your subject, but we'd recommend purchasing a purpose-built diffuser, too, as it works far better. As we discovered when conducting this test, in all areas including build quality, the kits are very similar, so for most photographers, the cheapest option may well be the best one. We've highlighted the major differences below, but in truth, they're all very similar products.

Elemental 5-in-1 (80cm)
www.studio-flash.com

Guide price: £26
Street price: £26

Better known for its excellent range of budget studioflash equipment, Elemental also offers a couple of 5-in-1 reflector kits that represent excellent value. This 80cm kit comes in its own black zip-up bag and, once removed, the 5-in-1 reflector looks and handles much like the similarly priced Interfit. The translucent panel is nicely manufactured and the coloured sleeve has a slot for the panel's tab to slip through when zipped up. The sleeve can be used to give a silver/black or gold/white effect, and is thick and well put together. This is a great budget option and excellent value for money.

Verdict

An excellent budget buy.

Build quality (panel)	★★★★★
Build quality (sleeve)	★★★★☆
Versatility	★★★★☆
Performance	★★★★★
Value for money	★★★★★
OVERALL	★★★★★

Interfit 265 (107cm)
www.interfitphotographic.com

Guide price: £43
Street price: £40

The white surface of the well-made translucent panel offers a 1/2-stop efficiency and has a thick black edge and small cloth tab for hanging off a hook. The sleeve is made from thick material and can be wrapped around to give silver/black or gold/white options. The zip has a smooth action and at its end, the sleeve has a gap for the tab to stick through. Interfit makes a large number of reflector kits, so you should have no trouble finding the most suitable size for you. Better still, they're available at an excellent price. A high-quality piece of equipment, supplied in a well-constructed zip-up black bag.

Verdict

An excellent, affordable kit.

Build quality (panel)	★★★★★
Build quality (sleeve)	★★★★☆
Versatility	★★★★☆
Performance	★★★★★
Value for money	★★★★★
OVERALL	★★★★★

Lastolite Bottletop 4896 (120cm)
www.lastolite.com

Guide price: £85
Street price: £80

This 120cm kit is the largest in the range, and also the biggest and most expensive 5-in-1 in our test. It's also different in a number of ways. First, the 5-in-1 kit is made up of a panel and two reversible elasticated sleeves: a gold/white and a silver/sunfire. This has a number of benefits: it's quicker to change from one to another as there is no zip, and you can fit one over each side of the panel, allowing you to have different combinations to suit your liking. The build quality is first-rate, and spare panels are available so you can place a sleeve on each and have two reflectors at the ready.

Verdict

Versatile and made to last.

Build quality (panel)	★★★★★
Build quality (sleeve)	★★★★★
Versatility	★★★★★
Performance	★★★★★
Value for money	★★★★☆
OVERALL	★★★★★

Flash accessories for portraits

There are a wide variety of lighting accessories available for your flashgun which, while not essential for general snaps, can make a difference when you're trying to be more creative with your photography. We highlight a selection of the best diffusers, softboxes and kits for your flashgun

WHILE SOME PHOTOGRAPHERS prefer to only use available light, a true master is able to sculpt light from many sources, with one of the most common being the good old flashgun. Flash is fantastic for supplementing light to get a better exposure, but they can also be used to override the ambient light for creative results. While a direct, naked flash is sufficient for some situations, many photographers frown on this basic approach as the light's rarely flattering and control is limited. So for professional results you need to start looking at adding some complementary accessories to your flash outfit to modify the light to suit the effect you want.

Before picking from the plethora of accessories available, you need to understand the difference between hard and soft light and know the flash effect you want to achieve. In basic terms, hard light produces strong shadows with sharp edges and high contrast, while one that casts weak shadows, with no definite edge, is soft light. You also need to decide if you want the light to be dispersed and natural-looking or harsh and more selective. The following selection covers every type of accessory your flashgun could ever need!

Sto-Fen Omni-bounce

Guide price: £17   **Street price: £11**
www.newprouk.co.uk

Some flashguns come supplied with a clip-on diffuser, but if yours doesn't, buy a Stofen. They are devilishly effective in softening the light from your flashgun, with many snappers leaving them attached for all their on-camera flash shooting. They're available for almost every flashgun. Well worth the modest outlay.

SCORE ★★★★★

Hama Uni Flash Diffuser

Guide price: £20   **Street price: £16**
www.hama.co.uk

A basic flash diffuser that has been made to fit most flashguns on the market. It can be secured to the flashgun with its own Velcro strap, making it suitable for use in the field. The price is a little high but it's worth keeping one in your camera bag should you have to use a flashgun unit you're not familiar with.

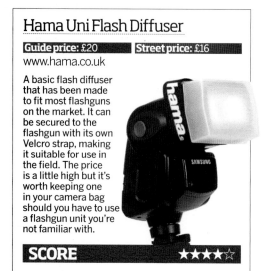

SCORE ★★★★☆

Lumiquest Softbox III

Guide price: £45   **Street price: £45**
www.newprouk.co.uk

The largest of the Lumiquest range, the Softbox III produces an extremely soft light that is no easy feat when you take the size and portability of it into account. One of the reasons for the great light is that the centre of the front panel is thicker than the edges, which reduces the possibility of a hot spot caused by the head of the flashgun.

BEST BUY

SCORE ★★★★★

Lastolite Ezybox kit (38cm)

Guide price: £170   **Street price: £160**
www.johnsons-photopia.co.uk

While many of the other products have a slight 'DIY' appearance to them, the Ezybox oozes quality and build stability like nothing else in this test. While the Ezybox is value for money for pros, its high price may prove too much for most enthusiasts, even though it promises such good performance.

BEST BUY

SCORE ★★★★★

Speedlight Pro Beauty Dish

Guide price: £80   **Street price: £80**
www.speedlightprokit.co.uk

When you see the dish in its pre-assembled state, you'd be forgiven for having low expectations. However, once you put it all together things start to look up and then the results blow you away. The value is outstanding, as is the quality of light it produces. One of the best accessories on the market!

BEST BUY

SCORE ★★★★★

Main types of flash accessories

Most flash modifiers fall into one of the following five categories, although some may also overlap

Diffusers:
This is a general term for anything that softens light and is usually in the form of an opaque or white surface, which is placed in front of the flash. Softboxes and standard diffusion domes are the most common type of diffuser.

Reflectors:
Bounced light has plenty of opportunity to spread out and, as a result, often softens the light. Reflectors come in white, silver and gold depending on how you want to alter the colour temperature of the light. Beauty dishes, although substantially bigger, also fall into this category.

Colour gels:
These serve one of two purposes – colour correction or colour effects. Colour correction gels are placed over the flash to match the colour of the flash with the temperature of the ambient lighting, such as tungsten or fluorescent. Colour-effect gels change your flash's colour for creative effects.

Honeycomb:
Also known as grids, these provide a smoother transition between shadows and highlights than a naked flash. The light falls off more gradually than other modifiers, in a similar way to a vignette, which can bring some impressive lighting effects to your images.

Snoots:
Designed like a cone, the snoot channels the stream of light from the flash allowing you to illuminate certain parts of the scene more selectively, much like a spotlight would. They are often used in combination with honeycombs for maximum creative effect.

Honl Flash Kit MkII

Guide price: £160
Street price: £160
www.flaghead.co.uk
Contains: Two straps, 1/4 grid, 1/8 grid, 8in snoot, 5in snoot, Gobo bounce card, colour correction kit, colour effects kit

It's not often that a range of products comes along and changes the way that photographers work. But the Honl kit has done just that. The snoots and bounce cards are made from high-grade webbing, which can take the rigours of heavy use. Many of these accessories are available separately but this bundle offers great value for money.
Bounce card The most obvious use for this card is to use the white side to bounce light off and to soften the light landing on your subject. But it can be used for much more than that. If you get two, you then have a simple set of barn doors that allow you to control the spill of the light across your image.
8in & 5in snoots The Honl snoots are very versatile pieces of kit, which lend themselves to a number of applications. They can be used closed to direct the light from your flashgun in a very direct, almost spotlight manner, so you can highlight one element in your camera's viewfinder. Alternatively,

you can open the snoot, which works in the same manner as a bounce card, directing the light up and forward towards your subject.
1/4 Grid & 1/8 Grid Spots These grids look and feel very robust and attach to your flashgun using the Speed Strap (included in the kit). Once attached, the strap's strong Velcro holds incredibly well so you'll have no worries about the grids slipping.
Colour Correction Gel & Colour Effects Kit Possibly the highlight of the Honl kit, these easy-to-use gels are fast becoming one of the most popular accessories to use for making flash photography more creative. The gels have Velcro edges and attaching them to the flashgun using the Speed Strap is easy and hassle-free as you just place the gel over the flash and push on the Velcro until it takes hold. Just like the Honl grids, the gels stay in place securely and cover the whole flashgun.

Verdict
The price isn't low but the quality of the kit is superb. The outfit slips easily into just about any camera bag, weighs next to nothing and is really simple to set up.

Build quality	★★★★★
Features	★★★★★
Performance	★★★★★
Value for money	★★★★☆

OVERALL ★★★★★

Interfit Strobies Portrait Kit

Guide price: £120
Street price: £110
www.interfitphotographic.com
Contains: Flashgun mount, globe, beauty dish, softbox, barndoors, snoot and honeycomb

The Interfit Strobies STR100 kit is a scaled-down version of larger studio accessories, so while the attachments are fairly sturdy, they aren't very compact or easy to transport, particularly the Globe option that is shaped like a small football. The accessories attach to a mount before they fit to a flashgun, so you'll need a separate mount if you wish to use more than one flashgun at a same time, which is highly likely.
Softbox The softbox is a miniature version of the one you get in studios and is also just as difficult to assemble. We would only recommend this softbox for a home studio as you wouldn't want to put it together more than once. That said, once assembled, the build quality is decent and as long as it isn't given too much abuse, it should give you a good few years of service.
Beauty dish The small beauty dish can be slipped on to the kit's standard mount and, despite its compact size, delivers an even spread of light. Unlike some

models, when attached, this lightweight dish won't make your flashgun feel top-heavy.
Globe diffuser This is an unusual piece of equipment that attaches to your flashgun via a supplied mount. For the best results, you will have to set your flashgun head to bounce (so it's pointing towards the ceiling) before attaching the diffuser. Once triggered, the dome fills with light and then emits the light in a spherical direction. Be careful when attaching the Globe, as one fall on to a hard surface will most likely crack it into pieces.
Barndoors Featuring four flaps, barndoors allow you to 'cover up' some of the light from your flashgun for more control over its distribution. When using the barndoors fully open, the light from the flashgun spreads over a wide area and makes an ideal accessory for a background light. The build quality is okay, but doesn't match the Honl kit.
Snoot & Honeycomb The snoot and honeycomb work in combination with each other. With the snoot fixing to the mount, it can be used on its own to create a spotlight. The honeycomb grid slides down the barrel of the snoot and is dense enough to block the light quite well.

Verdict
This kit has some useful applications and would prove a frugal and rewarding buy for the photographers taking their first steps with flashgun accessories.

Build quality	★★★★☆
Features	★★★★☆
Performance	★★★★☆
Value for money	★★★★☆

OVERALL ★★★★☆

Be sure to bracket!
Whether you use the grey card or not, in tricky lighting conditions, bracket your exposure by +/-1 stops using your camera's exposure compensation or AEB functions to ensure a correct exposure

Metered to perfection!
Scenes with strong backlighting can lead to exposure error. Use a grey card and you should have no problems.

How to use your metering & White Balance cards

The 18% grey card can be used to ensure perfect exposures when you're shooting in tricky lighting conditions. Both reference cards can also be used to set a custom White Balance, but how you do this depends on your camera (refer to your camera's manual). In the meantime, here is a brief explanation to get you started

DIGITAL CAMERAS USE sophisticated exposure systems with a choice of metering patterns to suit different lighting situations. The systems work on the assumption that the area of the scene being metered is a mid-tone, or 18% grey to be precise; the average if all dark, light and mid-tones were mixed together. It's the basis of all metering patterns and works surprisingly well, but can render incorrect exposures when the overall scene or subject is considerably lighter or darker than 18% grey. For example, very dark areas can fool the metering system into overexposing the image, while very light areas can fool the camera into underexposure, as the light meter will take a reading that renders it as a mid-tone.

As a camera is trying to render an image 'grey', it's your job to ensure you compensate to keep the tones true to life. You can do this by either using one of your camera's exposure override facilities, such as exposure compensation, the AE-Lock button or by metering from an area of the

scene that has a mid-tone. And that's where our grey card comes in. Using it is very simple as our step-by-step guide below illustrates.

The key thing to remember is that you need to place the grey card in similar lighting to your subject, for instance, don't place it in a shaded area if your subject is bathed in sunlight. Also, make sure that the card fills the metering area – we would recommend you use spot or partial metering as the card won't need to fill the entire image area – but any is suitable. You can either lock the exposure using your camera's AE-Lock facility or note the aperture and shutter speed, then switch to manual mode and dial in these settings. This latter method isn't suitable on days where lighting is variable. The card has AF reference lines to help your camera's autofocus lock on to it. However, you don't necessarily need it to be in focus to work correctly. The grey card (as well as the white card) can also be used to take a custom White Balance reading from, too.

1 Getting started If you're shooting portraits in difficult lighting conditions, such as backlighting, give your subject the grey card and ask them to hold it angled towards you.

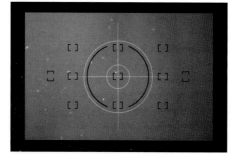

2 Take a meter reading Ensure that the entire metering area is filled by the grey card (in this instance we're using spot metering) and lock the exposure with the AE-Lock button.

3 Compose & shoot With this exposure locked, you can compose your scene and take your shots. When you check it on your LCD monitor, the exposure should be perfect.